Creating the
SOUL
BODY

Creating the
SOUL
BODY

The Sacred Science of Immortality

Robert E. Cox

Inner Traditions
Rochester, Vermont

Inner Traditions
One Park Street
Rochester, Vermont 05767
www.InnerTraditions.com

Library of Congress Cataloging-in-Publication Data
Cox, Robert.
  Creating the soul body : the sacred science of immortality / Robert E. Cox.
    p. cm.
  Includes bibliographical references and index.
  ISBN 978-1-59477-221-4 (pbk.)
  1. Immortality. 2. Consciousness. 3. Religion and science. I. Title.
  BL530.C69 2008
  299'.93—dc22

                                                                    2008001940

Printed and bound in the United States by Lake Book Manufacturing

10 9 8 7 6 5 4 3 2 1

Text design by Virginia Scott Bowman; layout by Replika Press Pvt Ltd.
This book was typeset in Garamond Premier Pro, with Delphin used as a display typeface.

To send correspondence to the author of this book, mail a first-class letter to the author c/o Inner Traditions • Bear & Company, One Park Street, Rochester, VT 05767, and we will forward the communication.

A stairway to the sky is set up for me . . . that I may ascend on it to the sky.

EGYPTIAN PYRAMID TEXTS, 1108 (ca. 2400 BCE)

Contents

Preface

This book is devoted to a reevaluation of ancient systems of religious-mythological thought and their relevance to our modern systems of scientific thought.

Throughout this book runs this theme: The ancients were much more intelligent than we have supposed them to be. In particular, the chapters that follow propose that many ancient cultures once shared a genuine spiritual science, a science of consciousness, which in certain ways rivals and even surpasses the most advanced physical theories of today.

In this volume we will focus upon a particular aspect of the ancient science dealing with the path of immortality—the step-by-step expansion of consciousness throughout the universe and even beyond the universe into the bosom of the infinite. In the process, we will see that the ancient Vedic, Egyptian, and Hebrew traditions shared a common map of this path, which, though expressed in arcane symbolic terms unique to each culture, was and is genuinely scientific.

More specifically, we will see that this map can be reduced to an exponential system of space-time scales, both macroscopic and microscopic, which can be used to predict accurately the most fundamental scales of cosmological organization discovered so far on the basis of general relativity, as well as the most fundamental scales of force-matter unification discovered so far on the basis of quantum theory.

The implications are quite profound both from a scientific point of view and from a cultural-historical point of view. How the ancients came to possess this knowledge remains a mystery of the highest order pertaining not only to the epistemological methods by which they obtained this knowledge, but also to the means by which different cultures, separated by serious linguistic, religious, cultural, and geographic boundaries, came to possess the same knowledge.

Yet our focus here is upon the substance of the knowledge—the science hidden behind the arcane myths, geometric symbols, and religious terms that the ancients used to express such knowledge. In this regard, we will draw upon primarily three ancient traditions that predate the birth of Christ and for which there are abundant surviving texts: the Vedic tradition of India, the Hebrew tradition, and the Egyptian tradition. We will also draw heavily upon the Hermetic texts written in Egypt during the Hellenistic era. Although these texts were written in Greek and contain many Greek philosophical ideas, the authors claimed to be presenting the philosophic spirit of ancient Egypt.

This is consistent with the spirit of the Ptolemies, the Macedonian rulers of Egypt at the time, who likewise sought to revive the ancient wisdom of Egypt. Upon assuming power in 332 BCE, after Alexander the Great had conquered Egypt, they ferreted out the secret scrolls of the Egyptian priesthood and made them available to the public for the first time in history. In its heyday, the Great Library of Alexandria purportedly held some seven hundred thousand scrolls, and scholars from all around the Hellenistic empire were invited to come and study their contents. Unfortunately, the Great Library was eventually destroyed, and the majority of the scrolls, which likely held a vast treasure of ancient wisdom, were lost.

The Hermetic texts, written during the peak of the Hellenistic empire, likely embodied many secrets drawn from the ancient Egyptian scrolls, expressed anew in Hellenistic language and thought. As such, they may offer a unique insight into the lost philosophic spirit of ancient Egypt, as the authors claimed. The texts reflect a prevalent view in the ancient world that earlier generations were wiser than the present generation. In fact, virtually all of the ancient cultures looked back with nostalgia on a previous age when the spiritual wisdom of humankind was greater than in their current time.

The ancients believed that this spiritual knowledge was most complete at the very dawn of civilization, and over the course of millennia it was gradually lost. For this reason, we will focus most closely upon the ancient Vedic, Egyptian, and Hebrew traditions because they claim great antiquity, dating back thousands of years before the time of Christ. The arguable facts that these traditions shared a common map of the path of immortality, counted exactly the same number of stages on this path, and understood these stages in the same way are consistent with the notion that there was once a great knowledge shared by all of humankind at the dawn of history.

Our goal here is to rediscover the lineaments of that ancient knowledge and attempt to translate it into the language of mathematics—the universal language of science—so that it can be evaluated in light of modern scientific discoveries.

Introduction

A SCIENTIFIC REVOLUTION IN
THE MAKING

At the present moment in history we stand on the brink of a scientific revolution that will likely determine the course of human thought for thousands of years to come. Theorists all around the world are currently collaborating on the development of a final scientific theory, a unified hypothesis of all the laws of nature, which promises to complete our scientific understanding of the universe. This prospective unified thesis has thus often been dubbed the "holy grail" of modern science.

The new theory is designed to study the behavior of the unified field, which acts as the source of all things in creation. Yet there is no direct, empirical evidence that the unified field exists; for all practical purposes, it is empirically hidden. There is no hope, even in principle, that the unified field or its elementary constituents will ever be observed empirically, either now or at any time in the future. As a result, its existence must be posited on an a priori basis, as we might posit an axiom in a theory of pure mathematics.

This amounts to an expansion of scientific thought such that the objects of scientific inquiry are no longer limited to the forms and phenomena of the observable universe. By consensus, the range of scientific thought has been expanded to include forms and phenomena that transcend all means of empirical observation.

METAPHYSICS VERSUS PHYSICS

To be honest, the pursuit of a unified theory more closely resembles an exercise in metaphysics than physics. *Physics* may be defined as the type of science that starts with empirical data and then attempts to derive the local laws of nature that govern that data. Newton first saw the apple fall and then deduced the law of gravity.

Metaphysics, on the other hand, may be defined as the type of science that starts with deductive assumptions regarding the hidden reality of the universe and then attempts to explain the empirical data on that basis. The term *metaphysics* means "that which goes beyond physics." Metaphysical theories tend to go beyond physical theories in the sense that they deal with hidden realities that transcend all means of empirical observation. Whether modern theorists are willing to admit it or not, the search for a unified theory represents literally an attempt to develop a metaphysical theory of the physical world.

In actuality, the quest for a unified theory is not motivated by any new empirical evidence. Instead, it is motivated by pure aesthetics—by the innate desire of the human mind to seek wholeness and unity in its understanding of nature. This desire is not new; it is as old as the hills. The ancients also sought to develop a holistic understanding of the universe by positing the existence of an empirically hidden field that acts as the source of everything. Like modern theorists, they also adopted a metaphysical approach to reach this understanding. This reminds us of Ecclesiastes 1:10: "Is there anything of which one can say, 'Look, this is new'? No, it has already existed, long ago before our time."

There are, however, profound differences between the ancient metaphysical theories and modern unified theories. These two types are rooted in mutually opposed paradigms or general ways of thinking about the world and everything in it.

THE WORLD IS AS YOU SEE IT

The old saying "beauty lies in the eye of the beholder" can be rephrased by saying that truth lies in the mind of the knower. The fact is that our preconceived notions of reality color strongly what we see as beauty and know as truth. This applies not only to individuals, but also to collections of individuals or social cultures. We tend to see the universe as a reflection of our own ideas about reality, as though we are gazing through a cosmic looking glass.

Our preconceived notions about reality serve as standards by which we judge things as real or unreal, true or untrue, beautiful or ugly, normal or abnormal—and these notions are largely conventional. They are shared by the majority of the people in a given culture. Here we are talking about general paradigms of thought or ways of thinking that largely determine how a given culture conceives the nature of life, the universe, and everything. Such paradigms tend to underlie the specific theories about reality developed within a given culture. This applies not only to modern scientific theories, but also to ancient religious theories.

MODERN AND ANCIENT PARADIGMS

For example, it can be argued that all forms of modern scientific thought are rooted in a general *objective paradigm,* which holds that all things in the universe, including all forms of consciousness, are rooted in insentient fields of force and matter operating mechanically. In modern science, the unity of these fields is called the *unified field.* This general paradigm is accepted as a simple truth by most scientists today. Any theory that falls outside this norm is thus viewed as a form of pseudoscience.

Yet the objective paradigm is a relatively recent development in human thought. For thousands of years prior to the advent of modern science, human thought was dominated by another general paradigm, which may be called the ancient *subjective paradigm.* This held that all things in the universe, including all forms of force and matter, are rooted in sentient fields of consciousness. In some traditions, these sentient fields were called the gods, and the unity of these fields was called God—but whatever they were called, the ancients invariably agreed that the universe has a sentient or conscious origin characterized by self-conception and free will, rather than mere mechanical action.

In the same way that the objective paradigm provides the basis for modern scientific theories, the subjective paradigm provided the basis for ancient religious theories. The difference between scientific and religious thought therefore boils down to a difference in opinion regarding the ultimate basis of creation. Modern theorists tend to presume that the universe has an insentient origin, called the unified field, while ancient theorists tended to presume that it has a sentient origin, called God.

A QUESTION OF VALIDITY

In both cases, the two paradigms represent general belief systems rooted in preconceived notions about reality. Which paradigm is more valid in a scientific sense cannot be answered because both paradigms are rooted in preconceived notions regarding the hidden origin of creation.

The only way to answer the question of validity would be to make two different assumptions regarding the nature of the unified field and then follow their logical consequences to develop two different types of theory. This would have more than just philosophical implications. The two opposing assumptions regarding the nature of the field would impact directly the type of models that could be used to represent its behavior.

For example, if we assume that the unified field possesses an insentient form of objective existence, then its elementary constituents would have to be modeled on analogy to insentient objects, such as vibrating strings, which are characterized by mechanical action and are governed by local laws of cause and effect. If, on the other hand, we assume that the unified field possesses a sentient form of subjective existence, then its elementary constituents would have to be modeled on analogy to sentient subjects, such as vibrating minds, which are characterized by self-conception and governed by free will.

In principle, a self-consistent theory could be developed on the basis of either assumption. Mere self-consistency, however, is not enough. To be considered a valid form of scientific knowledge, the theory must also be consistent with the empirical facts so that it can be used to predict the facts accurately. No matter what its starting assumptions might be, if one theory provides predictions that are more accurate and larger in scope than the other, then it would have to be accepted as a more valid form of scientific knowledge.

In this sense, we stand at a critical point in history. We now have the potential to develop two different theories of the unified field, each rooted in one of the opposite assumptions outlined above. This would allow us to test the objective and subjective paradigms. Whichever theory wins will likely determine the course of human thought for thousands of years to come. The question at stake is whether human society will continue to operate on the basis of the objective paradigm, which dominates modern civilization, or will revert to the ancient subjective paradigm that dominated the earliest civilizations on earth.

THE MASTERS OF INTUITION

Given the fact that there are legions of modern theorists who have already adopted the objective paradigm, it behooves us to take the road less traveled and adopt the subjective paradigm. In this respect, we are not alone. We stand with legions of ancient sages and seers who likewise operated on that theoretical basis.

Just as scientists are viewed as the knowledgeable authorities of today, so the sages and seers were viewed as the knowledgeable authorities of yesterday. They were the theorists of their time. Yet unlike modern theorists, who are trained to develop their powers of empirical observation and mathematical logic, the ancient sages were trained to develop their powers of intuition. In fact, they were viewed as the masters of intuition.

This training was no trivial affair. It often took the form of a lifelong discipline that involved practicing various meditation techniques, following rigorous dietary and behavioral regimens, and performing symbolic rituals—all of which were designed to heighten powers of intuition. The ultimate goal of this training was to enlighten the mind and enable the individual to apprehend, directly and intuitively, the hidden reality of the universe. Those who succeeded in this endeavor were held in the highest esteem by the ancient cultures. They were viewed as complete men whose minds were merged with the divine mind—the mind of God. Compared to ordinary men, such enlightened souls seemed immortal gods. The ancient Hermetic texts thus state:

> They received [divine] Mind, and so became complete men. . . . These, my son, in comparison with the others, are as immortal gods to mortal men. They embrace in their own mind all things that are, the things on earth and the things in heaven, and even what is above heaven, if there is aught above heaven; and raising themselves to that height, they see the Good. . . . Such, my son, is the work that Mind does; it throws open the way to knowledge of things divine, and enables us to apprehend God.[1]

In the earliest cultures, the enlightened sages played the role of seer-kings and seer-priests, and their words served to guide both the destiny of the state and the daily affairs of the people. Such individuals were viewed as embodiments of the gods or God on earth. This notion gave rise to the divine right of kings, which involved the propagation of what became known as holy bloodlines over the course of thousands of years.

The ancient leaders of society, whether they played the role of seer-kings or seer-priests, were renowned for their wisdom, which was born not of empirical experience or mathematical logic, but of pure intuition. The ancient sages claimed the ability to apprehend directly and intuitively the hidden reality of God (the unified field) and his influence upon the physical universe. Based upon this intuitive insight, they attempted to answer the ultimate question—what is the meaning of life, the universe, and everything—by developing various metaphysical theories that were often couched in religious terms.

THE ANCIENT SPIRITUAL SCIENCE

Here, we will discover that, hidden behind all the religious language and arcane symbolism used by the ancients, there was a genuine spiritual science that was once shared by many ancient cultures around the world.

This idea is not new. It has been advocated by a number of independent researchers and authors who have devoted themselves to a study of ancient texts and monuments. Most notably, Graham Hancock has promoted this notion in a series of popular books revolving around a mysterious sky-ground dualism found at many ancient sites. In *Heaven's Mirror* he makes this broad generalization:

> A great pan-cultural theory of the meaning and mystery of death and the possibility of eternal life illumined the ancient world. Linked to it was a science of immortality that sought to free the spirit from the gross encumbrance of matter. In its own way, this science was every bit as rigorous and empirical as astrophysics, medicine, or genetic engineering. Unlike modern science, however, it appears from the very beginning, to have been as old as the hills—fully evolved, with its adepts and teachers already present and at work at the dawn of history as far afield as northern Europe, Egypt, Mesopotamia, Vedic India, the Pacific, Japan, China, Southeast Asia, and the Americas.[2]

Our concern here is not so much with the historical origin of the ancient science, but with its substance. Yet there is a problem that must be overcome: Unlike modern scientific theories, which are typically expressed in well-defined mathematical formulas and published in peer-reviewed journals, the ancient spiritual theories were expressed in arcane symbolic formulas unique to each culture. To get at the essential teachings of the sages, we must therefore penetrate the veils of symbolism—something easier said than done. Unfortunately, the symbolic systems used by the ancients were a closely guarded secret. The religious meanings of the myths and symbols may have been available to the common people, but the deeper scientific meanings were the prerogative of a small group of spiritual initiates who used the knowledge for their own mysterious purposes, and sought to preserve it for future generations.

This was not a popular or public science; it was an elite or secret science, which was generally passed down along hereditary lines through strict oral traditions. The French mathematician and ardent Egyptologist Schwaller de Lubicz expressed it this way:

> The Ancients never "popularized" anything; to the uninitiated they provided only the minimal *useful* teaching. The explanation, the philosophy, the secret connection between myth and the sciences were the prerogative of a handful of specially instructed men. Did not Pythagoras wait twenty years before being admitted into the Temple? Did he not, in his own teaching, impose silence on pain of death? Therefore, this teaching was not written down.[3]

The myths and legends that surround the ancient science suggest that rather than being developed over time through experimentation, it was a body of knowledge received originally from a mysterious group of gods or from godlike sages who walked the earth during the predawn history of the human race. The myths go on to suggest that this ancient, revealed body of knowledge was then preserved over the course of millennia by the elite descendants or followers of the original sages, who eventually assumed the role of the royal and priestly classes during the historical epoch.

Apparently, it was this elite group, possessed of the science of their own "divine" ancestors, who administered the earliest civilizations on earth and shaped those civilizations for their own purposes over the course of thousands of years. Upon studying the sacred monuments of ancient Egypt, Schwaller de Lubicz commented:

> Obviously, no one would build such monuments, and in such great numbers, over thousands of years, for uncultivated peasants. The work is of necessity that of an elite, and, even more remarkably, an elite that never ceased to renew itself, an elite that seems to have been uniquely endowed with a wealth of scientific knowledge, including an understanding of the laws of Life. . . . We are dealing here not with an evolution of science, but rather, on the contrary, with an immutable basis . . . from the time of the earliest dynasties. . . . What we see is not the beginnings of research, but the application of a Knowledge already possessed.[4]

Modern physical science has persisted for a few hundred years and provided the basis for one of the most rapidly changing and turbulent periods in human history. By contrast, the ancient spiritual science persisted for thousands of years and served as the basis for some of the most stable and enduring civilizations the world has ever known.

THE LOSS OF SPIRITUAL WISDOM

Yet neither the original science nor the civilizations founded upon it were destined to last forever. The sages predicted that their spiritual wisdom would eventually be lost. Anticipating this event, the Hermetic sages cried out:

O Egypt, Egypt, of thy religion nothing will remain but an empty
tale, which thine own children in time to come will not believe;
nothing will be left but graven words, and only the stones will tell
of thy piety. And in that day, men will be weary of life, and they
will cease to think the universe worthy of reverent wonder and of
worship. . . . No one will raise his eyes to heaven; the pious will
be deemed insane, and the impious wise. . . . As for the soul, and
the belief that it is immortal by nature, or may hope to attain to
immortality, as I have taught you—all this they will mock at, and
will even persuade themselves that it is false.[5]

With the advent of the modern era, the memory of the ancient
spiritual science began to wane. It was replaced eventually by modern
physical science, which has little, if anything, to say about the immortality of the soul. In fact, the modern objective paradigm suggests that
consciousness does not and cannot survive the death of the body.

THE PROSPECT OF SPIRITUAL IMMORTALITY

Modern theorists generally believe that consciousness is created by the
activity of the brain and nervous system. There is no notion that individual consciousness is rooted in an all-pervading field of consciousness that is eternal and uncreated. As a result, it is presumed that when
the body dies, consciousness dies. In this case, dead means dead. That's
it—end of story.

Although thousands of well-documented near-death experiences are
often cited as proof that consciousness survives the death of the brain,
the scientific community remains largely unimpressed. The latest scientific conjecture regarding such visions of the afterlife is that they are
little more than euphoric, dreamlike states produced by declining oxy-
gen levels in the brain during the process of dying. As a result, scientists
continue to argue that near-death experiences are dependent upon brain
functioning—that is, upon the reduced levels of brain functioning that

occur while the brain is in the process of dying. Theorists who suggest otherwise are deemed unconventional at best, and "wacko" at worst.

The ancients, however, held a completely different view: All forms of individual consciousness are rooted ultimately in a universal field of pure consciousness, which does not die when the body dies. In this regard, the ancient spiritual science was rooted in a fundamental conservation principle, which involves the conservation of consciousness. By comparison, modern physical science holds onto the conservation of mass-energy, which states that mass-energy can be neither created nor destroyed; it can only change forms. This is consistent with the modern field-theory view of mass-energy.

Similarly, ancient spiritual science was rooted in the principle that consciousness can be neither created nor destroyed; it can only change forms. This is consistent with the ancient field-theory view of consciousness. Given this principle, we can assert that the type of consciousness possessed by the soul after death may be different from that possessed during life, but it is still a form of consciousness. This offers hope, at least in principle, that the soul might realize a form of spiritual immortality in which consciousness survives the death of the physical body.

Yet the prospect of spiritual immortality was not just a religious platitude to which the ancients paid lip service. It was the dominant force in the earliest cultures and civilizations. It guided not only the affairs and expenditures of the state but also the daily lives of the people. In fact, the attainment of spiritual immortality was deemed the ultimate purpose of life, the universe, and everything. In time, however, this driving purpose was destined to become lost. Even during the Hellenistic era, when the Hermetic texts were being composed, the general view was that the common human had given up on the hope of spiritual immortality and had surrendered to death. One Hermetic sage therefore cried out: "O men, why have you given yourselves up to death, when you have been granted the power to partake of immortality?"[6]

It can be said first and foremost that the ancient spiritual science was a science of immortality. It dealt with how the individual human mind can become identified with the divine mind—the all-pervading field of pure consciousness—and then expand its range of intuitive comprehension over the entire spectrum of creation and even beyond creation.

Secondarily, it was a science about the universe and everything. This follows naturally from the ancient notion that the ultimate field that created the universe and everything is none other than a field of pure consciousness. When the enlightened soul becomes identified with that field and expands its intuitive comprehension over the full spectrum of creation, it becomes a knower of the universe and everything. It then develops the ability to see what no physical eye can see, to hear what no physical ear can hear, and to know, directly and intuitively, what the ordinary human mind cannot know.

Such enlightened souls who possessed the eyes to see and the ears to hear the otherwise hidden universal reality were deemed sages or seers. It was on the basis of their all-embracing universal vision that the ancient spiritual science was formulated.

THE REVIVAL OF SPIRITUAL WISDOM

Although the sages predicted that their spiritual science would be lost, they also predicted that eventually it would be rediscovered. Toward this end, they wrote their sacred texts, mapped out their sacred lands, and designed their sacred monuments for posterity—for the sake of a future generation that might be more worthy to receive them. For example, the Hermetic sages prayed: "Ye holy books, which have been written by my perishable hands, but have been anointed with the drug of imperishability by Him who is the master over all, remain ye undecaying through all the ages, and be ye unseen and undiscovered by all men who go to and fro on the plains of this land, until the time when Heaven, grown old, shall beget beings worthy of you."[7]

Over the course of the last three centuries, many ancient texts, sites, and monuments, which were previously lost and forgotten, have been rediscovered. For the first time in history, we now have access to ancient sacred texts from all around the world. These were once the exclusive province of the elite classes and secretive cults and are largely written in a highly symbolic code language unique to the cultures from which the texts originate. Our goal here is to crack the code of the ancient spiritual science so that the science possessed by different cultures can be compared and evaluated in the light of modern empirical science. To accomplish this we must adopt a heuristic approach.

THE HEURISTIC APPROACH

The term *heuristic* comes from the same Greek root as *eureka,* which means "to find." In essence, a heuristic approach to problem solving involves a way of directing our attention fruitfully toward a solution by simultaneously drawing upon many analogies, models, and sources of insight, which may or may not, at first glance, appear to be related.

Thus good heuristics depend critically upon an appropriate choice of the various systems and sources of knowledge that will be brought to bear upon the problem-solving process. As such, the heuristic approach is more of an art than a science, for it requires some degree of intuition as to which seemingly disparate systems of knowledge might have relevance to a given problem.

In our heuristic approach to rediscover the lost ancient science, we will draw upon two very different and apparently unrelated bodies of knowledge:

- The body of ancient spiritual knowledge as recorded in sacred literatures all around the world
- The body of modern physical knowledge as recorded in peer-reviewed scientfic journals around the world

In particular, we will draw upon the sacred literatures of the ancient Vedic, Egyptian, Hebrew, and Hermetic traditions, for which there are abundant surviving texts, and the theories of quantum mechanics and general relativity, which are our most accurate modern scientific theories.

Although the heuristic approach often results in little more than a general rule of thumb that merely points the way to an actual solution, it can reduce dramatically the time required to reach a solution by eliminating the need to consider unlikely possibilities or irrelevant models.

A SPIRITUAL-SCIENTIFIC JOURNEY

We are on a quest to rediscover the lost spiritual science of the ancient seers. In the process, we will go on a long, spiritual-scientific journey—a journey of pure knowledge—that will take us throughout the boundaries of the known universe and beyond.

Hold onto your hats, because this journey will likely challenge your most cherished preconceived notions of reality. During the course of our travels, we will discover that the ancient spiritual science was a genuine *science* from which accurate, empirical predictions can be made about the overall organization of the universe. Yet rather than being taken from the perspective of ordinary, empirical observation, our journey will be taken from the perspective of enlightened consciousness on its way to obtain full immortality in the bosom of the infinite.

This perspective results in a completely different view of the universe than that provided by mere empirical observation. More specifically, it results in a layered vision of the universe as a living reality in which each and every thing, over the full spectrum of space-time scales, must be viewed as alive and endowed with consciousness. The ancients therefore conceived the universe as living and rooted in a universal field of consciousness. The layers of the living universe represent layers of consciousness, which can be understood as various universal fields of consciousness. The ancients compared the process of traversing these layers to the process of ascending (and descending) a divine ladder or stairway to the sky. Moreover, they understood this divine ladder or stairway as the path of immortality.

That path is the principle subject of this book. Our job will be to understand the path in light of modern scientific concepts rooted in a field-theory framework. This will involve translating some of the most abstract and profound spiritual ideas ever conceived by the human mind into a concrete model involving a spectrum of self-conscious fields, each of which is characterized by a particular space-time scale.

Although this might sound like a hopeless task, the fact is that the ancients have paved the way. We will see that they possessed a secret system of measured arrangement by which they estimated the space-time scales associated with the various layers. In this sense, the ancient system is mathematical; it can be translated into the language of mathematics—the universal language of science.

Upon inspecting this system and evaluating it in light of modern empirical evidence, we will discover that it can be used to predict accurately the most fundamental scales of cosmological organization discovered so far on the basis of general relativity as well as the most fundamental scales of force-matter unification discovered so far on the basis of quantum theory.

More important, we will discover that the ancient system can be used to predict accurately a hidden vertical symmetry between the two sets of scales, in accordance with the ancient principle "as above, so below." Given the fact that this symmetry remains unknown in modern theory, the only possible conclusion is that the ancients possessed a genuine spiritual science that rivals and in certain ways surpasses the most advanced physical theories of today.

The implications regarding the origins of human culture and the knowledge possessed by the earliest cultures are exceedingly profound. We are dealing here with a historical and scientific mystery of the highest order.

ORGANIZATION OF THE MATERIAL

Our journey will require some preparation. Before we can begin, we first have to clarify the ancient worldview and discuss the general principles upon which it was based.

We must examine the field-theory view of consciousness in more detail and develop a terminology appropriate to that view. In this regard, the ancients commonly referred to the fields of consciousness as universal gods. We can therefore characterize the ancient theory regarding these fields as a science of the gods.

The first few chapters that follow elaborate on a general field theory of consciousness and outline the mechanics by which individual human consciousness can be identified with the universal field of consciousness. According to the ancient teachings, this identification marks the onset of spiritual enlightenment. Yet the mere attainment of spiritual enlightenment marks not the end of the path, but the very beginning. It is only after enlightenment that the real journey begins—the step-by-step journey toward full immortality in the bosom of the infinite. That is the journey we will undertake, at least in principle, in this book.

To prepare for these travels, we first must enlighten ourselves—at least intellectually—regarding the nature of human consciousness and its relation to the field of pure consciousness. Once the general principles have been laid out and the ancient science of the gods has been outlined, we will begin our journey by examining the major milestones along the path.

This will culminate in a new (yet very old) picture of the universe and the role of human beings within it—something about which modern science is largely mute. Whether you agree with the interpretation presented here or not, it is hoped that you will enjoy the journey.

1
The Philosophy of Enlightenment

WHAT IS REAL?

For thousands of years philosophers have debated about what is real. Yet if you were to ask a common person on the street if the world that he or she sees is real, then the answer would be almost invariably yes.

The fact is that the human mind tends to assign external objective reality to its sensory perceptions. For example, take the perception of an apple: If an apple is placed on the kitchen table and we are then asked whether or not the apple is real or imaginary, almost everyone would agree that it is real because we can see it, touch it, smell it, taste it, and even hear its crunch as we bite into it. No one doubts the reality of the external world, because it is the realm of our common experience. According to the ancients, however, what we perceive as the external world is not external at all, but is rather an appearance in consciousness—a set of mental impressions created within our own mind. This may seem paradoxical, but such an understanding is consistent with modern scientific principles.

Take the process of visual perception. According to modern physics, an apple is composed of atoms. In order to see the apple, the atoms must emit electromagnetic waves that propagate from the apple to our eyes. When the electromagnetic waves impinge upon the retina of the eye, they induce certain structural and chemical changes. These changes, in turn, stimulate the nerve cells in the eye. Nerve impulses then travel along nerve fibers from the eye to the visual cortex of the brain, where they cause the cells of the brain to fire in certain patterns. Based upon this brain activity, a mental impression of the object is created in the mind.

At this point in the process, however, modern science must insert a big black box, indicating that the mechanics are unknown. We do not yet understand how brain activity structures a mental impression on the level of consciousness. All we know is that certain types of brain activity have the potential to give rise to certain types of mental impressions.

Once the mental impression has been created, it is then experienced as a pattern of color within the mind. We interpret this pattern of color intellectually as an apple on the table—but in truth, we never actually see the apple; all we see is a pattern of color created within our mind on the basis of brain activity.

This same process can be applied to all five senses: sight, hearing, taste, touch, and smell. In every case, the senses stimulate the brain, which then gives rise to a mental impression created within the mind. All we ever actually experience on the basis of sensory perception are our own mental impressions of the world; we never actually experience the world as it is in itself. Nevertheless, we externalize our mental impressions so that they are conceived as the objective realities of the world. In the final analysis, this represents a mistake of the intellect: The effect is mistaken for the cause.

In the Vedic tradition, this type of false attribution, where one thing is mistaken for another, was called superimposition (*abhasya*), which may be understood as a form of ignorance or illusion. The common analogy used to explain this concept concerns a snake and a rope: In a dark room we might see a coil of rope and mistake it for a snake. Because of this perception, adrenaline is pumped through the system, and we experience a state of fear. In truth there is no reason to be afraid. The fear has its source in the false notion that the rope is a snake. In this analogy, the coil of rope represents our mental impression of the world, while the snake represents our mistaken belief that this mental impression is an external object.

Plato used another analogy to explain the same concept: Since the time of their birth, a certain number of individuals are chained as a group within a cave, with the back of each of them facing the entrance. Each can see only the shadows cast upon the cave wall by the light coming through the entrance. Because of this, only the shadows of objects—never the objects themselves—can be seen. As a result, the people in the group take the shadows to be the actual objects of the real world. In this analogy, the cave represents the mind, the chains represent the senses, and the shadows represent the mental impressions of the external world created within the mind through the agency of the senses. There is no way—especially using philosophical arguments—to convince those within the cave that the shadows are not real; every person in the group literally sees them. Because "seeing is believing," the only way to dispel the illusion is to cut the chains and lead the individuals out of the cave into the light, so that they can see for themselves the otherwise hidden reality of the real world.

Thus, the radical solution proposed by the ancients involved breaking the attachment to the physical senses and transcending the cave of the human mind. Only then can we enter into the light of the real world—the world as it is in itself. Those who accomplished this miraculous feat were said to be enlightened, and were deemed true seers.

TWO DIFFERENT TYPES OF REALITY

Spiritual enlightenment occurs when the limitations of the human mind and senses have been transcended and the awareness begins to operate on the basis of the universal field of consciousness that underlies all things. Rather than being a matter of faith or belief, this is a matter of direct intuitive experience.

In an enlightened state, the reality of the world is experienced very differently from how it is experienced in an unenlightened state. It is no longer perceived by all senses as an external, objective reality. Instead, it is experienced for what it is: an internal, subjective reality or a mere appearance in consciousness.

In this regard, the enlightened sages distinguished between two different but interrelated types of reality: In Greek philosophy, the empirical appearance of the world, which is rooted in the experience of the empirical mind, was called the *physical Cosmos,* while the transcendental reality of the world rooted in the experience of the divine mind, or field of pure consciousness, was called the *metaphysical Logos.* Those who are enlightened see both: By means of the empirical mind they see the reality of the physical Cosmos, and through the field of pure consciousness they see the reality of the metaphysical Logos. The sober conclusion of such enlightened sages was that the metaphysical Logos serves as the hidden cause of the physical Cosmos. In other words, the Logos represents the world as it is in itself and the hidden cause of the mental impressions created within the mind.

THE METAPHYSICAL LOGOS

In the Greek tradition, the metaphysical Logos was viewed as the indestructible structure of divine wisdom inherent within the divine mind, and it was suggested that these pure ideas exist independently of the human mind. They were often described as the ideal forms or eternal archetypes that underlie all empirical appearances, and therefore represent the true form of everything prior to the appearance of mental impressions within the human mind.

These pure ideas were also described as forms of divine speech. In the same way that we can compare a sequence of ideas within the human mind to a form of mental speech, which we use to talk to ourselves, the Greeks compared the sequence of ideas within the divine mind to a form of divine speech, which God uses to talk to himself. For this reason, the term *logos* is often translated as "speech" or "word." The Logos was commonly viewed as embodying the word of God or the thought of God.

In the same way that a speaker is identified with his or her speech or a thinker is identified with his or her thoughts, the relation between God and the Logos was viewed as one of identity. This is precisely the view expressed in the opening passage of the Gospel of John in which the original Greek Logos is commonly translated as the Word. We can substitute the original term:

> When all things began, the Logos [Word] already was. The Logos dwelt with God, and what God was, the Logos was. The Logos, then, was with God at the beginning, and through him all things came to be; no single thing was created without him. All that came to be was alive with his life, and that life was the light of men. The light shines on in the darkness, and the darkness has never mastered it.[1]

We can translate this into more modern scientific terms. If we equate the subjective essence of God and the field of pure consciousness, then the elementary excitations of the field can be described as sonic and luminous in nature. Whereas the sonic modes constitute the sound of consciousness, the luminous modes constitute the light of consciousness. In the ancient Vedic tradition, the vibratory modes of pure consciousness were described as forms of transcendental sound (*param nada*) and transcendental light (*param jyotih*). Here, the sages were talking about virtual waves of sound and light—which transcend all means of direct empirical observation.

THE VIRTUAL REALITY OF THE LOGOS

In modern quantum theory, the universe is described as having a vibratory basis such that each elementary particle can be described equivalently as the wavelike excitation of a quantum field. This is called the *wave-particle duality*.

Yet two different types of particles and waves—*real* and

virtual—are described by the theory. A real particle or wave is one that can be observed empirically, at least in principle. A virtual particle or wave is one that cannot be observed empirically, even in principle. In spite of their nonobservable nature, virtual particles and waves are required by the principles of the theory. In fact, the theory holds that the vacuum of so-called empty space is filled with virtual particles and waves.

In practice, real particles and waves constitute the subject matter of physics and the real or observable reality of the universe, which the ancients referred to as the physical Cosmos. In theory, however, virtual particles and waves must also be accepted as inherent in the vacuum of empty space. Such particles and waves constitute the virtual or hidden reality of the universe, which the ancients referred to as the metaphysical Logos. In this way, the modern scientific distinction between what is real and virtual is reflected in the ancient philosophical distinction between the physical Cosmos and metaphysical Logos.

THE CAUSAL NATURE OF THE LOGOS

According to quantum theory, every atom in creation is subject to spontaneous jumps in its electron energy states, which result in the emission of real light. These are called spontaneous emissions. In the same way, every elementary particle in creation is subject to spontaneous fluctuations in its energy, momentum, and position states. These are called quantum fluctuations.

The actual causes of these emissions and fluctuations are unknown, but it is generally presumed that these causes are inherent in the virtual reality of the quantum vacuum. The Standard Model of quantum theory makes no attempt to describe these hidden causes explicitly. The emissions and fluctuations are simply accepted as the way things are—though they literally determine the empirical appearance of the universe.

Thus, from an ancient philosophical point of view, the hidden causes that determine ultimately the behavior of every atom and elementary particle in creation can be attributed to the metaphysical Logos—the virtual reality of the quantum vacuum. For this reason, the metaphysical Logos was viewed as the hidden cause of the physical Cosmos.

HIDDEN INFLUENCES

In the Vedic tradition, this hidden influence of the metaphysical Logos was called the *adrishta*—the unseen influence, and rather than being viewed as an objective influence coming from any physical source, it was seen to be subjective and arising from the will of the gods or God, the hidden fields of universal consciousness that underlie the observable reality of the universe.

Such fields correspond to universal vacuum states inherent within the unified field. According to the ancients, each of these fields, or vacuum states, is characterized by its own modes of transcendental sound and light, which correspond to the virtual excitations of the field. These virtual excitations represent the hidden or unseen influences that ultimately govern the behavior of all observable things.

In this regard, we can assume the existence of two different types of hidden influence: *local* and *nonlocal*. A local influence propagates at the speed of light, while a nonlocal influence propagates faster than light—at the speed of thought. These two types can be attributed to the modes of transcendental light and transcendental sound, respectively. The Standard Model of quantum theory deals exclusively with the local modes of the quantum vacuum. These are invariably modeled as transverse waves that propagate locally at the speed of light.

There is no notion in the Standard Model that the quantum vacuum is also pervaded by modes of transcendental sound (which would correspond to longitudinal waves that propagate nonlocally at the speed of thought). Yet the axiomatic formulation of quantum theory allows such nonlocal influences, at least in principle.

In the 1950s a mathematical proof was developed on the basis of the axiomatic formulation of quantum theory: Bell's Theorem, which pertains to any "hidden variable" theory that might hope to go beyond the Standard Model by providing an explicit description of the hidden influences that underlie the quantum fluctuations. Bell's Theorem proves that any such theory will necessarily be nonlocal and must include hidden, nonlocal influences within its formulation. In other words, if we want to describe the hidden causes of quantum fluctuations, then in addition to invoking hidden local influences, which propagate at the speed of light, we must also invoke hidden nonlocal influences, which propagate faster than light. The ancients referred to these two types of hidden (virtual) influences as modes of transcendental light and transcendental sound, respectively.

THE SUBSTANCE OF CONSCIOUSNESS

Like all real light waves, the local modes of transcendental light may be viewed as having transverse waveforms, and like all real sound waves, the nonlocal modes of transcendental sound have longitudinal waveforms. In spite of their differences in waveform (transverse and longitudinal) and speed (local and nonlocal), however, the ancients—especially Hermetic sages—held that these two types of modes are not separate. One sage described his initial experience of enlightenment this way: "I beheld a boundless view; all was changed into Light, a mild and joyous Light; and I marveled when I saw it. . . . And . . . from the Light there came forth a holy Word [Logos], which took its stand upon the watery substance; and me thought this Word [Logos] to be the voice of the Light. . . . They are not separate one from the other."[2]

This amounts to an intuitive cognition of the virtual quantum vacuum experienced as a field of pure consciousness. The modes of light and sound are said to have their basis in a watery substance, which serves as their underlying medium. This is consistent with the fact that in virtually all of the ancient traditions, the field of pure consciousness was assigned a fluidlike nature. For example, in the ancient

Egyptian tradition the field of pure consciousness was called the *nun,* the "watery abyss." The metaphysical Logos, which takes its stand upon the watery abyss, was called the Duat, or "underworld"—that is, the invisible virtual world that underlies the visible universe.

In the Vedic tradition, the field of pure consciousness was identified with God, the Supreme Being, in his form as Narayana, "the abode of the waters." The metaphysical Logos was called the Veda—the indestructible structure of pure knowledge inherent within the field of pure consciousness, which serves as the basis for the observable universe. The fluidlike substance of the field was called *dravya,* from the root *dru,* "to flow." A fluid is defined generally as any substance that has the ability to flow, but the fluidlike substance of pure consciousness was conceived not as a physical substance, but as a metaphysical one— literally, the substance of consciousness itself.

Although pure consciousness is not a material substance, the Vedic seers held that it could nevertheless be compared to a material substance in that it has the ability to move and flow: "It is pure consciousness, [which is] birthless, motionless, and nonmaterial, as well as tranquil and nondual, that has the semblance of birth, appears to move, and simulates a material substance."[3]

In the Hermetic texts the metaphysical substance of consciousness was called Mind—the very substance of God. "Mind . . . is the very substance of God, if indeed there is a substance of God, and of what nature that substance is, God alone knows precisely."[4]

In spite of its abstract and metaphysical nature, the substance of consciousness was compared to a fluid in that it has the ability to flow in both streams and waves.

THE HOLY GRAIL AND THE HOLY BLOOD

In the Rig Veda, the oldest and most authoritative of the ancient Vedic texts, the flowing essence of consciousness was called *soma,* the drink by which the gods attain immortality, and *amrita rasa,* "immortal blood." This has deep connotations to the myth of the Holy Grail.

The immortal blood corresponds to the fluidlike essence of consciousness, which may be compared to the waters of life. The immortal vessel that contains the waters of life or the immortal blood is none other than God—the field of pure consciousness. This is the essential meaning of Narayana. As the very substance of God, the immortal water or immortal blood was viewed as cosubstantial with the immortal God; the immortal blood and immortal vessel were viewed as one.

This notion is reflected in the myth of the Holy Grail, which can be translated from the French as "holy vessel" (*san greal*) or "holy blood" (*sang real*). According to this myth, the very sight of the holy vessel or taste of the holy blood is enough to render the wasteland whole and the soul immortal.

THE SUPERFLUID VACUUM

As we have seen, the ancient intuitive descriptions suggest that the modes of transcendental light and sound exist as correlated components of a single, unified wave field that may be compared to a metaphysical fluid field. There is one trouble spot in this theory, however.

We know that a classical fluid is incapable of supporting transverse waves of any kind and can support only longitudinal waves—like sound waves. At first glance, this would appear to contradict the notion that the fluid field of consciousness can support both modes of transcendental light (corresponding to transverse waves) and modes of transcendental sound (corresponding to longitudinal waves).

Nevertheless, there is a way around this dilemma. According to the ancients, the modes of transcendental sound and light are both quantum waves, which can be modeled as harmonic waves and represented by harmonic ratios. In the fifth century BCE, this notion was outlined originally in the harmonic theory of Pythagoras. Due to the harmonic ratios inherent within the field, the term *logos* is often translated as "ratio." The implication is that the fluid of pure consciousness must correspond to a *quantum fluid* rather than a classical one.

Quantum fluids were first discovered in the twentieth century, with one of the most common being a superfluid such as superfluid helium. This is created when ordinary fluid helium, which behaves like a classical fluid, undergoes a phase transition at very low kinetic temperatures. Unlike a classical fluid, a superfluid displays the property of quantum wholeness, meaning that it behaves as a single, nonlocally correlated quantum whole, rather than as a collection of individual fluid particles subject to random, independent motions. In this sense, a superfluid can be compared to the field of pure consciousness, which the ancients believed behaves as a single quantum whole, or a single conscious Being whose will simultaneously and nonlocally governs the behavior of all its parts.

Like an ordinary classical fluid, a superfluid is capable of supporting longitudinal sound waves. Unlike a classical fluid, however, superfluid sound waves also have transverse components resembling closely electromagnetic waves in the vacuum of empty space. The theoretical prediction of such transverse components was made in the 1950s, but the empirical verification of the prediction did not come until 1999, when the transverse components of superfluid sound in helium II were first detected in a laboratory experiment.[5] The researchers reasoned that because the transverse components must involve displacements of the fluid transverse to the direction of wave propagation, the components should define a polarization direction similar to that of electromagnetic waves.

The transverse components of superfluid sound were detected by rotating the polarization of the waves in the presence of a magnetic field. The researchers suggested that this is the acoustic analogue of the magneto-optic Faraday effect, whereby the polarization direction of an electromagnetic wave is rotated by a magnetic field applied along the propagation direction.

Therefore, we can argue that if the fluid of consciousness is capable of supporting both longitudinal sound waves and transverse light waves, as implied by ancient descriptions, then its behavior must resemble that of a quantum fluid such as superfluid helium. The ancient notion that these two types of waves are not separate from each other is consistent with the fact that the transverse and longitudinal waves in superfluid helium are complementary components of the same wave phenomenon. In other words, the ancient theory suggests that the field of pure consciousness behaves like a superfluid vacuum or a superfluid wave field.

The upshot is that the ancient intuitive descriptions of the field are consistent with both quantum theory and the theory of quantum fluids. Although these descriptions are couched in philosophic and spiritual terms, they appear to have a sound scientific basis—at least, if we accept the premise that the universe is rooted in an underlying subjective reality, an all-pervading field of consciousness.

Now that we have discussed the philosophy of enlightenment, we can ask how a person becomes enlightened. What are the mechanics involved?

2

The Mechanics of Enlightenment

THE AGE-OLD DILEMMA

The ancients drew a sharp distinction between those who were enlightened and those who were not. Whereas the enlightened mind has the ability to experience directly both the hidden reality of the Logos and the empirical reality of the Cosmos, the unenlightened mind is left with the empirical experience of the Cosmos alone.

Those who are unenlightened have no recourse except either to accept or reject the teachings of the enlightened sages on the basis of faith or belief. They have no way to confirm teachings on the basis of direct intuitive experience. This has been the age-old dilemma faced by sages throughout history: How do we convey the truth about the hidden, nonlocal reality of the universe to those who have no direct experience of that reality?

Like the people in Plato's cave, it is not easy for us to accept the notion that the concrete and tangible world that we perceive around us is but a shadow of reality. We see the world around us as very real, and no philosophical or theoretical arguments are likely to convince us otherwise. The sages concluded that ultimately, it was a waste of time to try to teach their "science" to the unenlightened. Rather, they provided various childlike, colorful stories in which the deeper scientific principles were personified and explained through the characters of gods and mythical individuals. The real science hidden behind the myths was reserved for those who attained enlightenment and who therefore had an experiential basis for understanding the teachings. In this way, the ancient spiritual science evolved into an initiatory tradition in which initiates were given knowledge in accordance with their experience. These initiates were classified into two groups:

- Those who were still striving to become enlightened
- Those who were already enlightened

Yet even among the enlightened, there were various degrees of enlightenment. Some enlightened individuals were viewed as masters.

PRACTICE AND THEORY

Those who were not yet enlightened were given what was called the lower knowledge pertaining to the various practices that serve to pave the way for the dawn of enlightenment. These practices included meditation techniques, ritualistic performances, dietary regimens, and codes of behavior, all of which were designed to purify the soul so that it would become a fit receptacle for the onset of spiritual wisdom.

Those who were already enlightened were given what was called the higher knowledge, which, instead of being related to any practice, was purely theoretical in nature. It pertained to the structures and dynamics of consciousness over a vast spectrum of space-time scales, and had to do with both how these structures and dynamics are related to the overall organization of the physical universe and the ultimate goal of enlightenment: to obtain full immortality in the bosom of the infinite.

In effect, the higher knowledge was designed to provide a road map for those enlightened souls who were on the path of immortality. The unenlightened, however, did not need this type of knowledge because they were merely on the preliminary stages of the path and had not yet begun the real journey. As a result, the higher knowledge was kept secret and reserved for the elite classes of enlightened sages. It may have been encoded in sacred texts and diagrams, alluded to in popular myths, and even mapped out on the sacred lands—but it was not made explicit to the unenlightened public.

In addition to these two types of knowledge, there was a third, intermediate type, which pertained to the actual mechanics of enlightenment: how the soul escapes from the bondage of ignorance and becomes free eternally.

THE STATE OF PURE IGNORANCE

The various practices prescribed by the sages were designed to deliver the soul to a unique state of consciousness, which can be characterized as a state of pure ignorance. It was also viewed as a state of pure consciousness. According to one Vedic text, there are at least 112 different ways to arrive at this state, at least temporarily.

One of the most commonly used methods involved the practice of meditation—like Transcendental Meditation as taught all over the world by Maharishi Mahesh Yogi in modern times. The purpose of these meditative techniques was to allow the mind to settle down to increasingly subtle levels of the thinking process so that it could fathom finer and more abstract thoughts. The process of transcending was often compared to following the sound of a struck bell as it fades into silence. When the most subtle level of the thinking process is transcended, we experience an unbounded state of silent darkness as tranquil as a waveless sea and as transparent as the night sky devoid of stars. In this state, there are no thoughts, no sensations, no emotions, and no active form of cognition. The entire world and everything in it, including all notions of time and space, are completely forgotten or ignored. For this reason, the sages often described it as a state of pure ignorance.

Yet this state of pure ignorance represents not a state of unconsciousness, but a state of pure consciousness in which consciousness is left alone without any object of cognition. All that remains is the subject of cognition—the knower. According to the ancients, this ignorant knower underlies all cognitions of the thinking human mind. The sages concluded that as a result, all conceptions of the unenlightened human mind are rooted in pure ignorance. By transcending the thinking process, the soul comes to know the truth regarding its unenlightened experience. It comes to know that all such experience is founded in ignorance.

The unbounded field of silent darkness experienced on the level of pure consciousness actually has an objective counterpart. It corresponds to the vacuum of outer space—the field of silent darkness that lies between all the stars and galaxies, and that appears to be empty or vacuous. The subjective cognition of the unbounded vacuum state during the practice of meditation occurs initially in a transient manner. It is cognized between two sets of thoughts. As the practice progresses, the thoughtless state is experienced for longer and longer periods. In the end, it becomes permanent.

The permanent realization of the thoughtless state marks a major milestone on the preliminary path to enlightenment: It marks the necessary precursor for the dawn of enlightenment. It can be compared to the darkest hour of the night before the dawn.

THE SLEEPLESS STATE

Those who have permanently realized the thoughtless state are not incapacitated; rather, they are dichotomized. Their awareness becomes twofold: On one hand, they experience the thoughtless state of pure consciousness, and on the other, they experience the ordinary process of thinking.

Permanent realization of the thoughtless state means that it persists along with all three ordinary states of consciousness: waking, dreaming, and sleeping. Those who realize the thoughtless state permanently were often called the sleepless ones. Unlike others, who experience a state of unconsciousness during deep sleep, the sleepless ones do not.

Instead, they experience the thoughtless state of pure consciousness even when the body and mind are asleep; they remain awake but devoid of thought. One Hermetic sage described his experience of the sleepless state: "My bodily sleep had come to be sober wakefulness of soul."[1]

In this sense, the sleepless ones experience a very different type of consciousness from ordinary people, which has nothing to do with faith or belief and relates only to direct experience.

THE DEATH OF THE INDIVIDUAL EGO

The sleepless ones were also described as egoless. The Sanskrit term for ego is *ahamkara*, "I do" or "I am the doer." This "doing" includes not only the action of the body, but also the action of the mind.

As long as the soul identifies with the activity of the human mind and body, it conceives itself as the thinker and doer. The thoughts of the mind are conceived as *my* thoughts and the actions of the body are conceived as *my* actions. According to the seers, all such notions of *me* and *mine* are manifestations of the individual ego, which binds the soul to the individual mind and body through a process of identification.

In order for the thoughtless state to become permanent, the soul's identification must shift. Rather than being identified with the human body and mind, which perform the process of thinking and doing, the soul must become identified with the field of pure consciousness, which is devoid of all thinking and doing. The permanent realization of the thoughtless state results in the death of the individual ego. Such souls no longer conceive the thoughts of the mind as *my* thoughts or the actions of the body as *my* actions. The egoless soul remains an uninvolved witness to the thoughts of the mind and the actions of the body, as though all thoughts and actions were carried out by an unseen hand—without any involvement on the part of the soul.

In the Vedic tradition, this was described as the desireless state of renunciation. Because it is established in the actionless state of pure consciousness, the soul has no desire to participate in the world from which it has become alienated. Effectively, it has renounced the world. The mind and body continue to participate in the world, but they do so completely on their own.

The ancients held that to become spiritually enlightened, first the individual ego must die—we must die to this world before we can be reborn in the other world. This means not that the physical body must die, but that the individual ego, which binds the soul to this world by means of desire, must die. The death of the individual ego is accomplished by the repeated experience of the state of pure consciousness in which all thoughts and desires are transcended. By repeated experience, the soul realizes that state eventually as its own eternal self. This realization, which happens in an instant, results immediately in the death of the individual ego. From that point forward, the soul becomes devoid of individual ego and all the desires associated with it; it simultaneously becomes egoless and sleepless.

THE SEA OF DEATH

The soul that is sleepless and egoless is caught in a state of limbo: It has died to this world, but is not yet reborn in the other world. While this is not particularly upsetting, it results in a rather dry experience of reality in which nothing in this world holds much interest.

Such a soul was said to be drowned in the sea of death. In actuality, it is drowned in the sea of pure ignorance. Upon looking at the world around it, the soul sees that everything has a beginning and end in the field of pure ignorance—the sea of death. As a result, the joys and pleasures of the world, which others hold so dear, become like dry sawdust in the mouth.

The old saying "ignorance is bliss" may hold true for all those who do not know what true ignorance is—but the soul that knows the state of pure ignorance experiences it not as a state of bliss, but as an abstract nothing. It is experienced as a sea of death. To escape from this state and realize eternal bliss, the soul must first cross the sea of death.

Yet this is easier said than done. The soul that is drowned in the sea of death is incapable of doing anything that might help it to cross that sea. The thoughts of the mind and the actions of the body are not its own, but are carried out by something or someone else. As a result, the egoless soul can do nothing, think nothing, and feel nothing—so how can it possibly cross the sea of death?

KNOWLEDGE AND IGNORANCE

The Vedic seers were well aware of this problem, but they had a solution presented in the form of a mysterious aphorism concerning the relation between knowledge and ignorance: "Knowledge and ignorance—whoever knows these two together, crosses over death by means of ignorance (*avidya*), and attains eternal life by means of knowledge (*vidya*)."[2]

What does this mean? The sea of death is crossed by means of pure ignorance—that is, by remaining awake in the state of pure ignorance without harboring any desire for the things in this world. Those who are capable of remaining awake in the state of silent darkness—whether waking, dreaming, or sleeping—will be delivered eventually to the other shore, the shore of eternal life, by the will of God, without any effort whatsoever on their part. Upon arriving at the other shore, they will attain eternal life by means of pure knowledge.

The solution is simple: The soul must wait in the state of pure ignorance, without any desire or sense of expectation, like a babe in the womb or a corpse in the tomb, until it is delivered from that state by the grace of God.

THE MYTH OF OSIRIS

Insight into these mechanics is provided by the Egyptian myth of Osiris. According to the Hellenistic version of the myth, the god-king Osiris was tricked by his brother Set and Set's conspirators to try out a specially constructed coffin to see if it would fit. Once Osiris climbed inside, the conspirators sealed him in it alive. He was doomed to death in the silent darkness of the coffin.

The coffin was then set afloat on the Nile River, where the currents carried it out into the Mediterranean Sea. It then floated across the sea to the shores of Byblos, an ancient port city on the coast of Lebanon, where the body of Osiris was eventually found and then resurrected. Upon this resurrection, Osiris renounced his worldly kingdom, ascended the stairway to the sky, and attained eternal life among the gods, where he became known as the Lord of Immortality.

This provides an example of the type of childlike myth offered by the sages to educate the unenlightened in their mysterious ways. The story, however, has a deeper meaning. The body of Osiris represents the individual ego (which here ruled over the land of Egypt as its king). The coffin represents the state of pure ignorance, the tomb of the individual ego, where it is destined to die in total silence and darkness. The Mediterranean Sea represents the sea of death, which Osiris had to cross to reach the other shore, the shore of eternal life. The currents in the sea, represent, in the story, the will of God that carries Osiris to the other shore. The currents serve to deliver the soul to eternal life without any action on the part of the soul. The resurrection of the body of Osiris represents the resurrection of the ego not as the individual ego, but as the universal ego—which is possessed by all enlightened souls.

The myth of Osiris therefore presents a spiritual allegory concerning the mechanics by which the soul becomes enlightened and endowed with a universal rather than an individual ego. This qualifies it to ascend the stairway to the sky and realize full immortality in the bosom of the infinite.

THE DOCTRINE OF SPIRITUAL REBIRTH

In many ancient traditions, becoming spiritually enlightened was compared to a process of spiritual rebirth. For this reason, the Vedic seers (*rishis*) were often called twice-born seers (*dvija-rishis*): First, they were born as ordinary human beings in this physical world, and then they were reborn as enlightened seers in the metaphysical world—the world of pure knowledge.

This doctrine can also be found in the Hermetic texts in which an entire chapter (Libvells XIII) is devoted to the subject of spiritual rebirth. The doctrine is presented in the form of a discourse between the immortal sage Hermes and his mortal son Tat.

First, Tat declares that, as his father has advised him, he has become alienated from the world and is now fit to receive the doctrine. This means that he has become egoless, that he has died to this world. Yet when Tat asks his father to explain the mysterious doctrine of spiritual rebirth, Hermes replies:

> What can I say, my son? This thing cannot be taught, and it is not possible for you to see it with your organs of sight, which are fashioned out of material elements. I can tell you nothing but this—I see that by God's mercy there has come to be in me a form which is not fashioned out of matter, and I have passed forth out of myself, and entered into an immortal body. I am not now the man that I was; I have been born again in Mind (*nous*), and the bodily shape which was mine before has been put away from me . . . To such eyes as yours, my son, I am not now visible.[3]

In response, Tat cries out in astonishment, for he can see his father clearly standing before him in a physical body, the same as always. Hermes goes on to explain that the immortal body is not composed of matter and cannot be seen by the physical eyes. It is an imperishable body of Logos that can be apprehended by itself alone. To realize the body of Logos, the soul must first be reborn as an immortal soul.

The text then tells us that Tat undergoes the process of spiritual rebirth, after which he proclaims: "Father, God has made me a new being, and I perceive things now, not with bodily eyesight, but by the working of Mind (*nous*). . . . Now that I see in Mind, I see myself to be the All. I am in heaven and earth, in water and air; I am in beasts and plants; I am a babe in the womb, and one that has not yet been conceived, and one that has been born. I am present everywhere."[4]

To this Hermes replies: "Now, my son, you know what the Rebirth is." The Hermetic doctrine, as we have seen, suggests that spiritual rebirth has nothing to do with faith or belief. It represents a profound transformation in consciousness, wherein the soul ceases to be identified with the mortal physical body and instead becomes identified with the immortal body of Logos—the body of pure knowledge inherent within the field of pure consciousness.

Because the Logos represents the all-pervading source of everything that exists, the reborn soul sees itself as present everywhere, in everything. It is no longer limited by the physical organs of sense, for it has developed the ability to see in Mind.

ENLIGHTENED PERCEPTION

The ability to see in Mind characterizes the nature of enlightened perception. Upon becoming identified with the field of pure consciousness, and having the veil of ignorance removed, the soul experiences a profound change in the self: That which was previously experienced as an empty field of silent darkness is now experienced as filled with modes of transcendental light and sound, which are both seen and heard. In other words, the emptiness is transformed into fullness.

Yet the modes of transcendental light and sound are not seen or heard by the physical organs of sense. Instead, they are perceived by the divine mind—the field of pure consciousness. According to the Vedic texts, this field contains all the qualities of the senses, even though it operates independently from the physical organs of sense. It has the ability to see without eyes, hear without ears, and so forth.

On the other hand, because the field of pure consciousness serves as the one eternal self of all beings, it can be said to have eyes, ears, heads, feet, and so on. It literally experiences the world through the senses of all beings. Regarding this extraordinary form of enlightened perception, the Vedic texts state:

> Its hands and feet are everywhere, its eyes and head are everywhere, its ears are everywhere, it stands encompassing all in the world. Separate from all the senses, yet reflecting the qualities of all the senses, it is the lord and ruler of all, it is the great refuge of all. . . . Grasping without hands, moving without feet, [the enlightened self] sees without eyes, hears without ears. He knows what can be known, but no one knows him.[5]

In order to know the enlightened self, the soul must become the enlightened self, for it can be known only by itself.

THE COSMIC WOMB

It can be said that the tomb of the individual ego also serves as a womb for the universal ego. The unbounded state of silent darkness serves not only as the death place for the individual ego, but also as the birthplace for the universal ego.

In the Vedic literature, this unbounded cosmic womb was personified as Aditi, the mother of all the gods and seers. The Sanskrit term *aditi* (*a* + *diti*) means "unbounded," but it can also be derived from *ad* + *iti,* which means "thus eating."

The unbounded state of pure ignorance was viewed as all-consuming, with the potential to consume the entire universe and everything in it, and reduce it to a mere nothingness, a mere emptiness. Yet from this emptiness is born the fullness of spiritual enlightenment. For this reason, the cosmic womb was viewed as the mother of all enlightened beings throughout the universe, whether they are conceived as universal gods or individual seers. It represents not only the end of all forms of individual life, but also the beginning of all forms of universal life—the type of life possessed by an enlightened soul. All such souls are deemed immortal. They may possess mortal bodies, which continue to operate in this world as before, but they also possess an immortal body of Logos.

THE DIAMOND THUNDERBOLT

The actual transition from mortality to immortality occurs in a single instant. It may take years or even lifetimes to prepare for this transition, but when it comes, it happens instantly—in a single flash of pure intuition.

The dawn of enlightenment requires the piercing of the veil of ignorance. The soul that is drowned in the sea of death, however, is incapable of piercing the veil on its own; it must rely on the will of God to deliver it from the cosmic womb at the appropriate time.

The Rig Veda presents an important myth—the story of the *vajra,* the diamond thunderbolt of Indra, the king of the gods—regarding this piercing of the veil. Indra represents the universal ego presiding over the visible universe and everything in it, and as such; he was viewed as the king of the gods, the one responsible for upholding the appearance of the visible universe.

The myth revolves around Indra's battle with a cosmic demon called Vritra (from the root *vrit,* which means "to cover or enclose"). From a subjective point of view, Vritra represents the veil of pure ignorance—the field of silent darkness that serves as the basis of the thinking mind. Objectively, he represents the veil of the physical vacuum—the field of silent darkness that serves as the basis for all the stars and galaxies. In both cases, this veil serves to cover, hide, or enclose the self-luminous field of pure knowledge from which is cognized the metaphysical Logos.

According to the myth, the enclosing demon Vritra was so powerful that he could not be destroyed by any of the individual sages or gods. Indra, the king of the gods, was deemed the only one who could vanquish him—with a special weapon called the vajra (a Sanskrit term that means both "diamond" and "thunderbolt"). The diamond thunderbolt of Indra was the only weapon capable of piercing the veil of silent darkness and thereby releasing the light and sound of consciousness, which was otherwise pent up and hidden by the veil. This divine weapon represents the flash of pure intuition that removes from the field the cover of silent darkness and reveals the transcendental sound and light that were there all along.

In silent darkness, the dawn of enlightenment begins with a swirling motion in consciousness—like a cosmic whirlpool—which catches the soul. It then delivers the soul to a previously unseen, luminous point value of consciousness. Upon reaching the point value and entering into it, a miracle occurs. The awareness turns inside out and simultaneously and instantly expands to infinity. This is accompanied by the simultaneous eruption of transcendental light (param jyotih) and transcendental sound (param nada). As a result, the veil of ignorance is pierced, and the cover of silent darkness is removed in a single, instantaneous flash of pure intuition.

This flash was compared to a thunderbolt (vajra) because it pierces the silent darkness with an instantaneous eruption of light and sound that reveals the infinite landscape of the self. It may be compared to a thunderbolt in the night, the pairing of light and thunder, which reveals the landscape of the earth. The flash was compared to a diamond (vajra) because the landscape of the self displays a transparent crystalline geometry, which resembles the transparent structure of a flawless diamond, infinite in extent. For this reason, the Vedic seers sometimes referred to the body of Logos as the immortal "diamond body" (*vajra-deha*).

With this flash of pure intuition, the field of pure ignorance is transformed into a field of pure knowledge, the field of death is transformed into a field of eternal life, and the field of emptiness is transformed into a field of fullness. It is only at this point that the soul actually becomes enlightened and is reborn immortally. It is only at this point that we can become an immortal seer of the Logos or the Veda.

THE CRYSTALLINE BODY OF LOGOS

The landscape of the self, which is revealed by the diamond thunder-bolt, rather than being a featureless continuum, is a quantized continuum, which contains its own ideal structure and dynamics. More specifically, it contains an ideal crystalline structure—literally, a structure of consciousness, a structure of pure knowledge.

This structure is ideal in the sense that it represents the most symmetrical pattern of periodic geometry that can be conceived intuitively in three dimensions, while allowing for these three dimensions to be complementary of each other. This follows from the notion that it is conceived by pure intelligence, which is the source of all order, symmetry, and coherence in nature. It is also conceived on the basis of pure subjectivity, which allows for complementary points of view on any subject.

The crystalline geometry of the Logos may be transparent and transcendental, but it can nevertheless be modeled and visualized by the ordinary mind. It corresponds to a unique crystalline lattice known in modern crystallography as the sodium-chloride lattice: the internal crystalline geometry of ordinary table salt. Yet the crystalline geometry of the Logos does not represent a physical lattice composed of material particles. Instead, it represents an infinite, metaphysical lattice composed of immovable point values of consciousness.

Because the lattice consists of two complementary sets of point values organized into face-centered cubic sublattices, it may be called the *transcendental superlattice,* whose unit cell is illustrated here.

The cubic cell represents a single cell in the infinite crystalline body of Logos, which the Vedic seers described as the imperishable diamond body (vajra-deha). This transparent, crystalline geometry represents the structure of pure knowledge that is cognized after all mental activity has been transcended and the knower, process of knowing, and known

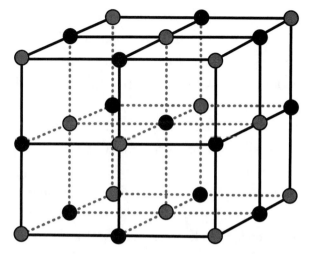

Fig. 2.1. This shows the unit cell of the transcendental superlattice, with the point values enlarged and their geometric relations indicated by lines. In actuality, the point values are infinitesimal and the entire lattice geometry is transparent.

have merged on the level of pure consciousness. The Vedic texts state: "When mental activity disappears, then knower, knowing, and known become absorbed one into another, [and take the form of] a transparent crystal, which assumes the appearance of that upon which it rests."[6]

That upon which the crystalline geometry of consciousness rests is none other than the underlying continuum of pure consciousness. Because both are transparent, the discrete crystalline geometry assumes the appearance of the continuum. In other words, it assumes the appearance of the self. The Vedic seers referred to this ideal form of pure geometry as the self-referral form (*svarupa*) of the self.

The Greek philosophers sought to study the ideal geometry of the self on the basis of pure intuition and reason. For this reason, two aphorisms were supposedly inscribed above the entrance to Plato's academy: "Know thy self" and "Let no one ignorant of geometry enter here." These two go hand in hand: By knowing the self, we automatically come to know the geometry of the self—that is, we automatically come to know the crystalline body of Logos.

Like an organic body, the crystalline body of Logos has a cellular structure, but in this case the cells are ideal and nonorganic—they have the form of perfect cubes within which sits an immortal point value of consciousness, the knower of the cell. In Sanskrit, the word for a cube is *aksha,* and the word for imperishable is *akshara,* which is derived from *aksha + ra,* meaning "that which illuminates the cube." The imperishable soul that sits at the center of the cube represents the illuminator of the cube.

When the veil of ignorance is removed and the soul takes its seat in the imperishable point value of consciousness, the soul becomes the illuminator of its own crystallographic cell, which is part of the infinite crystalline body of Logos. Although the crystalline body of Logos is immovable, it is pervaded by the movable substance of pure consciousness, which constitutes the immortal lifeblood (amrita rasa) of the self. It is also pervaded by the transcendental light and sound of consciousness, which exist in the form of spherical waves centered on every point value.

Whether this immortal reality was called the Logos, Veda, Duat, or Etz Chaim (Tree of Life) is immaterial. It was, is, and always will be the true abode of the enlightened soul. When the soul spirals onto the immortal point and the veil of ignorance is removed, it falls effectively through a "rabbit hole" and enters into a whole new world—the imperishable world of Logos. We want to see just how far the rabbit hole goes.

3

The Spectrum of
Consciousness

REALIZING THE FULL POTENTIAL
OF THE SOUL

Although the attainment of spiritual enlightenment may mark the culmination of individual evolution, it does not mark the end of universal evolution. A newborn enlightened soul is just a babe regarding knowledge, power, and presence. It may have realized the field of pure consciousness as its universal self and become identified with the immortal body of Logos, but it has not fully realized all the possible excitations of the field or the full extent of the metaphysical body.

Just as a newborn lion cub is still a lion, even though it does not yet possess the form or power of a full-grown lion, so a newborn enlightened soul is still immortal, even though it does not yet possess the omniscience, omnipotence, and omnipresence of the fully immortal Supreme Being. To achieve its full potential, the enlightened soul must "grow up" to become like its father. This means the soul must expand its knowledge, power, and presence over a vast spectrum of space-time scales until it becomes both smaller than the smallest and bigger than the biggest ideas of space and time. To know God fully, the enlightened soul must become like God. The Hermetic texts declare:

If then you do not make yourself equal to God, you cannot apprehend God; for like is known by like. Leap clear of all that is corporeal, and make yourself grow to a like expanse with that greatness which is beyond all measure; rise above all time, and become eternal; then you will apprehend God . . . make yourself higher than all heights, and lower than all depths . . . grasp in your thought all this at once, all times and places, all substances and qualities and magnitudes together; then you can apprehend God.[1]

In order to become like its father, the newly enlightened soul must ascend to the highest heights and descend to the lowest depths until it has fathomed fully the range of the divine mind. Only then will it develop the potential to grasp "all times and places, all substances and qualities and magnitudes together" in its all-inclusive awareness. Only then will it truly become like God, the fully immortal Being.

THE SCALES OF CONSCIOUSNESS

This leads to a discussion of the scales of consciousness, which the ancients used to map out the path of immortality. Each individual soul, including the enlightened soul, may be understood as operating on its own scale of consciousness as determined by its self-conceived ideas of space, time, and motion.

The mystery here arises from the fact that at the moment of enlightenment, awareness expands from point to infinity in an instantaneous flash of pure intuition. Why, then, does the enlightened soul need to expand its range of comprehension? It is already established in unbounded awareness; what more is there?

Insight is provided by the Vedic tradition in which the individual soul was called the *jiva* and the universal self was called the *atman*. These represent the point value of consciousness and the infinite value of consciousness, respectively. To realize the infinite self, the pointlike soul must expand to infinity. This is the innate potential of the soul.

"The jiva is extremely subtle like the point of a hair divided and sub-divided many times, yet it has the potential for infinity. He [the jiva] should be realized [as the atman]."[2]

Speaking mathematically, point and infinity may be viewed as the absolute limits of the field. When a person becomes enlightened, these two limits are grasped simultaneously and instantaneously in a single flash of pure intuition so that the innate potential of the soul is ful-filled. Yet this realization takes place abstractly on the level of pure intuition alone. We may compare this to remembering someone, but being unable to recall his or her name. You know exactly whom you are thinking of, but a name escapes you, and as a result, you are unable to represent that person on the level of the discursive intellect. It is only when you grasp the name that the intellect rests and the recall becomes complete.

Similarly, the initial flash of pure intuition, which extends from point to infinity, reveals abstractly the infinite landscape of the self. At that point, we come to know directly and intuitively the absolute limits of the field, though we may not grasp fully all the discrete steps that lie in between point and infinity. This kind of full understanding of the field by the discursive intellect requires step-by-step exploration of the full range of scales between point and infinity. We must fill in all the blanks between point and infinity. This involves a journey of pure knowledge over the full spectrum of consciousness.

THE HALF MEASURE

In this regard, the seers held that all enlightened souls begin their jour-ney at the midpoint—halfway between the infinite and infinitesimal. The Vedic seers referred to this unique scale of consciousness as the half measure (*ardha-matra*).

Starting at the half measure, the awareness expands simultaneously toward the infinite and contracts toward the infinitesimal—holding on to both the infinite and infinitesimal the whole time. In this way, we fill in all the blanks between point and infinity—that is, we fill in all the vibratory modes of consciousness that lie in between point and infinity on different scales—which can be understood as different scales of space and time or different wavelength and frequency scales. Expanding the earlier analogy, we can say that by grasping progressively all the vibratory modes of the field, we remember the "name" of the Supreme Being.

The sages referred to this expansion of vibratory consciousness over the full spectrum of scales as *ascending* and *descending:* By expanding the wavelengths of consciousness toward the infinite, the soul ascends, and by contracting the wavelengths toward the infinitesimal, the soul descends. The enlightened soul has the potential to both ascend and descend simultaneously, in a balanced manner.

Although we grasp point and infinity at the moment of enlightenment, the sequential process of expansion and contraction is endless. No matter how large a given wavelength might become, the infinite will always be larger. Similarly, no matter how small a wavelength might become, the infinitesimal will always be smaller.

The Vedic seers defined the ultimate reality as that which is simultaneously "smaller than the smallest, and bigger than the biggest" (*anor aniyam mahato mahiyam*). That is the ultimate goal toward which all conscious evolution tends and is present, paradoxically, at every step of the evolutionary journey.

REAL AND VIRTUAL WAVES

In modern scientific terms, we can say that the enlightened seers were actually seers of the vacuum. According to quantum theory, the vacuum state is not really empty; it is filled with virtual quantum waves, which transcend all means of direct empirical detection.

For example, the difference between a real electromagnetic wave and a virtual electromagnetic wave is that one can be empirically detected, at least in principle, while the other cannot. In spite of the fact that it cannot be detected, a virtual wave is required by principles of quantum theory. Moreover, quantum theory suggests that the so-called vacuum of empty space is filled with virtual quantum waves of all types. According to the ancient seers, these are hidden initially by the veil of pure ignorance that shrouds the mind. When our awareness becomes identified with the field of pure consciousness, and the veil of ignorance is removed, then the virtual quantum waves inherent within the universal vacuum are experienced as the waves of our own unbounded awareness and the transcendental light and transcendental sound of consciousness—the vibratory modes of our own being.

That which is experienced by the unenlightened soul as a silent and dark form of emptiness becomes experienced by the enlightened soul as a luminous and sonic form of fullness. The virtual light that shines in the awareness of such an enlightened soul is the light that shines in the darkness—the light, which the darkness has never mastered. This light serves as the "life" of the Cosmos, while the virtual or transcendental sound serves as the "life" of the Logos. Both are required to uphold the conception of the self as a living being, which is spiritual and material, metaphysical and physical.

According to the seers, the modes of transcendental light and sound are eternal. They existed before creation and during creation and they will continue to exist after creation. To grasp fully the reality of the metaphysical Logos, we must cognize the full spectrum of virtual waves. As the awareness of the enlightened soul expands over the spectrum, it does not create these modes. The expansion of consciousness involves merely remembering what had been forgotten due to the influence of ignorance.

This remembrance involves not a physical action, but an act of knowledge. The seers declared that it is through knowledge that the soul obtains full immortality in the bosom of the infinite. In this sense, the ancient spiritual science may be viewed as a science of the vacuum and its virtual modes over a vast spectrum of space-time scales.

HEAVEN AND EARTH

The half measure played an extremely important role in the ancient spiritual science, for it marks the boundary between heaven and earth. With respect to the spectrum of consciousness, the terms *heaven* and *earth* have a technical meaning.

All the virtual modes that lie above the half measure were viewed as part of heaven and all the virtual modes that lie below the half measure were viewed as part of earth. Therefore, the ancients viewed the spectrum as divided into two halves: the upper heavenly half and the lower earthly half. Each of these has direct relevance to human consciousness, because human consciousness was viewed as fluctuating around the scale of the half measure. In the same way that the human body stands upright with its feet planted on the earth below and its head in the sky above, so human consciousness stands at the juncture of heaven and earth.

Yet unenlightened human consciousness is unstable—it is not established on the scale of the half measure. Sometimes our awareness soars above, in the happiness of heaven, and sometimes it drags below, in the misery of earth. This qualitative description of the two halves of the spectrum as relating to happiness or misery is rooted in the Vedic notion: "The infinite is happiness. There is no happiness in anything small. The infinite alone is happiness. Seek to know the infinite."[3] That which engenders happiness may be viewed as good, and that which engenders misery may be viewed as evil. The unenlightened soul, subject to cyclic fluctuations of happiness and misery, is thereby snared in the Tree of Knowledge regarding good and evil. This represents a "fallen" state.

The enlightened soul, on the other hand, transcends the notions of good and evil. When the awareness becomes established firmly on the scale of the half measure, it grasps the balance between heaven and earth, happiness and misery, good and evil, and the infinite and infinitesimal. This occurs when the fluctuations of the human mind are transcended and we experience the state of pure consciousness. For this reason, the Vedic seers held that the half measure represents the scale of transcendence, the scale where the field of pure ignorance is first cognized as a precursor to the dawn of enlightenment.

The egoless soul that has realized permanently the state of pure ignorance may therefore be viewed as embodying the balance between heaven and earth. It has transcended all notions of good and evil. As a result, it is not plagued by any desire for happiness or any aversion to misery. At this stage, however, the soul is ignorant of the full extent of heaven and earth. Only after the veil of ignorance has been removed can the soul begin to explore the lineaments of heaven and earth within its awareness.

To grasp the heights of heaven and the depths of earth in a balanced manner, the soul must ascend and descend simultaneously. Further, it must descend below the half measure as far as it ascends above the half measure so that the scales of heaven and earth remain balanced in the soul's awareness. By doing this, the Tree of Good and Evil is transformed into the Tree of Eternal Life.

The half measure may be compared to the fulcrum of a cosmic balance that is upheld by all enlightened souls throughout the universe. This is the balance between the infinite and infinitesimal, or the large and the small, and is also the balance between heaven and earth, good and evil, happiness and misery. Although this balance is realized initially on the scale of the half measure, it has many manifestations on different scales of consciousness. To understand it fully, we must consider two innate powers of consciousness: those of analysis and synthesis.

THE ANALYTIC AND SYNTHETIC POWERS

We can say that all forms of knowledge are cognized by a simultaneous process of analysis and synthesis: a whole may be analyzed into its parts, and the parts may be synthesized into a whole.

The word *consciousness,* like the word *science,* comes from the Latin *scio,* which means "to know." Consciousness is characterized by the ability "to know"— and the powers of analysis and synthesis are innate in consciousness. The science that underlies the spectrum of consciousness involves the relation between these two powers, whose strengths vary as a function of scale: Although both are at work on every scale of consciousness, the strength of the analytic power grows as the scale of consciousness contracts toward the infinitesimal, while the strength of synthetic power grows as the scale of consciousness expands toward the infinite. This means that synthetic power dominates above and analytic power dominates below.

Speaking mathematically, we can say that the strengths of the two powers are related inversely as a function of scale. It follows that there can be only one scale in which the two powers are equal in strength and therefore balanced: the half measure, where the soul becomes balanced in preparation for enlightenment. The intuitive realization of that balance qualifies the soul for enlightenment and the resurrection of its ego as the universal ego, which serves to uphold the balance between heaven and earth over a vast spectrum of space-time scales.

The actual dawn of enlightenment occurs when the soul grasps simultaneously point and infinity as well as the half measure (that is, the midpoint between them), and takes its first step on the divine ladder. This first step involves both an ascent above the scale of the half measure and a descent below the scale of the half measure. By ascending as far as we descend, analytic and synthetic powers remain balanced in awareness.

In this way, the ascent toward the infinite is balanced by a corresponding descent toward the infinitesimal. In the Vedic literature, this process of simultaneous ascent and descent was compared to stringing two ends of a cosmic bow.

STRINGING THE COSMIC BOW

In this analogy, the two ends of the bow correspond to the two matched scales above and below, where the strengths of the synthetic and analytic powers are equal. By stringing together these two scales in the awareness of the self, the cosmic balance realized originally on the scale of the half measure is maintained at every step.

The larger the cosmic bow and the farther apart its two ends, the more powerful the bow becomes. The arrows shot from the bow correspond to the intentions of the soul. As the soul strings together in a balanced way ever more disparate scales of time and space, its intentions become more powerful and far-reaching. Eventually, the soul develops the ability to grasp at the same time the finest fabrics of creation, conceived by means of the analytic power below, and the largest wholes of creation, conceived by means of the synthetic power above. It then develops the ability to stir the finest fabrics of creation to fulfill its cosmic intentions.

In this way, the enlightened soul becomes a master of creation. Such a soul was deemed capable of performing what others would view as miracles. By its slightest intention, it can make the sun shine, the rains fall, and the winds blow—but its intentions must be in accordance with the will of God, the Supreme Being, who is none other than the soul's eternal self.

The balanced expansion of consciousness over the virtual spectrum involves more than just an expansion of knowledge. It also involves an expansion of power and presence. The enlightened soul develops not only the ability to grasp the smallest parts and largest wholes of creation on the level of knowledge; it also develops the power to marshal the parts into wholes by means of its cosmic intentions. This is possible because the presence of the soul extends over the entire spectrum—as the very self of all the parts and wholes. It can be said, then, that as the awareness of the enlightened soul expands over the cosmic spectrum, it becomes increasingly omniscient, omnipotent, and omnipresent—increasingly like God. The sages claimed that to know God, we must become like God, for like is known by like alone.

Yet this does not mean that the enlightened soul will ever actually become God. It will always be in the process of becoming God, because the expansion and contraction of consciousness is endless. The evolving soul will never fill in completely the blanks between point and infinity. God may be understood as the actualized totality of all possibilities, which the enlightened soul is ever striving to grasp. No matter how completely the soul might imagine that it has come to know God, the Supreme Being will always be more than what is known.

Nevertheless, at a certain stage the distinction between the enlightened soul and God becomes a matter of metaphysical hair-splitting. For this reason, the sages held that it is possible to attain union with God, whether viewed as a form of duality or nonduality. In the final analysis, however, it does not matter which is true. All of the sages agreed that the enlightened soul has the potential to become increasingly like God, which is the ultimate goal of the spiritual journey: to attain the omniscience, omnipotence, and omnipresence of God in the bosom of the infinite.

THE SONIC AND LUMINOUS HALVES OF THE SPECTRUM

The analytic and synthetic powers of consciousness have a concrete, dynamic manifestation as the modes of transcendental light and transcendental sound. Therefore, we can equate the analytic power of consciousness and the local, transverse modes of the field (transcendental light), and we can equate the synthetic power and the nonlocal, longitudinal modes of the field (transcendental sound).

By virtue of transcendental light, the universe is locally analyzed into its microscopic parts, and by virtue of transcendental sound the universe is nonlocally synthesized into its macroscopic wholes. Both are required to uphold the integrity of the universe over the spectrum of space-time scales. Without the light of consciousness, the universe would dissolve into a single, nonlocal wholeness, and without the sound of consciousness the universe would dissolve into its elementary constituents.

Although both powers are active on every scale of consciousness, the luminous, analytic power dominates below on microscopic scales and the sonic, synthetic power dominates above on macroscopic scales. Therefore, the overall spectrum is divided into two halves: the upper, sonic half, which embodies the nonlocal realms of heaven, and the lower, luminous half, which embodies the local realms of earth.

AS ABOVE, SO BELOW

The ancient notion that the cosmic spectrum is divided into two halves is consistent with modern theory. Over the course of the twentieth century, two great empirical theories have emerged: quantum theory and general relativity.

Quantum theory deals with the microscopic half of the universe, the realm of the elementary parts (or particles) of creation, and general relativity deals with the macroscopic half, the realm of cosmological wholes. Unfortunately, these two theories do not converge. In fact, they are fundamentally incompatible, both conceptually and mathematically—which is one of the reasons why theorists are now seeking a unified theory that might overcome this theoretical dichotomy between the small-scale and large-scale laws of nature.

The ancients also recognized that the laws of nature that govern the upper, macroscopic half of the universe (dominated by nonlocal, synthesizing laws) are different from those that govern the lower, microscopic half (dominated by local, analyzing laws). Rather than emphasize their differences, however, they chose to emphasize their similarities through the principle "as above, so below." This notion pertains to a hidden symmetry between the analytic and synthetic powers of consciousness: Although the two are opposite in function, the strengths of each are balanced around the scale of the half measure. This means for any given scale above the half measure, there will always be a corresponding scale below so that the strength of the synthetic power above and the strength of the analytic power below are equal in magnitude. In other words, the magnitude above will correspond to the magnitude below.

This principle was designed to illuminate a fundamental balance in nature, which is required to uphold the integrity of the universe over a vast spectrum of space-time scales. This characterizes the balance within the divine mind—the mind of God, who represents the Father of the universe. The Rig Veda puts it this way: "He who knows the Father of this [universe] as that which is Below associated with that which is Above, and that which is Above associated with that which is Below, he as it were, has the mind of a sage."[4]

Compare this estimation to a passage taken from the Emerald Tablet (Tabula Smaragdina), which is considered the oldest and most authoritative of the Hermetic texts: "That which is Below corresponds to that which is Above, and that which is Above corresponds to that which is Below, in the accomplishment of the miracle of one thing. . . . It is the Father of every completed thing in the whole world."

The principle "as above, so below" was a general theoretical notion that once pervaded the ancient world, from India to Egypt, and persisted for thousands of years. We can even include in the mix Taoist China, where the same theoretical principle was professed from the earliest periods. This principle suggests that there is a similarity or symmetry between the large-scale and small-scale laws of nature. Yet this does not mean that what is above is exactly the same as what is below. The analytic and synthetic powers associated with the matched pairs of scales are obviously different with respect to their functions—but they are similar with respect to their strengths.

In order to unify the two sets of laws under a single theoretical umbrella, we must consider both their differences and similarities using a balanced process of analysis and synthesis. It was on the basis of this type of knowledge, born of both analysis and synthesis, that the ancient science was formulated.

THE DIVINE LADDER

The expansion of consciousness over the spectrum of scales is discrete and step-by-step, rather than continuous. As we've discovered, in the Rig Veda, the expansion of consciousness was compared to ascending and descending a divine ladder whose rungs support all the worlds: "Those [steps] that are called descending are also termed ascending; and those that are called ascending are also termed descending; those [ascending and descending steps] . . . support these divine worlds as though they were yoked together on a pole."[5]

In ancient times, ladders were often constructed by tying sticks to a single pole, a practice still common in rural India. Ancients equated the process of ascending and the process of descending because the enlightened soul must ascend toward the infinite and descend toward the infinitesimal simultaneously in order to maintain the cosmic balance; for each step of ascent there must be a corresponding step of descent so that the knowledge of the microscopic parts and macroscopic wholes grow together.

We can find a similar notion in the book of Genesis in which, in a dream, the divine ladder is revealed to Jacob, the grandson of Abraham: "And behold a ladder set up on the earth, and the top of it reached to heaven: and behold the angels of God ascending and descending on it. And, behold, the Lord stood above it, and said, I am the Lord God of Abraham thy father."[6]

The Vedic and Hebrew sages very well might have conceived similarly the spectrum of consciousness and used the same analogy (the divine ladder) to describe it.

THE ANGELS OF GOD

The original Hebrew word translated as "angel" in the Genesis passage above is *malakh,* which means "messenger," a term commonly applied to the Hebrew prophets and sages. Hence, a more literal translation would have the enlightened prophets—the messengers of God—ascending and descending the divine ladder.

This is consistent with the fact that the earliest known school of Hebrew mysticism was *merkabah mysticism.* Although the original doctrine has been lost, this school supposedly taught that the soul could become immortal by ascending the divine ladder into the infinite bosom of God.

Although the concept of angels has become an integral part of our modern mythology, the common depiction of an angel as a spiritual being with wings is symbolic. The winged symbol is based on the notion that the enlightened soul can ascend through the heavens like a divine bird. The English word *angel* can be traced back to the Sanskrit Angiras, the name of a great Vedic seer who was credited as being the first to teach the science of immortality (*brahma vidya*) to mortal human beings on earth. Although the myth of Angiras is little known in the West, his name has been preserved in Indo-European languages all around the world: Linguistic scholars have argued that in Old Persian, the original Sanskrit word *angiras* became *angiros;* in ancient Greek it became *angelos;* in Latin it became *angelus;* and in English it became *angel*. It can be said, then, that Angiras served as the mythical prototype for what we now call an angel, or a messenger of God.

According to the Vedic texts, however, Angiras was no spiritual being with wings. He was a seer who was first born as an ordinary human being on earth and then was reborn as an immortal seer of the Veda. After this, he became liberated from the scale of human awareness; his awareness was free to expand and contract over the entire spectrum of consciousness. In the process, he cognized the science of immortality, which he then taught to his fellow human beings on earth. In this sense, he was viewed as a messenger of God who was free to ascend and descend the divine ladder at will.

THE STAIRWAY TO THE SKY

A similar use can be found in the Pyramid Texts, the oldest religious records ever found in Egypt. These texts, which date back to at least 2400 BCE, are filled with references to a mysterious divine ladder or stairway to the sky on which the soul could ascend to attain immortality among the gods:

A stairway to the sky is set up for me . . . that I may ascend on it to the sky.[7]

A stairway to the sky is set up for you among the imperishable stars.[8]

A ladder is set up for him that he may ascend on it.[9]

I ascend on this ladder, which my father Ra (the sun god) made for me.[10]

Although modern Egyptologists presume commonly that the stairway to the sky was ascended after the death of the physical body, the Hermetic texts, which claim to explicate the older, philosophic spirit of ancient Egypt, suggest that the enlightened soul has the potential to ascend to heaven without ever quitting the earth: "Man ascends even to heaven, and measures it; and what is more than all beside, he mounts to heaven without quitting the earth; to so vast a distance can he put forth his power. We must not shrink then from saying that a man on earth is a mortal god, and that a god in heaven is an immortal man."[11]

By traversing the path of immortality while possessing a physical body, the enlightened seers discerned the lineaments of heaven and earth within their ever-expanding awareness and thereby formulated the ancient science of immortality.

THE SYSTEM OF MEASURED ARRANGEMENT

All forms of science tend to employ systems of measurement. Such systems allow our qualitative experience of reality to be expressed in terms of quantities or numbers.

In this regard, the ancient science of immortality was no different. It was rooted in a "system of measured arrangement," which served to specify the scales of consciousness that constitute collectively the path of immortality. According to the Hermetic texts, as an enlightened soul ascends through the heavens, it measures them. These measurements, conducted in consciousness, provide the basis for a scientific description of the spectrum expressed in the language of mathematics, the universal language of science.

The Hermetic texts go on to suggest that the Egyptians possessed an ancient system of measured arrangement by which they mapped out the various layers of consciousness that constitute collectively the cosmic spectrum. This doctrine is presented in the form of a discourse between the Egyptian goddess Isis and her son Horus: "The space between earth and heaven is parted out into divisions, my son Horus, according to a system of measured arrangement. These divisions are variously named by our ancestors, some of whom call them zones, others firmaments, and others layers. They are the haunts of the souls that have been released from their bodies, and likewise of the souls that have not yet been embodied."[12]

The antiquity of this doctrine is emphasized by putting it into the mouth of the goddess Isis, the wife and sister of Osiris and one of the oldest deities in the Egyptian pantheon. It is further emphasized by having Isis state that the system was known even to her ancestors. It has to do with the layers of consciousness that serve as the haunts for disembodied soul. In other words, this philosophy pertains to the arrangement of virtual vacuum states inherent within the unified field, each of which may be viewed as having its own elementary constituents.

Although the actual system of arrangement is not described in detail, the notion that it represents a measured system implies that it can be described in terms of numbers or quantities.

THE CONCEPT OF SELF-REFERRAL MEASURE

The measurement systems employed in modern empirical science may be understood as forms of object-referral measure: a physical object, such as a ruler or clock, is used to measure other physical objects.

This type of system, however, cannot be used to measure the layers of consciousness, which correspond to virtual vacuum states, simply because these layers are nonphysical or metaphysical—and for all empirical purposes resemble empty space. To measure the metaphysical vacuum states, we must use metaphysical, rather than physical, rulers and clocks. Yet what does this mean? In order for the enlightened soul to measure the layers of consciousness, it must use the vibratory modes of its own consciousness as self-referral standards of measure.

These vibratory modes correspond to the waves of transcendental light and sound, each of which has a characteristic wavelength and frequency. In this case, the wavelength can serve as a metaphysical ruler and the frequency can serve as a metaphysical clock by which the lengths and frequencies of other waves can be evaluated or measured. In a self-referral measurement system, the empirical value of the wavelength or frequency is unimportant; what matters is the ratio between the standard of self-referral measure and what is being measured.

The Pythagoreans outlined the principles that underlie this type of measurement system in their theory of harmonics. To demonstrate the validity of their theory, they used vibrating strings and showed that if the tone produced by a vibrating string of length L is taken as the fundamental tone of a harmonic system, then (all other things being equal) the tone produced by a string of length 2L will correspond to the lower octave of the fundamental, while the tone produced by a string of length $\frac{1}{2}$ L will correspond to the higher octave of the fundamental. More generally, they argued that a vibrating string whose length is rationally related to the fundamental length L by any rational fraction of the form N℧/N, where N = 1, 2, 3, and so on, will produce a harmonic of the fundamental tone.*

---

*The N℧ indicates a variable that can differ from the value of N.

The ancient theory essentially related harmonic tones and measures of space corresponding to string lengths so that both the tones and the measures of space could be represented simultaneously by the same set of pure number ratios. The system was such that the actual empirical measure of the standard length L is unimportant; regardless of the value and whether it is expressed in centimeters or meters or some other unit, the theory holds true. Any string of arbitrary length L can be chosen as the fundamental standard of measure on the basis of which the harmonic system is defined.

This is a self-referral system of measurement: One aspect of a system is chosen as a standard of measure by which the entire system is measured in accordance with principles of ratio and proportion. In this type of measurement, no standardized physical rulers or clocks are required. The whole process of measurement can be performed intuitively, on the level of consciousness, by comparing one harmonic sound to another.

In the Vedic tradition the harmonic modes of transcendental sound that are inherent within the metaphysical Logos were viewed as forms of transcendental speech (*para vak*). In this regard, the seers held that there is a fundamental duality between space and speech; they were viewed as complementary aspects and were identified with each other: "That which is space is indeed speech."[13]

In the system of Vedic philosophy called Samkhya (enumeration) the relation between space and speech was clearly specified and the transcendental measure (*tan-matra*) of space was identified as none other than speech. In this regard, speech was defined as *shruti*, "that which is heard"—it represents a form of sound.

The Pythagoreans quantified this relation by equating string lengths (measures of space) and harmonic tones (measures of sound) in such a way that both measures can be represented by the same pure number ratio. Yet the principle that underlies the Pythagorean system was very ancient; it was professed by the Vedic seers long before the Greek civilization arrived on the scene.

It turns out that the ancient notion that the measures of sound and the measures of space are related intimately has been preserved in the modern English language. For example, the English term *meter,* which is derived from the Sanskrit word *matra,* "measure," indicates not only a linear measure of space, but also a measure of speech (as in a sonic meter). Similarly, the word *foot* indicates both a linear measure of space and a measure of speech (as in a sonic foot). Even the word *volume* is used to indicate both a measure of three-dimensional space and the decibel magnitude of sound.

The Hermetic texts tell us that the enlightened soul "measures" the heavens as it ascends through them. This means that the measured forms of divine speech or transcendental sound are "heard" by the soul in the upper half of the spectrum. Although the wavelengths of transcendental sound cannot be measured by any physical ruler, they can be used to measure themselves in accordance with principles of ratio and proportion. In doing this, the ancient seers discerned intuitively a system of measured arrangement inherent within the metaphysical Logos that represents not only a system of harmonic sound, but also a system of harmonic space.

THE EXPONENTIAL ARRANGEMENT

The ancient system of measured arrangement pertains to the organization of layers inherent within the metaphysical Logos. Each of these layers can be viewed as a frequency or wavelength band of consciousness, and each is associated with a fundamental wavelength or frequency on which is evaluated all other frequencies using self-referral measure through a harmonic system of analysis.

Yet a harmonic analysis is not sufficient to describe fully the overall arrangement of layers, which instead requires comparing the fundamental wavelengths associated with the various layers. This amounts to a type of meta-analysis, which transcends the internal harmonic system associated with each layer. The Vedic seers therefore declared that the layers are organized in an exponential fashion: "The layers that cover the worlds are each ten times thicker than the one before."[14] This means that the fundamental wavelength of each higher layer is ten times longer than the fundamental wavelength of the previous lower layer—consistent with the Greek tradition in which the Decad, the number 10, was viewed as the most holy number. In the Hermetic texts, the Decad is described specifically as the number by which the immortal soul is generated. In this case, each generation of the soul corresponds to its tenfold ascent through a given layer.

The implication is that the overall system of measured arrangement is exponential or logarithmic, rather than harmonic. Interestingly, the word *logarithm* was derived originally from the Greek terms *logos* (ratio) and *arithmus* (number). Logarithmic numbers are represented by exponential powers rather than harmonic ratios. In a base 10 logarithmic system, the increasingly large exponential numbers would be given this way: $10^0 = 1$, $10^1 = 10$, $10^2 = 100$, and so forth. The increasingly small exponential numbers are expressed thus: $10^{-1} = \frac{1}{10}$, $10^{-2} = \frac{1}{100}$, $10^{-3} = \frac{1}{1000}$ and so forth.

Given this type of scientific notion, it is now possible to present a diagrammatic representation of the ancient system of measured arrangement, expressed in terms of pure numbers. To illustrate the principle "as above, so below," the fundamental scales of the various layers are arranged in matched pairs, centered on the half measure. In this diagram, the characteristic scales are represented by pure numbers, with no associated units. The system has no empirical meaning; it represents a system of self-referral measure, rather than a system of object-referral measure. In order to create parameters for the system so that it can be evaluated empirically, we must assign to the numbers empirical units of measure, such as centimeters, meters, and so forth.

Since the first scale in the upper half of the spectrum is represented by $10^0 = 1$, it can be taken as the base unit of the spectrum. By assigning this particular scale an empirical unit of length, we can create parameters for the entire spectrum. Yet how can this be done? How

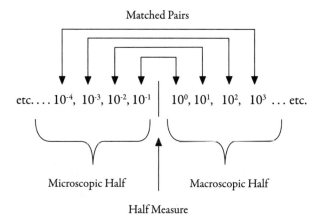

Fig. 3.1. The system of matched pairs

can we possibly assign an empirical unit of length to something that cannot be measured by any physical ruler? In the absence of the ancient teachings, we would be at a complete loss, but fortunately, the ancients provided the clues to solve this problem.

THE DIGIT OR THUMB MEASURE

Systems for measuring length have been around since the earliest periods of human civilization. For instance, during the course of the twentieth century, the meter was adopted as the base unit of length in the International System, and by a convention adopted in 1983, the meter is now defined in terms of the speed of light. More specifically, it is defined as the distance that light will travel during $\frac{1}{299,792,458}$ second.

In ancient times, there was also a widely accepted system of length measure that was shared by the Vedic, Egyptian, Hebrew, Greek, and Roman cultures—but this ancient base unit of length was defined in terms of the human body, rather than the speed of light. This meant that it represented literally a self-referral unit of measure. The *digit* came to be named from a Latin term that means "finger," yet this unit did not come from the Roman culture. In the Vedic culture, the digit was denoted by the Sanskrit terms *angula* (finger) and *angushta* (thumb).

The digit corresponds to the width of the human thumb, which is approximately 2 centimeters. Because the width of the thumb can vary from one person to the next, however, the ancient system was approximate; the base unit varied slightly from one culture to the next. In fact, memory of this system has been preserved in colloquial language: A system of approximate evaluation is commonly referred to as a "rule of thumb."

To simplify calculations and measurements, the ancients also used two other important units of measure called the cubit and half cubit, both of which can be expressed in terms of a number of digits: A standard cubit is equal to twenty-four digits and a standard half cubit is equal to twelve digits. Interestingly, the word *cubit,* meaning "elbow," is also of Latin origin. A standard cubit is equal to approximately the distance from the crook of the elbow to the tip of the middle finger. The standard half cubit is equal to approximately the distance from the base of the wrist to the tip of the middle finger. In the Vedic tradition, the cubit was called the *aratni* (elbow) and the half cubit was called the *vitasti* (hand span).

These units were also important in the Hebrew culture. For example, the Bible tells us that the dimensions of the Ark of the Covenant and King Solomon's Temple were measured carefully using an integral number of cubits or half cubits, and hence an integral number of Hebrew digits. Similarly, Egyptologists have shown that the base of the Great Pyramid was measured carefully using an integral number of Egyptian cubits, and hence an integral number of Egyptian digits.

In spite of the approximate nature of the system, each ancient culture developed its own standards. In the Vedic culture, the thumb of the king determined the standard digit—so that the king became the ruler of his kingdom, both literally and figuratively. There are indications that the Egyptians also employed this practice—though this standard digit was not always used. For example, in Vedic rituals designed to propitiate the gods, the person who sponsored the ritual and the one for whom the ritual was being performed, the *yajamana,* was deemed the ruler and contributed the thumb measure. In such cases, this measure was used to determine the dimensions of the sacrificial ground (*vedi*), the sacred fire altar (*agni*), the fire bricks (*ishtakas*), and even the utensils used to make the offerings. In every case, these were measured carefully according to the digit of the yajamana, and in this way, the ritual became attuned to that particular person.

Yet why did all of these ancient cultures choose the thumb width as their base unit of measure? Equally important, why did the ancients take such care to measure out the dimensions of their sacred constructions using an integral number of digits?

THE DIGIT AS THE BASE MEASURE OF THE SELF

As compared to all other living creatures on earth, the human body is unique in that it has an opposable thumb—a thumb that can grasp. Interestingly, the thumb represents the chief finger of the hand, which enables us to grasp the things in this world, and the digit represents the chief unit of measure, which allows us to grasp the measures of the things in this world. But there is more to it than this.

The digit was actually a sacred unit of measure, viewed so because it can be related to various bodies—the body of humans, the body of the altar, the body of the Cosmos, and the body of Logos—through a system of measured correspondences. The general idea was that all of these bodies, whether physical or metaphysical, share the same base unit of measure: approximately equal to the width of a human thumb.

We can gain insight into the meaning of the thumb measure through considering the Vedic system of *mudras* (hand gestures). Here, the thumb was used to represent the universal self, while the index finger was used to represent the individual self. For example, when seated in meditation, the sages often placed their hands on their knees, with their fingers arranged in a sacred mudra: They touched the index finger to the thumb, forming a circle. This particular mudra represents the union of the individual self (index finger) with the universal self (thumb)—the goal of the meditative process. The ancients believed that the human being is the only creature on earth that has the potential to realize the universal self. Moreover, this realization was related to the thumb measure. In the Vedic texts, the form of the universal self that is cognized when the newly enlightened soul takes its first step on the divine ladder was called the *angushta-matra purusha,* "the soul that has the measure of a thumb." Those who cognized the thumb-size soul as their very own self were said to become immortal: "The soul, the measure of a thumb, the inner controller, is perceived by the mind in the heart; they who know it become immortal."[15]

The thumb-size soul was also viewed as the inner controller of the human mind and body, because it represents the higher self of the human being. It would be a mistake, however, to imagine that the thumb-size soul has a form that resembles that of the human body. Instead, it consists of a point value of consciousness associated with spherically symmetric waves of consciousness, each of which has a wavelength on the order of a digit. These waves are sonic in character and operate nonlocally at the speed of thought, rather than locally at the speed of light. They manifest the fundamental tone of the first layer above the half measure—that is, in the sonic half of the spectrum. The transcendental sound produced by these waves represents the first and finest sound that can be heard by the divine ear.

THE DIVINE KA

For this reason, the Vedic seers equated this sound with the letter *ka,* the first consonant in the Sanskrit alphabet. First, it should be pointed out that the letters in the Sanskrit alphabet were arranged according to certain phonetic principles, and each letter was assigned a certain degree of openness (*vivritta*) or closure (*sprishta*) depending upon how it was produced by the vocal apparatus. In this system, the letter *ka* was assigned the maximum degree of closure. This follows from the fact that *k* represents a full guttural stop. Unless it is associated with a vowel—that is, *ka, ki, ku, ke,* and so forth—it cannot be pronounced at all. It represents the most constricted form of speech.

In the Vedic system of phonetics, the least constricted sound, and therefore the sound associated with the maximum value of openness, was assigned the letter *a* (pronounced as in father). According to the Agama (Revealed) texts of the tradition, which deal with the meanings of *mantras* (sonic formulas) and *yantras* (geometric formulas), the letter *a* symbolizes the immeasurable self of all the other letters. For this reason, the consonants of the Sanskrit alphabet are typically pronounced by associating them with the vowel *a,* so that they are pronounced as *ka, kha, ga, gha,* and so on.

The union of *k* and *a* produces *ka,* which symbolizes the union of the most constricted form of divine speech (*k*) with the infinite self (*a*) and represents the smallest wavelength of transcendental sound that can be "heard" by the infinite self. For this reason, the thumb-size soul was called the divine Ka, to whom an entire hymn is devoted in the Rig Veda.

A similar terminology was used in the Egyptian tradition: The inner controller of the human mind and body was also called the Ka, and was often represented by the human body in Egyptian iconography in order to indicate that it was the inner controller of human beings. The more technical hieroglyphic symbol for the Ka, however, was two outstretched arms bent upward at the elbows. The place where the two arms meet represents the heart, where the Ka, the thumb-size soul, is realized. The arms bent at the elbows symbolize the cubit, which is measured on the basis of the digit. The Ka may be viewed as the heart and soul of the cubit.

We can conclude, then, that the thumb-size soul was understood similarly in both the Vedic and Egyptian traditions, and that it was represented in both systems by the same phoneme: *ka*. We will discover other such linguistic correspondences later.

THE UNIVERSAL RULE OF THUMB

We are skirting the boundaries of a very deep science relating the digit, the smallest characteristic measure of the human self, to the divine Ka, the smallest characteristic form of the divine self. This science is based upon a correspondence between the measure of a physical object (the thumb) and the measure of a metaphysical subject (the soul).

Exactly how the ancients came up with this correspondence is unknown, but it serves as the key to assigning empirical units of measure to the spectrum of consciousness. If the thumb width (digit) is equal to the characteristic measure of the first layer above the half measure, which represents the base unit of the exponential system, then the parameters of the entire system of matched pairs is defined by:

$$10^0 = 1 \text{ digit} = 2 \times 10^0 \text{ centimeters}$$

This scheme suggests that the half measure is on the order of a half digit, or approximately 1 centimeter. This is the unit that lies halfway between 2×10^0 centimeters and 2×10^{-1} centimeters on an exponential scale. It follows that the system of matched pairs can be formulated most intuitively in terms of centimeters, rather than meters.

EMPIRICAL EVALUATION

Now that we have given the system parameters, we must evaluate its scientific validity. To do so, the characteristic scales must be interpreted so that they can be assigned meaning in the context of both ancient spiritual science and modern empirical science. The mathematical system of scales may be viewed as a translation system: it can be used to translate ancient spiritual concepts into modern empirical ones. As such, it is an important key to unlocking the secrets of the ancient science.

Before we can evaluate the system in terms of modern science, however, we first must determine how the ancient seers interpreted it themselves. This leads us to the next chapter, in which we examine the science of the gods.

4
The Science of the Gods

THE UNIVERSAL GODS

The ancients commonly held that God administers the universe by means of the gods—universal gods and celestial gods—who carry out divine will on different scales of time and space.

In the Vedic tradition, the universal gods (*vishva-devas*) correspond directly to the universal layers of consciousness that lie above the half measure. These are also known as immortal gods because they possess imperishable bodies of Logos (instead of perishable bodies of Cosmos).

Each universal god above (endowed with synthetic power) was viewed as "married" to its own creative power (*shakti*) below (endowed with analytic power); the gods and their powers are compared to husbands and wives or divine couples engaged in creative union. Therefore, the gods and their shaktis correspond to the sets of matched pairs outlined in chapter 3. The two sets of layers are compared literally to the fathers and mothers of creation. By means of their creative unions the divine couples conceive the universe, the perishable from the imperishable, as the divine embryo (*hiranyagarbha*) or cosmic egg (*brahmanda*) within the unbounded cosmic womb.

Although tradition held that both the gods and their shaktis are required to conceive the universe, the act of creation is initiated not by the shaktis, but by the gods above. Just as an egg in the female womb is incapable of developing into an embryo unless it is first inseminated by male seed, so the layers above were viewed as inseminating the layers below with the synthetic power of consciousness, so that the otherwise incoherent and local parts of creation might become nonlocally organized into coherent wholes—or conscious created beings.

In this sense, the gods above were viewed as stronger than their powers below, because they have the potential to infuse the analytic fields of force and matter with the self-organizing power of consciousness. The Hermetic sages taught a similar principle: "All the world which lies below has been set in order and filled with contents by the things which are placed above; for the things below have not the power to set in order the world above. The weaker mysteries, then, must yield to the stronger; and the system of things on high is stronger than the things below in as much as it is secure from disturbance and not subject to death."[1]

Even though the strength of the synthetic powers above may be equal mathematically to the strength of the analytic powers below, they were still viewed as stronger, because they have the potential to infuse with consciousness otherwise incoherent matter-energy. The universal gods and their shaktis represent all-pervading fields of consciousness that span a particular range of space-time scales. God, the Supreme Being, on the other hand, was viewed as the one eternal self of them all. Unlike the gods and their shaktis, who embrace a particular range of scales, the awareness of God spans the entire spectrum of scales, ranging from the infinitesimal to the infinite.

Unlike God, the Supreme Being, the gods were viewed not as fully omniscient, omnipotent, and omnipresent, but as limited aspects of the Supreme Being who possessed limited values of knowledge, power, and presence.

THE CELESTIAL GODS

The created offspring of the universal gods were known as the celestial gods. These represent the conscious forms of material existence that appear as the stars, solar systems, galaxies, and so forth—as those bodies that shine in the night sky. Unlike the universal gods, which are immortal, the celestial gods are mortal; they possess mortal bodies composed of ordinary matter-energy.

Unlike the mortal human body, the body of a celestial god may persist for millions or billions of years. As compared to human beings on earth, then, the celestial gods were viewed as relatively immortal—though, in the final analysis, their bodies are mortal; they were created at some point in time, and they will dissolve at some point.

Although a given celestial god may have a body that displays the form of a luminous sphere composed of matter-energy, that sphere is not insentient; it represents a celestial "godhead" that is filled with pure knowledge and self-organizing power. Each such celestial godhead provides an operative basis, or a point of view, for the universal gods and their shaktis within the physical Cosmos. Ultimately, however, all the gods represent different aspects of God, the Supreme Being, who is the very self of them all, whether universal or celestial.

THE LIVING UNIVERSE

According to the seers, the highest of the celestial gods has a cosmic body that corresponds to the body of the Cosmos as a whole. In the Hermetic texts, this great god was simply called Cosmos, the embodiment of the living universe: "Now this whole Cosmos—which is a great god, and an image of Him who is greater . . . is one mass of life; and there is not anything in the Cosmos, nor has been through all of time from the foundation of the universe, neither in the whole nor among the various things contained in it, that is not alive."[2]

The idea that the universe and everything in it is alive and endowed with consciousness is consistent with the ancient subjective paradigm, which suggests that everything in the universe has its ultimate origin in the field of pure consciousness. This includes not only the celestial bodies that appear as the cosmological wholes above, but also the elementary particles that appear as the microscopic parts below. In this regard, we must draw a distinction between the universal gods, which correspond to all-pervading fields of consciousness (or universal vacuum states), and the elementary constituents of those fields, which correspond to disembodied souls.

As we have seen, in the Vedic tradition, the soul was called variously the jiva or purusha, which in a disembodied state has the form of a point value of consciousness. These point values represent the elementary constituents of the universal fields of consciousness. Yet not all point values are the same. The Vedic texts tell us that there are two types of souls in the world, the perishable (*kshara*) and imperishable (akshara): "There are these two [types of] souls in the world—perishable and imperishable. The perishable consists of all the elements. The immovable multitude is called imperishable. But the highest soul is another, called the supreme Self. . . ."[3]

This very revealing passage suggests that the perishable souls—the perishable point values of consciousness—correspond to "all the elements" (*sarva bhutani*) of creation. In other words, they correspond to the elementary particles. In both classical and quantum mechanics, the elementary particles are treated as infinitesimal point particles, which are nevertheless endowed with certain properties, such as mass, charge, momentum, and energy. There is no notion that one of these properties is consciousness, so that an elementary particle can be conceived as an elementary soul—but that was precisely the position of the ancients: Each elementary particle was viewed as a perishable point value of consciousness.

The idea that these point values are perishable is consistent with quantum theory, in which the elementary particles are viewed as being created constantly and annihilated constantly at a frequency that transcends all means of empirical observation. In the Vedic texts, this constant process of creation and annihilation was called *nitya pralaya* and was attributed to the force of time:

Some men, knowing the subtle state of things . . . declare the creation and dissolution of all beings, from Brahma [the Cosmos] downward, as taking place all the time. The successive stages undergone by all changing things serve as an index of the constant creation and dissolution of those things, as carried out by the force of time. These [high frequency] stages [of creation and annihilation], brought about by the force of time . . . are not perceived [by ordinary men].[4]

The point values of consciousness caught up in this constant process of creation and annihilation were viewed as perishable souls, which constitute "all the elements" of creation. These correspond to the movable point values of consciousness from which is fashioned the perishable form of the Cosmos. The imperishable souls, on the other hand, correspond to the immovable point values from which is fashioned the imperishable form of the metaphysical Logos. This is none other than the crystalline structure of the transcendental superlattice, wherein each lattice point serves as the seat of an imperishable soul.

Unlike the perishable soul, which is movable, the imperishable soul is immovable; it does not have the freedom to move through space, and therefore has no interpretation as a particle or element of creation. Rather, the imperishable souls collectively form an "immovable multitude" (*kutastha*), which defines the quantum geometry of transcendental space itself. That crystalline geometry is none other than the transcendental superlattice, which represents the ideal form of the metaphysical Logos.

Although the imperishable souls are immovable, this does not mean that they lack freedom. They may be eternally frozen in place, but they are free to expand and contract their scales of subjective comprehension over the entire spectrum of consciousness. This amounts to a completely different type of freedom from that enjoyed by the perishable soul.

The field of pure consciousness includes both types of point values.

The Science of the Gods   77

In the passage quoted above, it is referred to as the highest soul, which serves as the one supreme self of all the point values—whether perishable or imperishable. By means of the perishable soul, the self obtains various points of view regarding the movable reality of the physical Cosmos, and by means of the imperishable soul, it obtains viewpoints regarding the immovable reality of the metaphysical Logos. In the final analysis, the same eternal self possesses both points of view.

That self, in turn, has various manifestations of space and time on different scales as all-pervading fields of consciousness, which can be viewed variously as universal layers, universal gods, or universal vacuum states. Each of these fields acts as the presiding deity, or self, of all the pointlike souls—both perishable and imperishable—that operate under its jurisdiction.

For this reason, the Hermetic texts tell us that the layers serve as the haunts of disembodied souls, the point values of consciousness, which provide the field with various points of view on its own reality. These souls constitute the conscious and living parts from which are composed both the physical Cosmos and metaphysical Logos. Their behavior is directed by the universal gods, and ultimately by God, the Supreme Being, who is the very self of them all.

THE CREATOR

The Vedic texts make a distinction between God, the Supreme Being, and God, the Creator. The Supreme Being was called Brahman (neutral gender), while the Creator was called Brahma (masculine gender). In effect, Brahma represents the living embodiment of Brahman.

The great god called Brahma in the Vedic texts is identical to the great god called Cosmos in the Hermetic texts. He represents the celestial embodiment of the entire living universe as a whole. Brahma was also called the *adi-purusha* (the first soul), because he was viewed as the first enlightened soul to be born at the beginning of creation—before anything whatsoever was actually created. Yet rather than being born from any mortal womb, he was born from the cosmic womb as a disembodied soul, a point value of consciousness, which nevertheless has the potential for infinity.

According to the Vedic creation myths, when Brahma was first born from the cosmic womb, or field of pure ignorance, he appeared as a thumb-size soul. Having come from the field of pure ignorance, the Creator was initially ignorant of who he was and why he had been born. Therefore, Brahma's first utterance was "Ka?"—Sanskrit meaning "Who am I?" For this reason, he was initially known as the divine Ka, and an entire hymn is dedicated to him in the Rig Veda.

The myth goes on to tell us that God, the Supreme Being, informed his firstborn son that he was destined to become the Creator of the universe. Having received this instruction, Brahma then tried to create the universe, but could not succeed—he did not have the necessary knowledge, presence, or power. Feeling that he had failed in his mission, he turned to his Father for advice, and received the instruction to perform *tapas*.

The Sanskrit word *tapas* means "heating," but it refers to the process of spiritual introspection whereby the senses are turned away from their objects toward the self. The instruction Brahma received therefore had to do with the process of transcendence whereby the space-time ideas associated with one layer are dissolved into the self so that a new, expanded set of space-time ideas can be conceived. The process of dissolving one set of ideas into the self to make way for a new set may be compared to a process of self-sacrifice: our preconceived ideas are offered to the fire of pure knowledge so that they are consumed and reduced to ashes. It is by means of tapas that the soul ascends from one layer to another.

In the beginning, the creative power of the Creator was weak because his awareness spanned only the first two layers of the cosmic spectrum, which lie immediately above and below the half measure. To realize his full creative power, he had to ascend and descend the divine ladder until his awareness reached the microscopic and macroscopic limits of creation. These limits mark the divine station of the Creator above and his shakti below. The Creator ascended the divine ladder by performing tapas. In the process, the universal gods—the dormant layers of consciousness—became warmed; the universal vacuum states became filled with the virtual excitations of light and sound, which were previously unseen and unheard.

The Vedic texts tell us that at this stage the universe existed as a "pure creation" (*shuddha srishti*), a virtual creation; no real forms of matter and energy were yet created. For empirical purposes, the universe at this stage would have resembled the vacuum of empty space—but the vacuum was not really empty. It was filled with virtual excitations of transcendental light and sound, which had been warmed or enlivened by the ascending and descending awareness of the Creator, the first enlightened soul in creation. We may compare the virtual creation to the warmed state of a seed prior to its actual sprouting. At that stage, all things existed only in a virtual or spiritual form, and the layers assumed the form of virtual vacuum states.

Upon arriving at his own divine station, the Creator became the embodiment of all the universal gods directly responsible for upholding the created appearance of the universe and of all the virtual vacuum states that exist on different scales of space and time. Having awakened or warmed the universal gods, the Creator then directed them to create the universe by transforming the virtual universe into the real universe. This was called the "impure creation" (*ashuddha srishti*).

Through his own divine will (which is nonlocal), by means of pure intention, he directed the gods to create the universe. In this way, the gods created all the material worlds and all the beings that inhabit them—the manifest from the unmanifest, or the real from the virtual. The Creator obtained the power to create when he ascended to his own divine station, because his awareness then embraced a vast spectrum of space-time scales. As a result, the analytic and synthetic powers of his awareness were enormous in strength—strong enough to conceive and create the entire universe. At that point, his awareness grasped simultaneously the whole blueprint of creation spanning billions of light-years, as well as all the microscopic parts of creation, by means of which that blueprint was to be executed over the course of billions of years.

This ancient Vedic myth has direct relevance to the enlightened human soul. Like the Creator, the enlightened soul is first born thumb-size from the cosmic womb. In order to grow to become like its Father, it must follow in the footsteps of the Creator. After being born, it must perform tapas and ascend the divine ladder, step by step, until it arrives at the station of the Creator. In the process, the enlightened soul experiences again the mechanics by which the universe was first created. By balanced ascending and descending of the divine ladder, it experiences the progressive enlivenment of the universal vacuum states, which correspond to the metaphysical layers above and below. Upon arriving at the station of the Creator, the enlightened soul becomes identified with the Creator, and conceives the entire universe as its own cosmic body.

This marks a major milestone on the path of immortality, which was emphasized by the ancient seers. At that point, the soul grasps the limits of creation as well as the largest and smallest space-time scales that have direct relevance to the creation of the universe.

THE CANONICAL SET OF THIRTY-THREE GODS

The station of the Creator marks the shore of this world. Beyond that lies the great mystery, which leads ultimately to full immortality in the bosom of the infinite. Upon reaching the station of the Creator, the enlightened soul becomes identified with both the full set of universal gods directly responsible for upholding the created appearance of the universe and the full set of celestial gods, who administer the universe as so many godheads.

According to the Vedic seers, the created appearance of the universe is upheld by a set of thirty-three universal gods and their thirty-three universal shaktis. These gods constitute the religious canon of the Vedic tradition and directly correspond to the first thirty-three layers above the half measure, while their shaktis correspond to the first thirty-three layers below.

If we accept this picture as authoritative, then for all empirical purposes we can restrict our analysis to the first thirty-three layers above and below the half measure. The universal rule of thumb can then be used to predict that the limits of creation are characterized by two matched scales on the order of 2×10^{32} centimeters and 2×10^{-33} centimeters.

THE WHOLE TREE OF LIFE

The Vedic notion of thirty-three universal gods is supported in the Hebrew tradition of kabbalah in which the cosmic body of Adam Ouila, who represents the first archetypal soul, is symbolized by the Etz Chaim, the diagrammatic Tree of Life.

This diagram, which lies at the very heart of the tradition, provides a geometric representation of the fundamental categories on the basis of which the universe is fashioned. The Tree of Life symbolizes the metaphysical Logos, the mere taste of which has the potential to render the soul immortal. In this regard, Adam Ouila, the first archetypal soul, provides a Hebrew conception of the universal being known in the Vedic tradition as Brahma, the first soul, and in the Hermetic tradition as Cosmos, the great god.

The wisdom associated with the Tree of Life suggests that the geometric elements of the diagram correspond to the "bones" of Adam Ouila. This has deep meaning. When the perishable body dies, the soft tissues of the body decay, but the bones remain. The bones may be viewed, then, as the imperishable elements of the body. This suggests that the geometric elements of the diagram correspond to the imperishable aspects of the Logos that uphold the perishable appearance of the Cosmos. These are none other than the imperishable layers of consciousness—which correspond to the universal gods.

The diagrammatic Tree of Life consists of thirty-two geometric elements: the ten *sephiroth* (spheres of splendor), represented by ten circles, and the twenty-two paths of wisdom, represented by twenty-two lines that connect the ten circles.

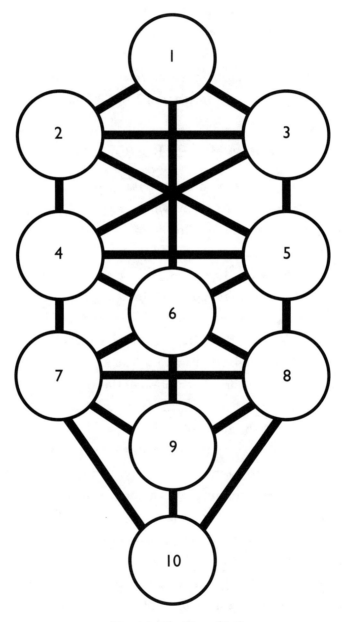

Fig. 4.1. The Tree of Life

The wisdom associated with this diagram relates to the "spine" of Adam Ouila. A spine may be compared to a ladder, with each vertebra corresponding to a rung. In this sense, the thirty-two elements on the Tree of Life may be compared to the first thirty-two layers above the half measure—that is, the rungs of the divine ladder that lead up to the station of the Creator.

Genesis tells us that God stands at the top of the divine ladder. With respect to the created universe, this God corresponds to the celestial godhead—the Creator of the universe—referred to in the tradition of kabbalah as Adam Ouila. This celestial godhead has the form of a sphere. The Hermetic texts tell us that the bodies of the celestial gods consist of only heads, and that a *head* means a "sphere." The Vedic seers referred to this cosmic sphere as the cosmic egg (brahmanda).

In the tradition of kabbalah, the celestial godhead is represented by the Tree of Life taken as a whole. In the same way that the "head" rests upon the thirty-two vertebrae of the spine, so the whole of the Tree of Life rests upon its thirty-two parts. The celestial godhead corresponds to the implied thirty-third aspect of the diagram—the whole. Interestingly, in the Vedic tradition, the thirty-third layer above the half measure was viewed as upholding the "shell" (*kapala*) of the cosmic egg—but the Sanskrit term *kapala* (shell) also means "skull." In this case, the thirty-two layers leading to the thirty-third layer may be compared to the thirty-two vertebrae of the cosmic spine, while the thirty-third layer may be compared to the cosmic skull that rests upon the spine.

As in the Hebrew tradition, there are certain doctrines in the Vedic tradition that give fundamental importance to the first thirty-two layers that uphold the created appearance of the universe. These layers constitute collectively the path of shakti—the path of analysis—which culminates in the realization of the thirty-third layer, viewed as the station of God, the Creator, the synthetic whole. The path of shakti may be compared to the path of subtle energy, up through the thirty-two vertebrae of the human spine, that eventually blossoms in the head.

This presents another take on the ancient notion that humans were created in the image of the Creator.

Therefore, we find that the Vedic and Hebrew sages are largely in agreement regarding the imperishable layers that uphold the perishable appearance of creation. In both cases, the canonical set of layers can be summarized by the mystical formula

$$32 + 1 = 33$$

The thirty-two aspects represent the thirty-two layers, which constitute the ascending path, while the thirty-third aspect represents the synthetic whole—the thirty-third layer, which constitutes the goal of the path.

This congruence between the Vedic and Hebrew traditions lends support to the notion that the created universe is upheld by a canonical set of thirty-three layers, both above and below. The question that remains is whether this understanding is genuinely scientific: Are we dealing with an actual science of the gods, or a mystical form of religious theology?

THE EVALUATION PROBLEM

The validity of a scientific theory rests upon its ability to make accurate empirical predictions. Whatever its assumptions or models, the validity of a theory will be determined by its predictive ability.

The Vedic and Hebrew sages may have expressed their theories of the universe using mystical formulas and diagrams conceived on the basis of a completely different paradigm from that used in modern science, but this does not necessarily mean that their theories were nonscientific. Just as the mathematical formulas of modern theorists must be interpreted in order to assign them empirical meaning, so the mystical formulas of the ancient sages must be interpreted.

Our interpretation of the mystical formula $32 + 1 = 33$ suggests that it pertains to the first thirty-three layers above and below the half measure, which form collectively the spectrum of creation. On the basis of the universal rule of thumb derived from the ancient teachings, we can assign these layers characteristic scales expressed in terms of centimeters. This amounts to an empirical interpretation of the formula. The ancient theory suggests that the thirty-three layers above and below represent the limits of creation. This can be interpreted to mean that they represent the largest and smallest distance scales that have any direct empirical relevance. The system of matched pairs predicts that these limits are on the order of 2×10^{32} centimeters and 2×10^{-33} centimeters, respectively. Given the fact that the ancient system is approximate, these are rough estimates. If they're accurate, however, then the spectrum of creation is huge. The theory suggests that the largest span of creation is on the order of some three hundred trillion light-years, while the smallest span is some twenty-five orders of magnitude smaller than the radius of an atom.

In both cases, these estimates fall outside the range of direct empirical observation. There is no telescope or microscope that can fathom these scales. So how can we possibly evaluate the system using empirical methods? We are faced with a serious evaluation problem.

THE SUPERUNIFICATION SCALE

It turns out that modern theorists are faced with a similar problem. In order to construct a unified theory, it must be formulated on the smallest scale of space and time in the universe that is empirically relevant. This is called the scale of superunification—the scale where all the laws of nature become superunified.

The problem is that this scale cannot be observed empirically, even in principle; it can only be estimated on the basis of logical inference. The general consensus is that the unification scale corresponds to the Planck scale, which is now considered the most important scale in all of physics. It was derived originally at the turn of the twentieth century by a German physicist named Max Planck, who used dimensional analysis of what are arguably the three most important constants in physics:

1. Newton's constant, which governs the strength of gravitational force
2. Planck's constant, which governs the quantifying of all force and matter fields
3. The constant speed of light, which governs the speed of all quantum waves

Planck found that these three constants could be arranged algebraically to define a fundamental distance, time, and mass scale. The problem is that the Planck scale represents an incredibly small time and distance scale that lies far beyond the reach of empirical observation. Due to its nonempirical nature, for many years it was viewed as nothing more than a figment of Planck's imagination—a purely hypothetical scale derived from the units of the fundamental constants. Few theorists took it very seriously.

As they began to search for a unified theory, however, the importance of the Planck scale became more widely recognized. It is now considered the most important scale in physics; any new, unified theory must be formulated to it. More specifically, it represents the scale by which all the fields of force and matter are predicted to assume the form of a single unified field, which represents the source of creation. It follows that the Planck scale may be viewed as the characteristic scale of the Creator below. In other words, it represents the microscopic limit of creation. The ancient science of the gods predicts that the microscopic limit of creation corresponds to the characteristic scale of the thirty-third layer below the half measure. The system of matched pairs provides an estimate of this scale as of 2×10^{-33} centimeters. By comparison, the Planck length is predicted to be 1.616×10^{-33} centimeters. The two predictions, derived on the basis of very different theoretical paradigms, agree to within a factor of 1.

This is our first real indication that the ancient system of matched pairs might be genuinely scientific. At this point, however, the jury is still out. One numerical correspondence, taken by itself, does not make a scientific theory. Further, there is still a problem regarding the predicted macroscopic limit, which is estimated to be 2×10^{32} centimeters—a distance that spans hundreds of trillions of light-years. This is much larger than any cosmological scale conceived in modern theory. As a result, there is no theoretical support in modern science for upper scale, which the ancients conceived as the station of the Creator above.

In order to evaluate fully the scientific validity of the ancient theory, we still have a great deal of work to do. Approaching the problem in a systematic manner, we can start from the beginning—from the scale of the half measure—and examine the most important matched pairs in the spectrum as outlined by the ancient science of the gods. To do this, we must consider the various wisdoms regarding the gods.

THE SCIENTIFIC WISDOMS

In many ancient traditions, the gods were viewed as organized into sets or groups that serve collectively to uphold various levels and forms of creation. In the Vedic tradition, the doctrines pertaining to the groups of gods were called *vidyas*, a Sanskrit term that means both "science" and "wisdom."

The ancient wisdoms are not easy to understand. At first glance, they appear extremely confusing and even contradictory. The problem is that each wisdom purports to present a picture of the whole—yet the number of gods, categories, layers, and so forth involved in the various wisdoms differ widely. From the perspective of the modern mind, which seeks a conclusive, well-defined model of reality, it would seem natural to presume that the ancients were in disagreement—but this would be a mistake. The ancients possessed an enlightened vision of the universe, which was highly subjective, allowing for complementary perspectives on the same idea. This notion is reflected by the Vedic aphorism, "The truth is only One, though the wise may speak about it differently."

Enlightened vision, however, is also holographic. A hologram is a record of coherent light, which can be used to project a three-dimensional image. Unique to a hologram is that the same image can be projected from every part of the record. The larger the part, the higher the resolution of the projected image; the smaller the part, the lower the resolution—yet in every case, the same three-dimensional image can be projected. The spectrum of layers may be compared to a cosmic hologram on the basis of which a three-dimensional image of the universe is projected in consciousness. In this case, the layers correspond to the parts of the hologram. As the enlightened soul ascends through the layers, it grasps larger parts of the cosmic hologram, corresponding to larger sets of layers. As a result, the projected image of the universe increases in resolution, but the same universal image is seen no matter how large a part of the cosmic hologram is grasped.

When the soul begins its journey, it tends to cognize a low-resolution picture of the whole, and at the end of its journey, it cognizes a very high-resolution picture. Yet the same universal image— the same whole—is cognized at every stage. The ancient wisdoms relate to these different holistic pictures of the universe obtained on the basis of different sets of layers. They were formulated in terms of different numbers of gods, categories, worlds, and so forth. As such, they are confusing to us and were also confusing to the ancient students of those wisdoms. For example, in one Vedic text, a discourse is presented between an inquiring student and his teacher. Bewildered by the various opinions of the sages regarding the number of worlds, gods, and categories, the student asks: "With what intention do the sages severally declare such a large variety of numbers?" The teacher replies:

> The categories being comprised in one another, O jewel among men, are enumerated as more or less according to the subjective viewpoint of the speaker. In a single category, whether it is viewed

as a cause or an effect, are found all the other categories. Therefore, we accept as conclusive whatever is stated by those sages, according to their own subjective viewpoint, who are seeking to establish a cause-effect relation, or a definite number of categories, there being a cogent reason behind every such assertion.[5]

The fact is that the ancient science was subjective; it was rooted in various subjective viewpoints on the reality of the universe, and each of those viewpoints was tied to a particular scale, or set of scales, of space and time. The wisdom pertaining to one set of scales may be different from that pertaining to another set, but in every case the wisdom was holistic.

In the remainder of this book, we will examine a number of the most fundamental wisdoms outlined in the Vedic, Egyptian, and Hebrew traditions—each of which utilized its own symbols, metaphors, models, and allegories. In the process, we will discover that when understood, the ancient wisdoms are very scientific. They accurately predict a hidden vertical symmetry in the overall organization of the universe, which is currently unknown in modern theory, but is nevertheless consistent with the empirical evidence. To begin, we shall start with the first wisdom, which has to do with the origin of the universe at the very beginning.

5
The First Wisdom

THE BIG BANG

Modern theory tells us that the universe began several billion years ago with a cosmic explosion from an infinitesimal point of nothingness. In the process, all forms of space, time, matter, and energy were created simultaneously—literally from nothing. This is called the theory of the Big Bang.

Although this theory is enormously popular, it amounts to little more than a modern creation myth. There is no doubt that it can be used to explain many circumstances that are otherwise unexplainable, but its starting premise is flawed logically. The dictates of pure reason tell us that something cannot be created from nothing. In order for the universe to be created, it must have been made from something, though modern science is mute as to what that mysterious something might have been. If we assume the Big Bang is a starting premise, the subsequent explanation of creation can be expressed logically, though it is rooted in an unexplained miracle.

THE FIRST VIRTUAL CREATION

The ancients avoided this trap by suggesting that the universe was created by God, or the field of pure consciousness.

This field is eternal: It existed prior to creation; it exists now, during creation; and it will continue to exist after creation. Prior to creation, however, the field was dormant, as if it were in a state of deep sleep; it was covered by a veil of pure ignorance. At that time, the layers of consciousness, universal gods, or universal vacuum states were all present, but they were "asleep"—that is, nonactive.

The Vedic seers held that the creation of the universe is cyclic, that the universal gods, like all living beings, experience cycles of waking and sleeping. When the gods sleep, creation is dissolved, and when they wake up, creation is initiated. Moreover, they held that these cosmic cycles of waking and sleeping, or creation and dissolution, span hundreds of trillions rather than a few billion years. For them, these cycles are governed by the force of time, which manifests the will of God, the Supreme Being.

When we as human beings begin to wake from the state of deep sleep, we experience an intermediate state during which we are neither fully asleep nor fully awake. It is a dreamlike state filled with forms of virtual reality, which respond to our slightest intentions and present our ideas in living color. The seers held that when the universal gods begin to wake, they experience a similar cosmic dreaming state characterized by virtual forms of reality. This is where the ancient theory of creation begins.

As in modern theory, the ancients held that the creation of the universe starts from a single point—but this was not viewed as a point of nothingness. Instead, it was seen as a point value of consciousness viewed as the seat of the first semiawakened soul, which was destined to become the Creator of the universe: When the Creator was first born from the cosmic womb, or the field of pure ignorance, he was in a cosmic dreaming state and was therefore semiawakened. He did not experience the empirical forms of reality that we associate with the waking state; rather, he experienced the virtual forms of reality that we associate with the dreaming state.

In the beginning, this cosmic dream was formless. It involved the cognition of the universal fields of transcendental sound and transcendental light associated with the first matched pair of layers located immediately above and below the half measure. Prior to this initial cognition, these fields were dormant, hidden by the veil of pure ignorance so that they were reduced to abstract fields of silent darkness. It was only when the Creator emerged from the cosmic womb, and then took his first step on the divine ladder, that the veil of ignorance was removed and the universal fields of light and sound shone forth in an instantaneous flash of pure intuition.

In the first hymn of the tenth mandala of the Rig Veda,[1] this initial emergence of light from the darkness was compared to a great fire: "The great fire at the beginning of the dawn has emerged, and issuing forth from the darkness has come with radiance." The hymn goes on to tell us that this great fire "filled all dwellings with shining light." These are none other than the dwelling places of the imperishable souls that constitute collectively the metaphysical Logos. They correspond to the crystallographic cells of the transcendental superlattice, each of which serves as the abode for an imperishable point value of consciousness.

The hymn further explains that this great fire was the "embryo of heaven and earth." It represents the first virtual form of the universe conceived within the cosmic womb on the scale of the first matched pair of layers immediately above and below the half measure. It was not insentient; it was personified as Agni (fire), the first ministrant priest, who is described as "all-knowing"[2] and is cognizant of the path of the fathers that leads to the gods.[3] This personified conscious fire represents the first virtual embodiment of the Creator at the dawn of creation.

As we have seen, this first virtual form of creation embraced initially the first two layers above and below the half measure. The layer below, which represents the luminous body of the Creator, was dominated by transcendental light and filled with local analytic power, and the layer above, which represents the Creator's sonic soul, was dominated by transcendental sound and filled with nonlocal synthetic power. The first virtual embodiment of the Creator involved the union of his luminous body and his sonic soul, the first matched pair of layers in the cosmic spectrum.

The emergence of the great fire at the dawn of creation was the first virtual Big Bang and marked the onset of the virtual creation (shuddha srishti) wherein the universal layers, universal gods, or universal vacuum states, would become enlivened progressively as the awareness of the Creator simultaneously ascended and descended through them in sequence. It was only after the Creator had ascended to his own divine station that the virtual creation began to be transformed into the real creation. Only then did the virtual particles and waves begin their transformation into the real particles and waves from which was fashioned the empirical universe.

The real creation followed in the footsteps of the virtual creation. It started from the beginning, on the scale of the first matched pair of layers immediately above and below the half measure.

THE FIRST UNIVERSAL LIGHT

The ancient theory outlined above suggests that the oldest form of real light in the universe was created on the wavelength scale of the first layer below the half measure. Real light means observable light—the type of light that can be detected empirically.

The universal rule of thumb can be used to estimate this scale as 2×10^{-1} centimeters, or approximately 2 millimeters. This amounts to a deductive prediction rooted in ancient principles and related to the oldest form of universal light that can be detected empirically. Is there any evidence, however, that this prediction holds true?

It turns out that there is. Electromagnetic waves with a wavelength that is roughly two millimeters lie within the microwave frequency band. Unlike visible radiation, microwave radiation is not visible to the human eye; therefore, the waves are hidden from direct human perception—but they are not hidden to electromagnetic instruments.

According to the history of science, microwaves were first discovered during the first half of the twentieth century and were employed for practical use beginning around the time of World War II. Since then, microwaves have become a part of our daily lives; we use them to cook our food and talk on our cell phones. Toward the middle of the twentieth century, when microwave antennas were first developed, scientists began to point them at the starry heavens, and therefore made a remarkable discovery: They found that the universe is pervaded by a uniform, homogenous, isotropic radiation field characterized by microwaves. This became known as the cosmic microwave background radiation (CMBR).

Oddly, the CMBR has no known empirical point source; it is not emitted by the stars or galaxies or any of the charged particles floating in space. It appears to be a fundamental feature of the cosmological vacuum itself. Its origin was initially a mystery. Theorists eventually concluded that it represents the leftover remnants of the big bang, the hypothetical event that, billions of years ago, created everything from nothing in a huge cosmic explosion. Consequently, the CMBR is considered currently to be the oldest form of real light in the universe. This is consistent with the ancient theory, which suggests that the oldest form of real light in the universe should lie in the microwave frequency band. Yet the prediction derived from the basis of ancient principles is quite specific, predicting that the CMBR should have a characteristic wavelength of about 2 millimeters—the characteristic scale of the first layer below the half measure. Here, we can learn if this prediction holds true.

The CMBR is known to have a blackbody spectrum, which consists of electromagnetic waves of different wavelengths and frequencies, but the intensity of the blackbody radiation can be plotted out in the form of a spectral intensity curve as a function of wavelength. In each such spectrum there will be a maximum in the curve that corresponds to a particular wavelength, which characterizes the spectrum.

We know that the maximum of the spectral intensity curve for the CMBR occurs at a wavelength scale of 1.86 millimeters. The prediction derived on the basis of ancient theory is 2 millimeters, which agrees with the empirical facts to within a factor of 1. This suggests that we are dealing with a highly scientific system that is capable of making accurate empirical predictions.

No doubt, the ancient system is couched in religious-spiritual terms—but we can see that when it is interpreted properly, it has predictive power. So far we have seen that it can be used to predict accurately the scale of superunification as well as the characteristic wavelength scale of the oldest form of light in the universe. Are these just coincidences, or are we dealing with a genuine spiritual science, which was known to the ancients thousands of years before the first modern scientist was born?

THE FIRST UNIVERSAL SOUND

Now let us turn our attention to the first universal sound: According to our interpretation of the ancient science, it should be characterized by longitudinal sound waves that have a wavelength on the scale of the first layer above the half measure—that is, 1 digit, or approximately 2 centimeters.

We should understand, however, that the first universal sound does not represent a sound wave in air or any other physical medium. Instead, it represents a sound wave in consciousness, which propagates nonlocally at the speed of thought, rather than locally at the speed of sound. This means that it will be undetectable by any empirical means—which presents a serious problem: How can the prediction be evaluated empirically?

The ancients provided the answer. According to the Vedic seers, the first universal sound represents the first shruti—the first sound that was "heard" by the Creator at the beginning of creation. More specifically, it represents the smallest wavelength of transcendental sound that can be heard by the divine ear—the ear of pure consciousness.

To evaluate the wavelength of this sound, the ancients used a fundamental anthropomorphic principle. The Bible tells us that humans were created in the image of the Creator, and similar anthropomorphic principles can be found in virtually all of the ancient traditions. In this instance, they suggest that the smallest wavelength of transcendental sound that can be heard by the divine ear should correspond to the smallest wavelength of physical sound that can be heard by the human ear. Although a wavelength of transcendental sound cannot be measured practically, it can be measured in principle by drawing upon the correspondence between the human ear and the divine ear. This leads to the prediction that the finest physical sound that can be heard by the human ear should have a wavelength on the order of 1 digit. We can evaluate this empirically.

Modern acoustics tell us that the highest frequency that can be heard by the average adult human ear is roughly 16,000–20,000 Hertz (cycles per second). At 70 degrees Fahrenheit, which we may take as the ideal temperature for human life on earth, the speed of sound in the ambient air at sea level is 344 meters per second. The highest frequency that can be heard by the adult human ear will therefore have a characteristic wavelength that is roughly 1.72–2.15 centimeters. The average of this range is 1.94 centimeters. One digit is estimated to be approximately 2 centimeters, which means that the highest frequency of sound that can be heard by the adult human ear has a wavelength that is more or less equal to 1 digit—as predicted on the basis of ancient principles. Is this, however, just another coincidence?

To calculate the smallest wavelength of audible sound that can be heard by the human ear, we must know the speed of sound in air. Yet there is no archaeological or textual evidence to suggest that the ancients knew this figure. Nevertheless, it appears that they knew, directly and intuitively, that the smallest wavelength of physical sound that can be heard by the human ear corresponds to the smallest wavelength of transcendental sound that can be heard by the divine ear.

According to the ancient "system of measured arrangement" that wavelength is on the order of 1 digit.

We can demonstrate the validity of this prediction with respect to the human ear, but not to the divine ear. If, however, we accept the principles of the ancient science as authoritative, then the two sounds should correspond.

THE SILENT DARKNESS OF THE HALF MEASURE

If the finest audible sound that can be heard by both the human ear and the divine ear has a characteristic wavelength of roughly 1 digit, then this implies that any sonic impulse with a wavelength smaller than that will be experienced as silence, rather than a sound.

This silence is characteristic of the half measure, which represents the scale of the field of silent darkness that serves as the boundary between heaven and earth and which, from the system of matched pairs, is about 1 centimeter. On the scale of the half measure, all perceptible forms of light and sound are transcended. When awareness becomes established on this scale, the field of pure consciousness is experienced as a field of silent darkness. It is only when awareness takes its first step on the divine ladder, by ascending to the first layer above and descending to the first layer below that the universal sound becomes heard and the universal light becomes seen.

The Vedic seers used an acoustic analogy to describe the silence of the half measure. The Upanishads, the Vedic texts that specifically deal with the eternal self, tell us that it corresponds to the silence that arises when the tones of a struck bell fade away. According to modern acoustics, the final audible tones of a struck bell are manifested by the highest harmonics of the bell, which have the smallest audible wavelengths. Because the half measure is roughly $\frac{1}{2}$ digit (approximately 1 centimeter), it transcends the smallest wavelength that can be heard by the human ear. As a result, when the smallest audible tones of the struck bell fade, the awareness is led to the silence of the half measure.

This principle was employed in ancient meditation practices and is used in the practice of Transcendental Meditation. According to Maharishi Mahesh Yogi, who has popularized this ancient practice in modern times, it involves following a mental sound to its source in silence—that is, initiating a particular sonic formula (mantra) on the level of the mind and then allowing that sound to fade away into silence. Doing this leads the awareness to the scale of the half measure, to the field of silent darkness that serves as the boundary between heaven and earth, to the midpoint between the infinite and infinitesimal. On that scale, all perceptible impulses of the mind are transcended. Therefore, it is experienced as a state of no thought. The field of silent darkness may be filled with sonic and luminous impulses, but they are imperceptible and are thereby hidden from view.

It is only when that state becomes established permanently and the soul takes its first step on the divine ladder, ascending to the first layer above and descending to the first layer below simultaneously, that the universal light and sound of consciousness become cognized. This results in the soul cognizing the same universal fields of transcendental light and sound experienced by the Creator at the dawn of creation. At this point, it becomes reborn as an enlightened, universal soul.

THE SCIENCE OF SACRED RITUAL

The utility of a scientific theory lies in its practical applications, and the ancient science was no different in this regard—but the practical applications of the ancient science were rooted in a completely different paradigm than those of modern science.

Whereas the material technologies of modern science are designed to engineer the local laws of nature, the spiritual technologies of the ancient science were designed primarily to engineer the nonlocal laws of nature. These technologies involved the practice of sacred rituals. As we have learned, the ancients required that the dimensions of their sacred altars, temples, arks, and pyramids be measured using an integral number of digits. Although these were material constructions, they were designed for spiritual purposes and were typically associated with ritual practices involving specific actions of the body accompanied by the recitation of specific sacred sounds to invoke the gods.

Human speech involves the production of sound waves in air, which impinge upon the human ear and are then "heard" by the mind. As we have discussed, the smallest impulse of audible sound that can be heard by both the human and divine mind has a wavelength of roughly 1 digit. The fact that sacred constructions were measured purposefully in terms of an integral number of digits implies that they were designed to "resonate" with the smallest wavelength of physical speech that can be heard by the human mind as well as the smallest wavelength of divine speech that can be heard by the divine mind.

This wavelength scale represents the sonic foundation of heaven and the quantum of divine speech on the basis of which all higher (larger) forms of divine speech are measured. Because the higher wavelengths of divine speech are related harmonically to the quantum of that speech, sound waves that are roughly 1 digit are capable of resonating throughout the entire upper half of the spectrum—which the ancients viewed as heaven. By invoking the digit in their expressions of sacred speech and in their sacred constructions, the ancients sought to invoke heaven on earth. They sought to attune their own physical bodies as well as the body of the sacred altar with that of Logos.

In ancient times the performance of such sacred rituals was deemed essential to uphold on earth the balance of human life, both individual and collective. In addition, such rituals were deemed essential to upholding the balance in nature so that the rains would come on time, the crops would fructify, and so forth. This balance was seen as a blessing of the gods, who ultimately control all things in the universe by means of the adrishta—the unseen sonic influence that manifests the will of the gods or God. In order to obtain this blessing, the ancients believed in the importance of worshipping the gods by reciting sacred sounds and performing sacred rituals using carefully measured instruments, materials, and altars, which were designed to resonate with the fundamental mode of the adrishta—that is, their measurements were based roughly on 1 digit.

Such rituals were designed to establish a harmony between heaven and earth; so that the unseen influence of the gods in heaven could be manifested on earth in a beneficial, harmonious way. Unfortunately, over the course of time, the science that inspired these ancient rituals originally was lost, and as a result, they became ineffectual. In the earliest cultures on earth, however, such rituals served as an important practical application of the ancient spiritual science: They were designed to engineer the field of pure consciousness for the benefit of humankind on earth.

When the ancient spiritual science was lost and the reasoning for the rituals was reduced to religious platitudes and dogma, the effectiveness of its practical application was also lost. As a result, the harmony between the gods in heaven and human beings on earth began to erode. The gods departed, leaving humankind to its own devices, for better or worse. Rather than relying upon spiritual technologies to engineer the nonlocal and unseen forces of nature, human beings then began to rely upon physical technologies to engineer the local and observable forces of nature. This has had its benefits: by developing material technologies on the basis of physical science, our physical lives have become more comfortable and convenient. Yet in the absence of any real spiritual technologies based upon a genuine spiritual science, our spiritual lives have suffered greatly; we have forgotten completely the gods, and the notion that the human soul is immortal or might hope to become immortal is now looked upon as a delusion, which no sensible person would take seriously. Even though our physical lives have become better, our spiritual lives have become worse.

The ideal state would be to have both physical technologies and spiritual technologies in our lives. There is no reason to abandon physical science or its material technologies—but physical science must be supplemented with a complementary spiritual science and its technologies. In this way, we could have our cake and eat it too; we could engineer both the local and nonlocal forces of nature for our benefit. Whether or not this will come to pass remains to be seen. The signs indicate that it will, but whether we will follow those signs is another matter.

6

The Standard
Cosmological Model

THE IDEAL NATURE OF
HUMAN EXISTENCE

The idea that the human mind and body resemble the divine mind and body amounts to a profound anthropomorphic principle, which pervaded the ancient science. We have already seen that it can be used to predict accurately the smallest audible wavelength that can be heard by the human ear. Yet why does this principle work? As we have seen, the sound waves that are heard by the human ear correspond to sound waves in the ambient atmosphere of the earth. If the earth's atmosphere were to have a different air density, then the speed of sound in air would be different, as would the wavelengths associated with a given frequency of audible sound.

In this case, the prediction regarding the smallest audible wavelength, based upon the measured arrangement of the matched pairs of layers in the metaphysical Logos, would no longer hold true. This wavelength would have a size different from 1 digit.

Yet this is not the case. The particular air density in which human beings have evolved carries the smallest audible wavelength: roughly 1 digit. This raises a fundamental question regarding the ideal nature of both the human being and our planet. According to the ancients, human beings are unique among all created beings in the sense that they are suited ideally for the realization of spiritual immortality. Moreover, this realization was deemed the ultimate purpose of creation. In order for human beings to evolve, however, they need a more or less ideal environment—an ideal planet.

Of all the planets within our solar system, only Earth provides the ideal environment for such evolution. When scientists search the starry heavens for possible signs of intelligent life, they look typically to other solar systems similar to our own that might include a planet similar to our own. It is accepted that the conditions required for the evolution of organic life, including humans, are very specific. Not just any planet will do; it has to resemble our own. If the human represents an ideal organic being capable of realizing the very purpose of creation, then the planet upon which human beings evolve must be ideal.

THE STANDARD BIOLOGICAL BODY

As we have seen, the parameters of the system of matched pairs was established in terms of the digit—the width of a human thumb. Based upon the notion that a human is created in the image of the Creator, the ancients used this particular part of the human body as a standard of measure to determine the dimensions of both the Cosmos and the Logos in accordance with principles of ratio and proportion.

The fact that this scheme can be used to make accurate, empirical predictions regarding the overall organization of the universe suggests that the human body presents a more or less ideal reflection of the whole. Put another way, we might say that the human body represents a standard biological body on the basis of which we can measure both the Cosmos and Logos. This notion of the standard biological body means that the human body—specifically, the human thumb, which forms the parameters of the system of matched pairs—can be used as a standard of measure to determine the overall dimensions of the physical

Cosmos and the characteristic dimensions of the various layers within the metaphysical Logos.

THE FATHERS OF HUMANKIND

The ancients held that the human body was the gift of the gods, who were the fathers of humankind. These include universal gods, who correspond to the metaphysical layers, and celestial gods, who correspond to the celestial bodies that shine in the sky.

The celestial gods, who have presided over the evolution of human life from the very beginning, are not just abstract disembodied beings; they have concrete bodies that correspond to our sun, solar system, galaxy, local universe, and superuniverse—each of which represents a conscious celestial being with powers of consciousness that far exceed those of ordinary human beings on earth.

In the same way that the Cosmos as a whole was viewed as an embodiment of the first archetypal man (Adam Ouila), who is our Father in heaven, so also, our sun, solar system, galaxy, and so forth were viewed as relatively immortal men who are our fathers in heaven. The Hermetic texts tell us: "We must not shrink then from saying that a man on earth is a mortal god, and that a god in heaven is an immortal man."[1]

The celestial gods were viewed as immortal as compared to human beings, because unlike the human body, their celestial bodies endure for billions of years. They were compared to humans because the enlightened soul of a human being and that of a celestial being are akin to one another in the sense that both are born from the same cosmic womb—the field of silent darkness that exists on the scale of the half measure. This means that the wisdom cognized by the human soul when it takes its first step on the divine ladder is the same as the first wisdom cognized by the celestial gods billions of years ago.

The difference is that the celestial gods, for billions of years, were born for a specific purpose: to uphold and preside over the appearance of the created universe within their own sphere of influence. Unlike the human being, who is born from a mortal womb as an unenlightened being and is reborn subsequently from the cosmic womb as an enlightened being, the celestial gods were born not from any mortal womb, but from the cosmic womb as already enlightened beings who immediately cognized the first wisdom and proceeded to ascend to their own cosmic stations. They then began the work of creation in accordance with the will of the Creator, who preceded and presides over them. This means that they began to create their own celestial bodies, which would serve as "worlds" for all embodied beings—including human beings. The Vedic seers held that this gradual process of creation took place over the course of billions of years.

Although modern science tells us that the universe evolved as a result of chance and circumstance, the ancient science tells us that it evolved under the nonlocal guidance of divine will, which was and is directed toward a teleological purpose: the redemption of souls that have become lost and have fallen into the clutches of mortality. It is the old story of the prodigal son who became lost. The father pined for him, doing all within his power to bring his lost son back into the fold. The lost son is none other than the unenlightened soul. The universe was created—and will continue to be created, cycle after cycle, over the course of eternity—to recover the souls that have lost their way and fallen into the clutches of mortality.

In order to be redeemed, the lost soul must first be born from a mortal womb, and then reborn from the cosmic womb. According to the ancients, there is no more favorable mortal womb for this purpose than that of the human being, who is suited ideally for the realization of immortality. To provide the conditions for this spiritual redemption, material worlds must be created from which conscious, material beings can evolve. That is the job of the celestial gods, who are controlled ultimately by the universal gods, who serve as their inner controllers. In the same way that the son is created in the image of the father, so is a human created in the image of his or her celestial fathers—the gods that shine in the sky.

STANDARD CELESTIAL BODIES

If the human being is suited ideally for the realization of immortality, then the celestial gods that have presided over the evolution of the human body, mind, and soul since the very beginning must also share in that ideal.

This has a concrete meaning. If the human body serves as a standard biological body by which the dimensions of the Cosmos and Logos can be determined systematically, then the celestial bodies of the gods, who are directly responsible for the evolution of the human body, must represent standard celestial bodies. This presents a radically new cosmological concept, which deserves some explanation.

Modern astrophysical observations have revealed that there are many different types of stars in the universe, some of which are similar to our own sun and some of which differ from our sun, both in size and behavior. In recent years, it has been shown that there are solar systems associated with some of these stars that may or may not be similar to our own. There are also many types of galaxies, some of which are similar to ours and some of which are different. At this point in history, we do not know if we are alone in the universe. According to the ancient seers, we are not. For example, the Vedic texts are filled with stories of enlightened sages traveling to different worlds within our far-flung galaxy, visiting places inhabited by human beings like ourselves. Yet the texts also make clear that the seers did not visit these worlds by traveling in spaceships. Instead, they used the spiritual power of their own consciousness. If we take these stories at face value, it follows that the ancient seers did not have to speculate about other forms of life in the universe; such life was part of their direct experience.

As far as modern theorists are concerned, however, the question of the existence of other intelligent beings in the universe is still unresolved. It is recognized generally that the conditions required for the evolution of organic life within a given solar system are quite specific.

The solar system must be similar to our own, which is suited ideally for the evolution of various forms of organic life, including human life. If the human represents an ideal organic being, then our sun, solar system, and galaxy must likewise be viewed as ideal celestial beings, which have also been created in the image of Cosmos, according to principles of ratio and proportion.

THE STANDARD COSMOLOGICAL MODEL

In the chapters that remain, we will discover that the ancient science of the gods was formulated in terms of a standard cosmological model: It was expressed specifically in terms of our sun, solar system, galaxy, and visible universe, which can be understood as standard cosmological bodies that represent our own celestial fathers—the celestial gods that have presided over the evolution of human life on earth from the very beginning.

The hypothesis here is that these celestial bodies, like the human body, should more or less reflect ideally the system of measured arrangement inherent within the metaphysical Logos. According to the ancients, the characteristic measure of the human body is the digit, the thumb measure. Yet the celestial gods do not have organic bodies, with limbs, arms, legs, and fingers. They take the form of spheres, the characteristic measure of which is its radius. Just as the system of measured arrangement is reflected by the width of the human thumb, which represents the characteristic measure of the standard biological body, so should it be reflected by the radii of the celestial bodies, which represent the characteristic measures of the standard cosmological bodies.

As we have seen, the digit represents an approximate unit of measure that can vary from one person to the next. The same holds true for the sizes of the standard cosmological bodies. Given the fact that there are some twenty trillion stars in the visible universe, it may turn out that there are many solar systems scattered throughout the universe that support human life. These stars and solar systems may have celestial bodies that vary somewhat in size—but just as the width of a human thumb varies only slightly from one person to another, so the size of the standard cosmological body varies only slightly. We adopt as a general principle that to be considered standard, the sizes of the cosmological bodies should be on the same order of magnitude. Any cosmological body that does not meet this standard may be viewed as immature—that is, still in the process of evolving; aged, or past its prime and in the process of decay; or deformed, perhaps by some cosmic accident such as a collision between stars or galaxies.

We can assume that none of these nonstandard conditions are suited ideally for the evolution of human life. This does not necessarily mean that organic life cannot evolve under such conditions, but it does imply that the resultant forms of organic life will likely be nonideal.

THE BIG PICTURE

The concept of a standard cosmological model may seem exceedingly humancentric, but it is consistent with the teachings of the ancients regarding the ideal nature of the human being and his or her unique position in the overall scheme of creation.

If the ultimate purpose of creation is to produce human beings who have the potential to realize their immortal status and become like God, then we might ask why human beings have not evolved on every planet or in every solar system. The answer requires a bigger picture.

The conditions required to realize the ultimate purpose of creation are not local—that is, they are nonlocal. The influences that ultimately govern the behavior of every elementary particle in creation correspond to nonlocal influences which, carried by the modes of transcendental sound, serve to correlate the behavior of one element here and the behavior of other elements there, no matter how far apart these elements might be in space. This means that everything in the universe, whether it displays an ideal or nonideal form, must play some part in the realization of God's will.

As human beings with limited intelligence and knowledge, it is impossible for us to understand fully the workings of God's will, because he works in mysterious ways on the basis of nonlocal omniscience. What appears to be a matter of chance and circumstance from our very limited and local perspective is not at all, in the final analysis, a matter of chance and circumstance. It is all part of a divine plan, which is continuously evolving under the guidance of the nonlocal will of God.

Divine will is expressed on different scales of time and space and originating from different locations within the universe through all the celestial gods—in fact, through every individual soul or point value of consciousness in existence. The ultimate purpose of creation may be to make human beings who have the potential to realize their immortal status, but this is not its only purpose. God has in his care all souls—not just human souls. Each type of soul requires its own conditions to evolve toward the ultimate goal. As a result, many different conditions must be created within the universe to further the ultimate purpose of creation. Some of these are more or less suited for the evolution of human life, and some are not.

According to the ancients, everything within the universe—down to the smallest elementary particle—is alive and endowed with soul. To provide conditions favorable for the evolution of all beings, and not just human beings, different types of stars, solar systems, galaxies, and so forth have been created to serve as "worlds" for those beings. The seers held, however, that of all the different types of life within the universe, human life here and now is suited most ideally for the realization of immortality.

Therefore, birth in a human womb was considered the highest blessing of God, and the sages bemoaned the fact that this blessing is often squandered in the pursuit of transient sensory pleasure, rather than the pursuit of immortality. Further, although they realized that their science of immortality, or science of the gods, would eventually become lost over the course of time as humankind became increasingly addicted to the material pursuit of sensory pleasure, they also held out hope that in the end the direction of time would be reversed by the will of God, and their teachings would be rediscovered and understood in their true scientific light.

To demonstrate the scientific validity of the ancient spiritual teachings, we need a standard cosmological model so that the measures of the celestial bodies related directly to the evolution of human life can first be predicted deductively and then evaluated empirically. This is the only way to demonstrate concretely the scientific validity of the ancient teachings. Having discovered what is meant by a standard cosmological model, we are now ready to proceed with an examination of the second wisdom, which pertains to the first of the great celestial gods, whose body shines in the sky as our very own sun: the solar wisdom.

7

The Solar Wisdom

ADITYA, THE SUN GOD

In the Vedic tradition, our sun was called Aditya, the son of Aditi. As we have seen, Aditi represents the unbounded cosmic womb experienced on the scale of the half measure. The first great celestial body to be born from that womb corresponds to a star or sun. For this reason, Aditya, the sun that shines in the sky, was viewed as the firstborn son of Aditi.

Yet there was a deeper wisdom regarding the celestial body of the sun. It was viewed as the manifestation of twelve universal gods called the *adityas,* the first twelve gods in the Vedic canon, which correspond to the first twelve layers above the half measure and constitute collectively the sonic soul of the sun. Aditya, the sun that shines in the sky, may be understood as the celestial manifestation of the twelve adityas— the first twelve vacuum states in the upper half of the spectrum, which predominate with nonlocal synthesizing power.

THE TWO FORMS OF SOLAR WISDOM

The twelvefold wisdom regarding the sun has both a higher and lower form. The higher wisdom pertains to the twelve adityas above, which constitute the sonic soul of the sun, while the lower wisdom pertains to their twelve shaktis below, which constitute collectively the luminous soul of the sun. From a practical point of view, these two forms of solar wisdom were used to determine the virtual influences coming from the sun. The nonlocal sonic influences emanating from the sun were conceived in terms of the twelve adityas above, and the local luminous influences were conceived in terms of their twelve shaktis below.

These may also be viewed as inner and outer wisdoms, respectively. The inner wisdom is related to the inner circle of the sun, which has twelve divisions related to the twelve adityas, and the outer wisdom relates to the outer circle of the zodiac, which has twelve divisions related to the twelve shaktis.

THE NONLOCAL INFLUENCE OF THE SUN

The inner circle of the sun corresponds to the spherical body of the Sun, which appears as a luminous circle in the sky. The outer circle of the zodiac corresponds to the apparently circular path of the sun around Earth during the course of a solar year.

The nonlocal sonic influences have little to do with the position of the sun with respect to Earth: because these influences travel faster than light—at the speed of thought—they manifest nonlocal correlations, which have no local cause-effect interpretation. Such a cause-effect relation occurs when some event "there" has the potential to affect another event "here" through an influence that travels at the speed of light. Because they travel faster than light, the sonic emanations of the sun do not manifest these types of local relations. As a result, considerations of "here" and "there" do not play an important role.

Most important to consider with respect to the sonic influences that come from the inner circle of the Sun is the sonic wavelength and frequency. These properties are expressed according to the layered structure of the Logos. The wavelengths and frequencies are quantized on the basis of the characteristic scales of the first twelve layers above the half measure (the twelve adityas). The inner solar wisdom is therefore vertical and not horizontal, and pertains to relative space-time scale, rather than relative space-time position.

THE LOCAL INFLUENCES OF THE SUN

The outer solar wisdom, on the other hand, is horizontal, rather than vertical. This means that the local luminous influences that come from the sun are highly dependent on the position of the Sun with respect to Earth.

These influences correspond not to the real electromagnetic waves emanated by the sun, but to the virtual electromagnetic waves that pervade the universe. Though these waves are virtual, they nevertheless have the potential to manifest local cause-effect relations and to influence locally the spontaneous emissions and quantum fluctuations displayed by every atom and elementary particle in creation. The sonic influences have a similar potential—but unlike luminous influences, they are nonlocal, and therefore have little to do with relative position.

The Vedic seers referred to the virtual light of consciousness as transcendental light (param jyotih). Therefore, the science of jyotih (light) was called Jyotish (pertaining to the light)—Vedic astrology. As in the Western traditions of astrology, with the twelve signs of the zodiac, the Vedic seers divided the apparent circular path of the sun around Earth into twelve divisions, each consisting of 30 degrees. In Jyotish, these twelve divisions were called *rashis,* a Sanskrit term meaning a "collection of rays." These represent the rays of virtual light that emanate from the so-called fixed stars—the stars and galaxies that are so distant from the earth that they appear to be fixed or unmoving. According to the seers, the rays coming from the distant universe carry different qualities depending upon the region from which they come. These qualities were symbolized by the signs associated with each rashi: the bull, the lion, and so forth. In this regard, the Greek and Vedic astrologers were largely in agreement: Both used the same signs or symbols for the twelve divisions. For example, in the Vedic tradition, the sign of Taurus was called Vrishabha (the bull) and the sign of Leo was called Simha (the lion).

Although the qualities of the rays coming from the distant

universe were viewed as static or fixed, these could nevertheless be modified by the transit of a celestial body, such as the sun, through that sign. In this case, the virtual light associated with the sun would mix with the virtual light coming from the distant universe and therefore give rise to a new, qualified form of light. The same holds true for all the planets and celestial bodies within our solar system, but because the sun is the chief of the celestial bodies, its modifying effect upon the universal light was deemed exceedingly important. Unlike that of the planets, the modifying effect of the sun extends over the full range of the twelve universal shaktis, which, as we have seen, correspond to the first twelve luminous layers below the half measure. Although these layers are organized vertically on different space-time scales, they have an outer or horizontal representation in terms of the twelve rashis, or divisions of the zodiac.

THE PREDICTIVE NATURE OF THE SOLAR WISDOM

The Vedic seers used these correspondences to develop a profound predictive science. They held that all events on Earth are largely governed by the sonic and luminous influences coming from the various celestial bodies—including the Sun—in immediate proximity to Earth. These celestial bodies were viewed as the visible bodies of celestial gods.

Whereas the sonic influences are largely determined by the space-time scales on which the awareness of a given celestial god operates, the luminous influences are determined largely by the position of the celestial body during its transit through the twelve rashis. Because the sun represents the chief celestial god within our solar system, the predictive science was based largely upon the solar wisdom, which pertains to the twelve adityas above and their twelve shaktis below. We will soon see that this same wisdom can be used to make accurate predictions regarding the radius of the sun and the radius of the elementary particles that compose the body of the sun.

THE BIRTH OF RA

In the Egyptian tradition, the sun that shines in the sky was identified with Ra, the creator sun god. According to a prominent Egyptian creation myth, Ra—born of Nun, the unbounded watery abyss, the unbounded cosmic womb that exists on the scale of the half measure—was the first celestial god to be born at the beginning of creation.

The myth describing the birth of Ra uses two potent symbols corresponding to the luminous body of the sun and the sonic soul of the sun: the luminous mound or island that emerged from the watery abyss and the *bennu* bird (the Egyptian phoenix), which, prior to the emergence of the luminous mound, hovered over the watery abyss with no place to land.

When the luminous mound appeared, the bennu bird perched upon it, and then uttered a cry that gave rise to all that exists. This represents the union of heaven and earth, the union of the sonic layers above, which are endowed with nonlocal synthesizing power, and the luminous layers below, which are endowed with local analyzing power. Their union created a conscious material being—Ra, the celestial sun god.

THE INNER CIRCLE OF THE DUAT

In the Egyptian tradition, the inner circle of the sun was represented by the inner circle of the Duat. The hieroglyph used to represent this concept was that of a circle inside of which was a five-pointed star. The circle represents the celestial body of the sun, which resembles a luminous circle in the sky, and the five-pointed star represents the solar or stellar "person" that dwells within the circle.

The five appendages of the five-pointed star correspond to the five human appendages: the head, two arms, and two legs. Following this was the notion that the solar person dwelling within the solar body is similar to the human person dwelling within the human body. The Hermetic texts verbalized this by comparing a human being to a mortal god on earth and a god to an immortal man in the heavens.

THE TWELVE DIVISIONS OF THE DUAT

Yet the Egyptians possessed a deeper wisdom concerning the inner circle of the Duat: it had twelve inner divisions that correspond to the first twelve layers above the half measure, identified by the Vedic seers as the twelve adityas.

We find, therefore, that the Vedic and Egyptian seers agreed regarding the inner reality of the sun. Both viewed the inner circle of the sun or the inner circle of the Duat as having twelve inner divisions. Further, we should not ignore the fact that these twelve divisions are related to the circle of the sun. According to the ancient science of the gods, the universal gods determine their own celestial manifestations. By virtue of their nonlocal synthesizing power, they determine the cosmological wholes that are created from the microscopic parts of creation.

THE SOLAR RADIUS

The whole of the sun appears in the form of a sphere or circle whose characteristic measure is its radius. If the solar whole is determined by the twelve adityas—the first twelve layers above the half measure—then its radius should correspond to the characteristic scale of the twelfth layer above the half measure.

The universal rule of thumb provides an estimate of this scale as 10^{11} centimeters. This leads to an accurate prediction regarding the radius of the sun, derived on the basis of the ancient science of the gods: According to modern astrophysics, the radius of our sun is indeed roughly 10^{11} centimeters.

To reach this prediction, we need only rely upon the ancient science of the gods, which gives the sun a twelvefold inner nature. We can interpret these twelve inner aspects in terms of the first twelve layers above the half measure whose parameters have been set using a universal rule of thumb. Because the upper layers are dominated by synthesizing power, it follows that they should determine the size of the solar whole. This represents the spherical body of a single being—the celestial sun god, whose awareness serves to correlate nonlocally into a single whole all the microscopic parts of its body.

The methodology is simple, but the question remains: Why does it work? The fact is that there are many stars or suns in the galaxy with radii different from that of our own. Some are considerably larger than that of our sun and some are considerably smaller. Further, we do not know if these other stars possess solar systems that include a planet similar to our own—a planet upon which human life has evolved. All we know is that the solar system associated with our sun provides suitable conditions for the evolution of human life.

This goes back to our concept of a standard cosmological model. Because our sun represents a celestial god that has presided over the evolution of human life from the very beginning, it must share the same ideality possessed by the human being. This means that the dimensions of its celestial body, like the dimensions of the human body, must reflect the layered organization of the metaphysical Logos. Whereas the characteristic dimension of the human body corresponds to the digit, tied to the first layer above the half measure, the characteristic dimension of the solar body corresponds to its radius, tied to the twelfth layer above the half measure.

But why are there twelve layers? What is it that makes the twelvefold formulation of the sun ideal and scientific? To answer this question, we must invoke the principle "as above, so below."

THE SOLAR-NUCLEAR CORRESPONDENCE

According to the principle "as above, so below," there should be a correspondence between the twelfth layer above the half measure and the twelfth layer below. In the same way that the twelfth layer above determines the size of the solar whole, the twelfth layer below should determine the size of the solar parts—the material particles from which the solar body is composed.

No matter what their relative size, all stars or suns are composed of similar material particles. Modern theorists tell us that these consist primarily of hydrogen and helium nuclei, which have been stripped of their orbital electrons by the intense heat of the sun. Because these nuclear particles make the largest contribution by far to the total mass of a sun or star, they may be viewed as the characteristic particles or parts from which the solar body is fashioned. Like the solar whole, the solar parts may be viewed as having a spherical form so that we can express their characteristic measure as a radius. Just as the radius of the solar whole is determined by the characteristic scale of the twelfth layer above the half measure, so the radius of the solar parts should be determined by the characteristic scale of the twelfth layer below the half measure.

The universal rule of thumb suggests that this radius should be roughly 10^{-12} centimeters. This leads to a prediction regarding the radius of the nuclear particles from which is composed the body of our sun or any star. Once again, it turns out that this prediction is accurate: Based upon careful quantum experiments and theoretical calculations, theorists have estimated the radius of the atomic nucleus to be about 10^{-12} centimeters.

Therefore, we find that when interpreted properly, the ancient science of the gods can be used to predict accurately both the radius of the sun and the radius of the atomic nuclei from which the sun is composed. This demonstrates that solar wisdom is much more than just an abstract form of mystical wisdom; it represents a profound form of scientific knowledge regarding the organization of the Cosmos and its relation to the layered structure of the metaphysical Logos.

We are now in a better position to understand the standard cosmological body: it represents a celestial sphere that displays a balance between the synthetic and analytic powers of consciousness. This balance is manifested by the matched pairs of layers within the metaphysical Logos. In order to uphold this balance, the size of the whole above and the size of the parts below should correspond to matched pairs in the ancient system. All stars or suns possess similar-size solar parts, but they do not always possess the same radii. Stars that have radii different from that of our sun may be viewed as nonideal or nonstandard in the sense that they do not uphold the balance between part and whole or the analytic and synthetic powers of consciousness.

According to the ancients, this balance is required for the realization of spiritual immortality, which they deemed the ultimate purpose of creation. It is also required for the evolution of human life, the unique form of organic life that is suited most ideally for this realization.

A SIMILARITY IN FUNCTION

The correspondence between the sun and the atomic nucleus goes beyond the characteristic radius of each and also pertains to their behavior. Under ordinary conditions, electrons orbit around the nucleus. Similarly, planets orbit around the sun.

Just as the atomic nucleus serves as the nucleus of an atomic system, so the sun serves as the nucleus of our solar system. This analogy was not lost to the physicists who first began to study the behavior of atoms. The first atomic models compared an atom to a miniature solar system: the orbiting electrons were like orbiting planets and the nucleus was like the sun. Later, a more abstract model was developed involving quantum wave function—but the classical analogy is still taught in high schools all around the world.

This solar-nuclear correspondence presents a concrete example of the principle "as above, so below." The behavior of the solar whole may not be exactly the same as the behavior of the solar parts, but the two behaviors correspond to one another.

THE SOLAR CUBIT

A star such as our sun may be viewed as a standard of cosmological measure, both literally and figuratively. Such stars serve as the celestial "rulers" on the basis of which evolves the standard human body.

The conscious awareness of a standard star, which is used to manipulate its environment, corresponds to the excitations of consciousness measured on the basis of the first 12 + 12 = 24 layers above and below the half measure. Similarly, the active part of the human body, which is used to manipulate its environment, corresponds to the portion of the arm extending from the crook of the elbow to the tip of the middle finger—measured on the basis of 12 + 12 = 24 digits.

The unit of measure consisting of twenty-four digits represents the human cubit, which was used by the ancients as an earthly standard of measure. The corresponding cosmological unit consisting of twenty-four layers represents the solar cubit, which can be used as a standard of measure in heaven. Both represent rulers that can be divided into two halves—half cubits—of twelve digits or twelve layers each. This illustrates the sacred nature of the ancient system of measure: The standard human cubit used to measure things on earth, corresponds to the standard solar cubit used to measure things in heaven.

THE SOLAR WORLD

The solar wisdom pertains not only to the spherical body of the sun, but also to the spherical body of the solar system as a whole. This may be understood as the solar world within which dwells the sun god.

In modern astrophysics, the solar world is called the *heliosphere,* which corresponds roughly to a spherical region of space filled with the material emanations of the sun. These emanations characterize the solar wind, which consists of high-energy, charged particles emitted by the sun. The solar wind is used by modern theorists to define the heliosphere—a roughly spherical region of space that extends beyond the orbit of Pluto and is filled with the solar wind.

The surface of the heliosphere defines the boundary of our solar system. More specifically, it is used to define the boundary between the vacuum of interplanetary space and that of interstellar space: the *heliopause,* which is so named because it represents the surface of the heliosphere on which the solar wind stops or pauses. This marks the point where interplanetary space—filled with the solar wind—comes to an end and where interstellar space—more or less devoid of the solar winds—has its beginning.

In this sense, the surface of the heliosphere marks an important transition between two different types of cosmological vacuum states, each of which differs with respect to its particle density.

THE SIXTEENFOLD PERSON

In the Vedic tradition, the heliosphere was viewed as the celestial embodiment of a sixteenfold person: the *sodashi-kala-purusha* (the soul with sixteen aspects). This person represents the more expanded self of the sun, which extends to embrace the entire solar world. In this regard, the heliosphere may be viewed as the celestial body of the sixteenfold solar person.

Like the twelvefold person in the sun, this sixteenfold person was viewed as a celestial god who from the very beginning has presided over the evolution of human life. This implies that the body of the heliosphere, like the body of the sun, should represent a standard cosmological body whose overall dimensions are related more or less ideally to the layers of the metaphysical Logos.

The sixteen aspects of this expanded solar person correspond to the first sixteen layers above the half measure—which the Vedic seers divided into four sets of four layers each. These were called the four quarters (*padas*) of the sixteenfold purusha. The famous "hymn to the soul" (*purusha sukta*) in the Rig Veda tells us that three of these quarters attained great immortality, while the other quarter is cyclical and remained behind to support the birth and death of all mortal beings. The three quarters that attained great immortality correspond to the first twelve layers above the half measure, which support the inner circle of the sun itself, and the quarter that remained behind corresponds to the subsequent four layers, which support the cyclical orbits of the planets around the sun. As described by the text, these planets serve to support the birth and death of all mortal beings.

THE RADIUS OF THE HELIOSPHERE

The ancient wisdom suggests that the body of the heliosphere was created in the image of the first $12 + 4 = 16$ layers above the half measure. Just as the radius of the sun is determined by the scale of the twelfth layer above the half measure, so the radius of the heliosphere can be determined by the scale of the sixteenth layer above the half measure.

The ancient universal rule of thumb gives this scale as about 10^{15} centimeters—which leads to a prediction regarding the radius of the heliosphere, derived on the basis of the ancient principles. The modern theoretical prediction, derived from careful observation and calculation, is that the radius of the heliosphere is indeed roughly 10^{15} centimeters. This provides yet another confirmation of the scientific nature of the solar wisdom.

THE SCALE OF ELECTRO-WEAK UNIFICATION

If the heliosphere represents a standard cosmological body, then it should embody a balance between the synthetic and analytic powers of consciousness. Unlike the sun itself, in which the balance is expressed in terms of the first twelve layers above and below, the balance that upholds the heliosphere should be expressed in terms of the first sixteen layers above and below.

We have seen that the scale of the sixteenth layer above marks an important transition between two different cosmological vacuum states. The principle "as above, so below" suggests that the scale of the sixteenth layer below should mark an important transition between two different quantum vacuum states. Because the sun acts as the primary source of visible light within the solar system, we can propose that this lower transition scale should have something to do with the electromagnetic vacuum, which acts as the source of all visible light in the universe. The universal rule of thumb suggests that this quantum transition scale should be about 10^{-16} centimeters. Is there any indication in modern theory that this represents a fundamental transition scale in the quantum vacuum?

In fact, there is. It turns out that 10^{-16} centimeters is one of the most important scales in the Standard Model of quantum theory: the scale of *electro-weak unification* in which the electromagnetic force field becomes indistinguishable from, and hence unified with, the weak force field. On this scale, ordinary electromagnetic waves are transformed into electro-weak waves and the electromagnetic vacuum is transformed into the electro-weak vacuum.

This confirms our hypothesis: Just as the scale of 10^{15} centimeters marks the boundary between two different cosmological vacuum states, so the scale of 10^{-16} centimeters marks the boundary between two different quantum vacuum states—in accordance with the principle "as above, so below."

THE UPPER AND LOWER SCALES AS UNIFICATION SCALES

The solar wisdom specifies two important scales below the half measure corresponding to 10^{-12} centimeters and 10^{-16} centimeters. We may view both of these as particle unification scales—but they pertain to particles of matter and force respectively.

We may view the scale of 10^{-12} centimeters as the scale of *nuclear unification* in which protons and neutrons (both of which are matter particles) are unified in the form of a single atomic nucleus. The scale of 10^{-16} centimeters, on the other hand, is the scale of *electro-weak unification* in which electromagnetic and weak particles (both of which are force particles) are unified in the form of a single electro-weak particle. We can view the upper scales as unification scales, but instead of giving rise to microscopic particles, they give rise to cosmological wholes represented by the sun and the heliosphere. On the scale of 10^{11} centimeters, all the particles from which the sun is composed are correlated nonlocally into a single whole: the sun. On the scale of 10^{15} centimeters, all the particles from which the heliosphere is composed are similarly correlated nonlocally into a single whole: the heliosphere.

The difference between the two types of unification above and below is that the lower scales are dominated by the local analytic power of consciousness, which gives rise to the conception of microscopic parts, while the upper scales are dominated by the nonlocal synthesizing power of consciousness, which gives rise to the conception of macroscopic wholes. Yet both involve a form of unification.

SPIRITUAL WISDOM AND SCIENTIFIC KNOWLEDGE

We are beginning to see that the ancient wisdoms are much more than they appear to be. Though they are expressed using arcane symbols and religious terms unique to each culture that gave rise to them, they were rooted in a genuine scientific understanding of the universe on the basis of which we can make accurate empirical predictions.

The key to a scientific interpretation of these ancient wisdoms lies in the system of matched pairs with parameters established by the universal rule of thumb. This allows the ancient wisdoms to be expressed in the language of mathematics, the universal language of science. Without this system we would be totally lost, like sojourners lost in a bewildering forest without a map. This explains precisely why the ancients developed this system: to provide a map for the soul seeking knowledge about the meaning of life, the universe, and everything.

In ancient times, this map was given to aspiring souls as they needed it. Though today, we can evaluate and understand the teachings of the seers in the light of modern science, in ancient times, such science did not exist. As a result, common men and women had no idea what the enlightened seers espoused; the seers' teachings were as foreign to the common person then as abstract algebraic formulas of quantum theory are to the common person today. Rather than create confusion in the minds of the common people, the seers kept secret their real science and instead taught colorful myths and stories that commoners could grasp, even if only symbolically. Since these early times, however, the human mind has matured in its analytic capabilities.

Though we may not be enlightened to the point of experiencing directly and intuitively the cosmic realities the seers believed, we at least have a well-developed system of empirical knowledge. On this basis, we can tie the seers' spiritual concepts to scientific concepts and thereby gain some understanding of the ancient wisdom. Here, rather than creating anything new, we have translated the ancient spiritual wisdoms into modern scientific language—the language of mathematics. We can follow in the footsteps of the ancient seers as they traversed the path to immortality so that we can translate their spiritual wisdom into a form of scientific wisdom.

Yet our journey has just begun. As the enlightened soul ascends and descends through the first sixteen layers above and below the half measure, it communes with the solar being and its solar world—but it does not stop there. It continues on its journey until it communes with the galactic being and its galactic world. The knowledge derived on that basis may be called the galactic wisdom.

8

The Galactic Wisdom

THE GALAXIES

Since time immemorial, the hazy swath of millions of stars visible in the night sky has been called the Milky Way. During the course of the twentieth century, astronomers realized that these stars form but a small part of our own vast Milky Way Galaxy. It turns out that our galaxy, in turn, is but a small part of the visible universe, estimated to contain some two hundred billion galaxies and twenty trillion stars.

A galaxy is a large collection of stars in space having a distinct identity and resembling a luminous island. Galaxies are often classified according to their different shapes. The most conspicuous of these are the spiral galaxies, which tend to present a beautiful rotational symmetry. They are also classified in terms of their size. The largest known galaxies are the huge elliptical ones that lie at the center of dense clusters of galaxies. Some of these have a diameter on the order of six million light-years, while the smallest galaxies may have a diameter of only a few thousand light-years. The third way that galaxies are classified is in terms of their mass, which is directly related to the number of stars they contain. In this classification scheme, the mass of our own sun is used as a standard; galactic masses are typically expressed in terms of solar masses. The least massive galaxies may contain only a few million solar masses—and stars, while the most massive contain several trillion.

Fig. 8.1. Atlas Image mosaic courtesy of 2MASS/UMass/IPAC-Caltech/ NASA/NSF.

The Milky Way Galaxy is a typical spiral galaxy containing some two hundred billion stars and has a diameter of approximately one hundred thousand light-years. Our solar system lies about two-thirds of the way from the galactic center toward the edge of the luminous disk, and is part of one of the spiral arms. Shown here is an infrared image of the Milky Way Galaxy taken by NASA's Background Explorer (launched in 1989).

Although it is generally believed that galaxies were first discovered during the twentieth century, there is textual evidence to support that the ancients knew about them thousands of years ago.

AN ANCIENT DESCRIPTION OF THE MILKY WAY GALAXY

The ancients were careful observers of the heavens, for they believed that the celestial bodies (celestial gods) in heaven play an important role in determining the destiny of everything on earth. Though they were renowned for their astronomical and astrological knowledge, however, standard interpretations of the ancient texts suggest that they had no idea of the existence of galaxies or that our own solar system is part of a vast galaxy, but here we may find out otherwise.

The enlightened seers did not have to rely upon powerful telescopes to observe the heavens. We must remember that they had the potential to expand their awareness by ascending the divine ladder and mentally embracing all things in heaven and on earth. These seers possessed the eyes of pure consciousness, which enabled them to see the universe on different scales of time and space. What's more, the awareness of the ancient seers was not restricted to what they could observe from the earth; though they were earthly, their awareness soared in the heavens. On the basis of their nonlocal powers of vision, they conceived themselves as citizens of not only this small planet, but also the universe.

In this regard, the Vedic seers viewed the earth-world—the place where embodied beings dwell—as the galactic world, the *jambu-dvipa,* or "island of created existence." Most scholars presume that this refers to our planet, but the geography of jambu-dvipa, described in the ancient texts, bears no resemblance at all to Earth. In the Vedic texts,[1] the earth is described as a luminous island floating in the cosmic waters. It supposedly has a shining central mountain composed of luminous gems, which serves as the exclusive abode of the celestial gods. Surrounding this mountain is a vast, luminous plain consisting of *varshas,* or celestial regions, which serve as abodes for various types of embodied beings both human and fantastical having no counterparts in the flora and fauna of our planet.

The term *varsha* means a "shower"—a shower of raindrops or of stars. According to the texts, the varshas wrap around the central mountain in a hemispherical manner; they are organized as a function of distance from the center. The varsha in which human beings dwell is called *bharata varsha,* a term often likened to the subcontinent of India. A careful reading of the texts reveals that bharata varsha was viewed as lying about two-thirds of the way between the center of the divine mountain and the edge of the luminous plain—precisely where modern astronomers place our solar system, which lies about two thirds from the center of the galaxy toward the edge of the galactic disk.

Although scholars have labored to match this ancient description of jambu-dvipa with the geographical features of Earth, they conclude generally that the ancient description is the product of mythical fantasy and symbolic obfuscation, which bears no resemblance at all to the geography of Earth. On the other hand, we can argue that the ancient description is consistent with the geography of a spiral galaxy such as our own. From the picture and description of the Milky Way Galaxy, we can conclude that it resembles a luminous island floating in the vastness of intergalactic space. Moreover, the central bulge of the galaxy may be compared to a shining central mountain that looms over a vast luminous plain, and the luminous gems that, according to the ancient texts, compose the central mountain may be none other than the luminous stars that make up the central bulge.

From modern astrophysics we know that the stars are packed so tightly in this central bulge that the conditions there are doubtless highly unfavorable for the development of organic life, due to intense radiations coming from all sides. This is consistent with the ancient description, which suggests that the divine mountain is the exclusive abode of the celestial gods (stars) and not of organic beings such as plants, animals, and humans. The texts state that all living or organic beings dwell in the luminous plain that surrounds the central mountain. This corresponds to the galaxy's galactic disk that surrounds the central bulge. Moreover, the texts state that this plain is organized in the form of varshas (showers), which wrap around the central mountain. These may correspond to the various star showers inherent within the spiral disk.

We know for a fact that in one of these showers lies our own solar system, where human beings have evolved. We also know for a fact that other stars scattered throughout the galactic disk have their own orbiting planets similar to those we know to be orbiting our sun. We do not know whether some of those distant planets support some form of organic life, but the general consensus is that Earth is unlikely to be the only planet in the galaxy that supports life. After all, the galaxy holds some two hundred billion stars; the idea that only our solar system supports life seems highly unlikely.

According to the Vedic texts, each varsha has the potential to support its own life forms: The solar systems that lie within the star shower known as bharata varsha have the potential to support human forms of life—yet the seers claimed that other varshas have the potential to support nonhuman, highly intelligent life, though we might view this life as alien. In fact, the ancient texts are filled with stories of enlightened seers traveling from one varsha to another by means of their innate spiritual powers (as opposed to space vehicles). It is said that these spiritual powers enabled them to fly through the sky, suspend their breath, and render their bodies both invisible and impervious to the elements. Although such stories might seem the product of a mystical imagination, they are no more fantastic than the notion that the human soul can become enlightened and immortal and expand to embrace the universe as a whole.

We therefore find that the ancient descriptions of jambu-dvipa are consistent with the modern scientific understanding of our galaxy. From this we can conclude that the ancient seers were aware of galaxies, including our own. In addition, they possessed a profound galactic wisdom—that is, an understanding of how our galaxy is organized on the basis of the metaphysical layers.

THE ELEVEN RUDRAS AND THE GALACTIC RADIUS

As we have learned, the first twelve gods listed in the Vedic pantheon were called the twelve adityas—the twelve solar gods—representing the first twelve layers above the half measure, which determine the size of our sun as represented by the solar radius.

The next eleven gods were called the eleven *rudras*. The Sanskrit word *rudra* is derived from *rud*, "to make cry or weep," and *ra*, "to illumine or shine." The rudras may be understood as the universal gods or metaphysical layers through which the Creator weeps luminous teardrops out of compassion for all created beings so that they might have worlds in which to live and evolve—these teardrops are the planets and stars that make up the galaxy.

The rudras represent the universal gods that preside over all forms of interplanetary and interstellar space characterized by relations among planets and stars within the galaxy. By means of their synthetic powers, they serve to bind all the planets and stars within the galaxy into a single nonlocally correlated whole that corresponds to the overall form of the Milky Way Galaxy itself. The chief of the eleven rudras, known simply as Rudra, corresponds to the highest of these universal gods. Just as the chief of the twelve adityas, known as Aditya, has a celestial body that corresponds to the luminous body of our sun, so Rudra has a celestial body that corresponds to the luminous body of our galaxy. Further, whereas Aditya represents the solar embodiment of the twelfth layer above the half measure, Rudra represents the galactic embodiment of layer $12 + 11 = 23$.

As the characteristic measure of the twelfth layer determines the radius of our sun, the characteristic measure of the twenty-third layer determines the radius of our galaxy as measured from its center to the edge of the luminous disk. The universal rule of thumb gives this measurement as 10^{22} centimeters, which leads to a prediction regarding the galactic radius. This prediction, obtained on the basis of the ancient science of the gods, is consistent with that provided by modern physical science, which estimates the galactic radius to be roughly 10^{22} centimeters. Once again, this confirms the scientific nature of the ancient wisdom.

CHURNING THE MILKY OCEAN

The Vedic texts provide not only a geographical picture of the galaxy, but also a mythological account as to its origin. Recorded in the Puranas, this myth describes the creation of the galaxy in terms of the Samudra-Manthan, the ritual churning of the milky ocean.

According to this myth, the galaxy existed initially in a formless state described as a luminous or milky ocean and representing the field of pure consciousness filled with virtual light. To create the spiral form of the galaxy, this milky ocean had to be churned, leading to "curds" and "whey." In this analogy, the lumps of white curd correspond to clumps of luminous stars and the transparent whey corresponds to the regions of interstellar space that lie in between.

The myth tells us that both the gods (*suras*) and antigods (*asuras*), which have opposite natures, churned the milky ocean. The suras and asuras represent the two sets of metaphysical layers above and below the half measure, and therefore are endowed with the synthetic and analytic powers of consciousness, respectively. The churning process is compared to a tug of war between the gods and antigods: Supposedly, the suras and asuras tugged on the ends of a cosmic rope, which was compared to a cosmic serpent representing the swirling streams of consciousness within the milky ocean. These streams were wrapped around the central axis, where the galactic mountain was to be. The result of this churning process: The created galaxy obtained a spiral form, like a coiled serpent.

The myth goes on to explain that the ultimate purpose of the churning process was to obtain the amrita rasa—the nectar of immortality, which has the potential to render the soul immortal. In other words, the galaxy was created to fulfill the ultimate purpose of creation: to provide worlds in which mortal souls could evolve to become immortal souls whose bodies are pervaded by the amrita rasa, the "immortal blood."

THE KALA-KUTA POISON

According to the myth, however, there was a problem. The first product of the churning process was a deadly black poison—the *kala-kuta* poison, characterized by *tamas,* "darkness" and "inertia." It had the potential to stupefy all souls and fill them with inertia to the point where they became unconscious. In order for conscious, material beings to evolve, this poison had to be neutralized.

The suras and asuras called upon the great god Shiva, who was immune to kala-kuta's stupefying effects. Shiva neutralized the poison by swallowing it—but the kala-kuta became lodged in his neck. Shiva is therefore often depicted as having a blue-black neck.

THE UNIVERSAL FORM OF SHIVA

Shiva is understood traditionally as the higher self of Rudra, the chief of the eleven rudras. While the body of Rudra corresponds to the visible form of the galaxy, the body of Shiva extends beyond the galaxy and is truly universal.

According to tradition, Shiva represents the universal embodiment of tamas, the darkness and inertia that serves as the source of all forms of observable matter in the universe. The texts state that the universal body of Shiva is dark but covered by a fine white ash, so that it appears white—which corresponds to how Shiva is depicted traditionally. This luminous white ash makes up the shining stars and galaxies that cover the darkness of the universal vacuum.

Shiva was immune to the kala-kuta poison—a manifestation of tamas—because of his own nature. Therefore, he could swallow it without being rendered unconscious. The universal form of Shiva extends over a vast spectrum of space-time scales. His white, ash-covered torso corresponds to the visible galaxy consisting of luminous stars. His blue-black neck corresponds to the galactic field of tamas (darkness and inertia) that pervades and extends beyond the visible form of the galaxy. The neck of Shiva may be compared to a dark spherical halo that surrounds the luminous form of the galaxy. In this surrounding region of darkness, there are no luminous stars or conscious embodied beings; they have all been swallowed in the field of tamas—the field of darkness and inertia that arose as the first product of the churning process.

Just as the neck lies above the torso, the head lies above the neck. Shiva's head corresponds to the vastness of intergalactic space that lies above and beyond the dark galactic halo. Shiva was therefore viewed as the embodiment of the visible, material universe as a whole.

THE GALACTIC FIELD OF TAMAS AND ITS TWENTY-THREE EVOLUTES

If the first twenty-three layers above the half measure uphold the luminous body of the galaxy, then the dark galactic halo—the galactic field of tamas—is upheld by the twenty-fourth layer. We find support for this in the system of Vedic philosophy called Samkhya, "enumeration."

The purpose of Samkhya was to enumerate the fundamental categories (*tattvas*) involved in the creation of the universe. The classical version of this system had to do with the creation of the galaxy from an underlying field of prime matter (*pradhana*), which was dominated by the quality of tamas—the same as the qualities of the kala-kuta poison. According to the texts, tamas represents the stupefying quality of consciousness, which has the potential to render the mortal soul (the movable point value of consciousness) ignorant and inertia-filled. Such ignorant point values correspond to the particles of matter from which are made the material bodies of all created beings. In this case, the inertia associated with such particles is none other than their mass.

The ancient theory suggests that all of the observable matter particles that compose the galactic body are but the evolutes (*vikrities*) of an unobservable field of prime matter—made up of particles of tamas or dark matter. The theory states that the elements of tamas themselves are unobservable by empirical means, but they can be inferred by their empirical effects. For this reason, the field of tamas was also called *anumana,* the inferred entity.

The classical theory enumerates twenty-four categories of matter: The field of tamas itself was counted as the twenty-fourth category, and the other twenty-three categories were viewed as the evolutes (vikrities) of the field. These categories were represented traditionally by the first twenty-four consonants of the Sanskrit alphabet, which also served to represent the first twenty-four universal gods of the Vedic pantheon—and hence, the first twenty-four layers above the half measure.

Therefore, there is a direct correspondence between the twenty-three categories of observable matter outlined in the theory of Samkhya and the twenty-three layers that serve to uphold the visible form of the galaxy. In this case, the twenty-fourth category corresponds to the twenty-fourth layer, which serves to uphold the galactic field of tamas, the dark matter halo likened to the neck of Shiva.

According to the ancient seers, this underlying field of dark matter serves as the hidden foundation (*bhumi*) of the galaxy and was the first product of the churning process on the basis of which the observable form of the galaxy evolved—but we can determine here whether or not this ancient galactic wisdom has any support in modern theory.

THE RADIUS OF THE DARK-MATTER HALO

When modern scientists realized that our own solar system is but a tiny part of a huge spiral galaxy, they began to map out, count, and classify the stars that constitute the galaxy, but because the galaxy had some two hundred billions stars, this was a huge undertaking that took many years to complete.

Once the number of stars and their relative sizes were determined through meticulous astronomical observations, theorists began to estimate the total mass of the galaxy, taking into account the mass of all the visible stars and the mass associated with the thin gas of charged particles that pervades interstellar space. Having obtained this estimate, theorists sought to confirm their findings using the laws of gravity. As it turns out, there are a number of smaller, satellite galaxies in the vicinity of our galaxy, and the projected motions of these can be determined by astronomical observations. Theorists concluded that like the motions of the planets around the sun, these satellite galaxies should be governed by the laws of gravity, which depend upon the mass of our galaxy. Yet there was a serious problem: When theorists inserted the estimated mass of our galaxy into the gravitational formulas, the results were inconsistent with the projected motions of the satellite galaxies. After rechecking the empirical data, they finally concluded that their estimate of the galactic mass was off by as much as 90 percent.

How could this be? Meticulously, they had taken into account all observable forms of matter in the galaxy, including both the visible population of the stars and the low-density population of particles distributed throughout interstellar space. Nevertheless, to explain the motion of the satellite galaxies, about ten times more mass was required. In the end, the theorists concluded reluctantly that an unknown type of matter possessing mass or inertia must pervade the galaxy. Unlike the observable forms of matter, however, this mysterious form must be non-luminous, or dark, and it was therefore called dark matter. Is it possible that this represents the discovery (or rediscovery) of the galactic field of tamas known to the ancients thousands of years ago?

Over the next few years, theorists began to investigate what kind of particles might correspond to dark matter, and it was soon determined that none discovered so far on the basis of quantum theory were acceptable candidates. At present, the most promising theory is that the particles of dark matter correspond to *wimps,* weakly interacting matter particles, which have only a gravitational interaction with ordinary matter based upon their mass. Although the mass of an individual dark-matter particle is predicted to be very small, we can reason that because the so-called vacuum of interstellar space is filled with dark matter, the total mass of all dark-matter particles throughout the galaxy exceeds that of all the visible particles. In this case, dark matter represents the dominant form of matter within the galaxy.

Unfortunately, dark matter particles have yet to be detected empirically. Their existence can be inferred from astrophysical calculations involving gravitational interactions, but at this point, no one has figured out a way to observe directly or detect dark matter particles in a quantum experiment. This is consistent with the ancient theory, which suggests that dark matter particles can be inferred, but not actually observed from their empirical effects. Modern astrophysics tells us that the dark matter field is spherical in shape, extends beyond the visible form of the galaxy, and is called the dark-matter halo. We can see that it corresponds directly to the dark neck of Shiva, which extends above his galactic torso.

Now we are in a position to make another prediction: If the twenty-fourth layer above upholds the spherical form of the dark-matter halo as a whole, then the radius of that halo should be determined by the characteristic scale of that layer. The universal rule of thumb gives this as 10^{23} centimeters—a prediction regarding the radius of the dark-matter halo and derived from the ancient science of the gods.

Although the dark-matter halo is invisible, theorists have used various models to calculate its radius, with the most widely accepted suggesting that the radius of the dark-matter halo is indeed approximately 10^{23} centimeters. Once again, the predictions derived on the basis of modern science and ancient science agree to within 1 order of magnitude.

THE SCALE OF DARK-MATTER UNIFICATION

Given the fact that the theory of Samkhya describes accurately the nature of dark matter as characterized by the qualities of tamas—darkness (non-luminosity) and inertia (mass)—as well as the fact that the twenty-four categories of the theory can be used to predict the radius of the dark-matter halo, we cannot ignore the conclusions of the theory regarding the relation between dark matter and ordinary matter.

According to this theory, the particles of dark matter represent the particles of prime matter from which are produced all observable forms of matter through a process of combination and permutation. This means that on a certain microscopic scale of consideration, all observable particles of matter may be viewed as composite—that is, composed of even more elementary dark matter particles. The scale by which ordinary forms of matter are resolved into their dark matter constituents may be called the scale of dark-matter unification.

If the radius of the dark-matter field as a whole is determined by the scale of the twenty-fourth layer above, then in accordance with the principle "as above, so below," the scale of dark-matter unification should be determined by the scale of the twenty-fourth layer below. The universal rule of thumb gives this as 10^{-24} centimeters. Unfortunately, this particular scale falls in a range of microscopic scales known in quantum theory as the Great Desert because virtually nothing is known about the quantum particles, if any, that exist in that range. At present, the most advanced particle accelerators are able to probe space-time-energy scales only to about 10^{-22} centimeters. As a result, our direct empirical knowledge regarding the microscopic parts of creation extends no farther than the scale of the twenty-second layer below the half measure. The scale of the twenty-fourth layer below the half measure lies beyond our empirical reach, and there is currently no way to verify empirically the prediction about the dark-matter unification scale.

Yet the real test of any scientific theory lies in its ability to make theoretical predictions in advance of their confirmation. On the basis of the ancient galactic wisdom, we can determine in advance that the scale of 10^{-24} centimeters represents the scale of dark-matter unification in which all observable matter particles become resolved into their prime constituents—dark-matter particles. Although it is unlikely that this prediction will be confirmed by any direct empirical observation, it could be confirmed, at least in principle, by an appropriate mathematical theory of dark matter rooted in inferences drawn from empirical observations. Such a confirmation would go a long way toward establishing the scientific validity of the ancient wisdom. Whether this will come to pass remains to be seen.

THE GALACTIC CUBIT

Previously, it was argued that our sun represents a standard star on the basis of which we can evaluate other stars. Similarly, it can be argued that our galaxy represents a standard galaxy on the basis of which we can evaluate other galaxies. In both cases, these cosmological bodies represent standards of cosmological measure described in terms of the cubit.

The cubit represents a standard of measure that involves 12 + 12 = 24 units. As we have seen, with respect to the human body, the cubit is represented by 12 + 12 = 24 digits. With respect to the solar body, it is represented by 12 + 12 = 24 layers that exist above and below the half measure, each of which is associated with its own unit of measure (corresponding to its characteristic scale). With respect to the galactic body, the cubit is represented by the first 12 + 12 = 24 layers that lie above the half measure. The first set of twelve layers represents the solar layers upholding the inner circle of the sun, and the second set of twelve layers represents the interplanetary and interstellar layers upholding the inner circle of the galaxy, which is marked by the dark-matter halo.

Therefore, the twenty-four galactic layers may be viewed as forming a standard cosmological measure called the *galactic cubit*. It is on the basis of this that all galaxies can be evaluated as either standard or nonstandard.

THE METRICAL MODEL

The ancient sages were fond of such numerological correspondences. Things that share the same numbers were often viewed as related. The Pythagoreans went so far as to claim that all things could be understood in terms of pure number (*arithmus*) alone.

One of the principal applications of this notion was in the Pythagorean theory of harmonics in which measures of space (represented by string lengths) and measures of sound (represented by harmonic tones) were represented simultaneously by the same pure number ratios. Although modern scholars tend to presume that the Pythagoreans invented the theory of harmonics for aesthetic purposes—so that pleasing musical scales could be developed—the fact is that the ancient theory was given cosmic significance. The Greek philosophers often used harmonic ratios to explain their theories of creation, which often involved the music of the spheres.

It is now known that the Greek and Vedic traditions were related closely: not only was the ancient Greek language related to Vedic Sanskrit but also the pre-Christian myths, gods, and religious practices of the ancient Greek tradition were related to those described in the Vedic texts. The same holds true with respect to Greek philosophy: both Greek and Vedic philosophers held that there is an intimate relation between space and speech or space and sound. The Greeks formulated this relation in terms of their harmonic theory, while the Vedic philosophers formulated it in terms of their metrical theory.

The theory of Vedic metrics involves creating measured forms of speech in which the expressions are restricted to a certain number of syllables. To this end, the Vedic seers prescribed the use of particular sonic meters involving a specific number of syllables. Although most modern scholars presume that they did so for aesthetic purposes—to give the expressions of speech a pleasing cadence—the Vedic meters, like the Greek ratios, were given cosmic significance and were often used by the Vedic seers to describe their theories of creation.

The Sanskrit term for a syllable is *akshara,* yet this same term also means "imperishable." The Vedic Upanishads tell us "space is woven warp and woof by the akshara"—that is, all forms of observable space are woven by the imperishable modes of divine speech (aksharas) inherent within the Veda or Logos. These modes of speech are organized fundamentally on the basis of the metaphysical layers, the imperishable foundations of the universe. Although various forms of metrical speech have been used for thousands of years by poets all around the world, the fact is that the Rig Veda, which is the oldest and most authoritative of the Vedic texts, represents the most ancient example of metrical speech that has ever been found. According to tradition, the Rig Veda encodes within itself a profound hidden science pertaining to the relation between the Veda (Logos) and the Vishva (Cosmos).

This hidden science is nongrammatical: It is expressed in terms of number and sequence, as opposed to grammatical rules. The Rig Veda itself tells us that it encodes hidden grades of measured speech, which are *na ingayanti,* not analyzable on the basis of grammar. These hidden grades of speech are metrical and involve measured forms of speech that are characterized by a particular number of letters, syllables, words, and so forth, arranged in a particular sequence. Thus we can see that numbers were very important: They were used as potent symbols to relate otherwise disparate concepts and ideas through numerological correspondence. Of particular importance were those assigned to the seven principal Vedic meters listed in the tenth mandala of the Rig Veda.

These were assigned the numbers 24, 28, 32, 36, 40, 44, and 48, which represent the number of syllables or aksharas allowed for each meter. The first and smallest of the Vedic meters was called the *gayatri,* and the last and largest of the Vedic meters was called the *jagati.* Whereas the gayatri was associated closely with the celestial sun god, the jagati was associated with the vast galactic word in which dwell the suns or stars. The word *jagati* is derived from *jagat,* "world," an association that is made clear by the ancient wisdoms, which involve various sets of imperishable layers that exist both above and below the half measure.

For example, we can see that the solar wisdom pertaining to the circle of the sun involves a total of 12 + 12 = 24 layers, which were symbolized by the twenty-four imperishable syllables of the gayatri. Similarly, it has been shown that the galactic wisdom pertaining to the circle of the galaxy involves a total of 24 + 24 = 48 layers, which were symbolized by the forty-eight imperishable syllables of the jagati.

In this way, the Vedic seers used the seven meters to formulate their solar and galactic wisdoms, as well as all the other wisdoms in between. Yet it would be a mistake to imagine that this is the only possible interpretation of the Vedic meters. The seers were fond of creating complex forms of measured speech that encode multiple complementary meanings. They strove to create not uniquely defined formulas, which have a single meaning, but rather variously defined formulas, which have the potential to encode many things at once. Through this means, the sonic, geometric, and numerical formulas served to reflect the nature of pure subjectivity—the innate potential of consciousness to conceive simultaneously the same subject from multiple complementary points of view.

THE ANCIENT EGYPTIAN MAP

The Egyptian seers possessed a similar galactic wisdom, and used it to map the ancient divisions of Egypt so that this land could be fashioned in the image of heaven.

According to myths recorded in the Edfu Temple Texts (composed during the time of the Ptolemies, the Macedonian rulers of Egypt, when, for the first time, secret scrolls were being ferreted from their hiding places all over Egypt and put on public display), the land of Egypt was originally surveyed during the period known as *zep tepi* (the first time) by a mysterious group of seers called the builder gods or seven sages. The Texts imply that this survey was designed to map the land for future generations so that Egypt could be fashioned in the image of heaven and thereby become a kingdom of heaven on earth. This notion is reflected in the Hermetic texts: "Do you not know . . . that Egypt is an image of heaven, or, to speak more exactly, in Egypt all the operations of the powers, which rule and work in heaven have been transferred to the earth below? Nay, it should rather be said that the whole Cosmos dwells in our land as in its sanctuary."[2]

The ancient name for the land of Egypt was Khem, meaning "black land." This is quite strange given the fact that Egypt is largely covered by white sand. Most scholars presume that "black land" had its origin in the alluvial black mud deposited along the banks of the Nile during the seasonal floods. While this may be partially true, however, we might see a deeper symbolic significance to the term, which pertains to the galaxy's hidden black ground (bhumi) underlying its visible white form. Just as the hidden black land of Egypt is covered by billions of grains of shining, white sand, the hidden black foundation of the galaxy is covered by billions of shining, white stars.

The central myth regarding the land of Egypt revolves around two kingdoms: the kingdom of Set, which lies in the dry desert regions along the Upper Nile, and the kingdom of Horus, which lies in the fertile delta regions along the Lower Nile. As we have seen, Set was the brother of Osiris who usurped his brother's kingdom, and Horus was the son of Osiris who inherited his father's kingdom. According to this myth, the land of Egypt was viewed as divided into two kingdoms: the unrighteous and unfertile kingdom of Set, and the righteous and fertile kingdom of Horus, and according to tradition, these two kingdoms were subdivided into various minor kingdoms, called *nomes*. The system of nomes appears to be very ancient; as far as scholars can tell, it was already in place by the time the first historical dynasties appeared around 3200 BCE.

Although many believe that the system of nomes evolved on the basis of political and secular forces during the predynastic period, this flies in the face of how the ancient Egyptians viewed their kingdoms. They were seen as spiritual kingdoms, not as secular ones. The pharaoh, who ruled over the land of Egypt as a whole, was viewed as the embodiment of God, and the nomarchs, who ruled over the various nomes, were viewed as embodiments of the gods. This is consistent with the fact that each nome was associated with its own spiritual cult and set of deities.

To understand the spiritual geography of Egypt, we cannot ignore the central role of the Nile River. The nomes were mapped out and counted in sequence along the course of the Nile. In essence, the flow of the Nile toward the Mediterranean Sea represents the flow of consciousness from the more limited realms of material existence, represented by the kingdom of Set, to the more unlimited realms, represented by the kingdom of Horus. This understanding is consistent with the myth of Osiris, in which the king's coffin floats down the

Nile into the Mediterranean Sea on his preliminary journey to attain immortality.

The kingdom of Set was formed by the first twenty-two nomes counted from the source of the Nile, and Horus was formed by the last twenty nomes counted toward the mouth of the Nile. These 22 + 20 = 42 nomes correspond directly to the first forty-two layers in the upper half of the spectrum, each of which supports an entire spiritual heaven, or spiritual kingdom. This implies that the twenty-two nomes in the kingdom of Set correspond to the first twenty-two layers above the half measure, and the twenty nomes in the kingdom of Horus correspond to the next twenty layers—the twenty-third to the forty-second. The twenty-third nome, the first nome in the kingdom of Horus, was assigned a unique and special significance: This was the nome where Horus subdued Set finally and became the ruler of all of Egypt. It thus represents the nome where the two kingdoms became unified into a single united kingdom.

To celebrate the importance of the twenty-third nome, the Egyptians located there their oldest and most sacred seat of wisdom: the temple complex of On (Heliopolis), which is now believed to lie buried under the streets of Old Cairo. There they also constructed their most sacred monuments: the Sphinx and the Great Pyramid. The ancient Egyptian name for this nome was Ineb-Hedj, the "white fortress," which appears to be an allusion to the Great Pyramid, the most prominent monument constructed in the nome. In ancient times, the pyramid was encased in white limestone and likely resembled a great white fortress. There may be a deeper, heavenly significance to this name, however.

Just as the luminous bulge of the galaxy resembles a shining white mountain (a fortress of the gods) looming over a vast white plain composed of billions of shining stars, so the Great Pyramid, resembled a shining white mountain looming over the vast plain of the Giza plateau, composed of billions of sand particles. As a symbol of the central galactic mountain, the Great Pyramid was likely viewed as the central abode of the gods, and the Giza plateau was viewed as an abode for ordinary living beings, the servants and worshippers of the gods. This is consistent with the Vedic description of the galaxy.

We cannot ignore the fact that the Great Pyramid and the Giza plateau were located in the twenty-third nome, which corresponds to the twenty-third layer in the upper half of the spectrum—the layer that supports the visible form of the galaxy as a whole. Just as the luminous form of the galaxy rests upon the hidden dark-matter field, which constitutes its underlying foundation, so the visible form of the Giza plateau rests upon the hidden black land of Egypt, which constitutes its underlying foundation. In this case, the twenty-third nome symbolizes the visible form of the galaxy as a whole.

THE BA OF OSIRIS

In the Vedic tradition the sequence of layers above the half measure was represented symbolically by the sequence of consonants in the Sanskrit alphabet. The thumb-size form of the enlightened soul, cognized on the scale of the first layer, was known as the divine Ka, the same designation as the first consonant of the alphabet. The twenty-third consonant of the Sanskrit alphabet, *Ba,* symbolizes the twenty-third layer above the half measure. The galactic form of the soul, cognized on the scale of the twenty-third layer, may thus be called the divine Ba.

It turns out that the phonemes *ka* and *ba* were also used by the Egyptians to refer to two important forms of the soul. The Ka was the form of the soul closest to the human condition. The Ba was the higher form of the soul, which was viewed as capable of ascending beyond this world into the fathomless realms of heaven. In Egyptian iconography, the Ba was thus represented by a bird with a human head.

The Egyptian sages held that in order for the soul to ascend beyond this world into the bosom of heaven and attain immortality, the Ka had to become united with the Ba. Drawing upon the Vedic alphabetical model, this can be interpreted to mean that the enlightened human soul (the divine Ka) must expand and become united with the enlightened galactic soul (the divine Ba) before it can ascend beyond the galactic world (the real earth world) into the vastness of intergalactic space.

The union of the Ka and the Ba thus provides a spiritual representation of the union of the two lands: the land of Set, which is cognized over the spectrum of the first twenty-two layers, and the land of Horus, which is cognized over the spectrum of the subsequent twenty layers. These two are united on the scale of the twenty-third layer (represented by the twenty-third nome)—which is also the layer where the Ka is united with the Ba. In support of this interpretation, the Egyptian texts state specifically that the Great Pyramid was constructed to house the Ba of Osiris, the Lord of Immortality. In this case, the house of the Ba corresponds to the visible form of the galaxy—the luminous body of the divine Ba.

This leads to the speculation that in ancient times the Great Pyramid may have been used as an initiation chamber wherein the king or pharaoh went to have his human Ka united with the galactic Ba—the Ba of Osiris—in a sacred ritual conducted by the high priests of On. By virtue of this initiation, the pharaoh was assigned a galactic state of consciousness, and was viewed as a fit embodiment of God to rule over the united kingdom of Egypt, the image of heaven on earth.

The fact that the Vedic alphabetical model can be used to illuminate the secret meanings of the Egyptian Ka and Ba suggests that the ancient spiritual science was expressed initially in a universal phonemic language prior to the emergence of, or perhaps in addition to, specific grammatical languages. This conjecture is supported by the biblical myth of the tower of Babel, which suggests that at one time, all men spoke a common language that was eventually lost, leading humans to speak in different tongues.

THE HEBREW MODEL OF GALACTIC WISDOM

The ancient Hebrew sages possessed a similar galactic wisdom. As we saw earlier, the diagrammatic Tree of Life consists of thirty-two geometric elements, known as the twenty-two paths of wisdom and the ten sephiroth, or spheres of splendor. With respect to the metaphysical layers, the twenty-two paths of wisdom correspond to the first twenty-two layers above the half measure, which lead to the realization of galactic consciousness.

In the Egyptian tradition, these twenty-two layers were represented by the twenty-two nomes that made up the kingdom of Set. Therefore, they correspond to the twenty-two paths of wisdom that lead to the seat of galactic wisdom. This was represented by the twenty-third nome, the first nome in the kingdom of Horus, where the oldest and most authoritative seat of Egyptian wisdom was located. Yet the twenty-third nome also served as the royal seat of the united Egyptian kingdom. Interestingly, in the diagrammatic Tree of Life, the twenty-third element, which is represented by the lowest of the ten sephiroth, is traditionally called Malkuth, the Kingdom, which is none other than the galactic kingdom upheld by the twenty-third layer above the half measure.

Upon completing its preliminary tour of galactic life by ascending through the first twenty-two layers, represented by the twenty-two paths of wisdom, the enlightened soul finally graduates from this initiatory school of wisdom, and becomes identified with the galactic being, the ruler of the galactic kingdom and everything in it. This represents the first real cognition of the kingdom of heaven and marks the first real stage of divine rule and wisdom at which are recognized all the higher spiritual worlds. At that stage, the human Ka becomes united with the galactic Ba and the soul becomes the very embodiment of the divine Ka-Ba, the first two phonemes in the body of Hebrew wisdom known as kabbalah (KBLH).

As we have noted, the earliest version of kabbalah was called merkabah mysticism; the Hebrew term *merkabah* means a divine "throne-chariot." This term was used in the Hebrew scriptures to refer to the divine chariot that Ezekiel saw in his vision and that carried him into the heavens. The doctrine of merkabah mysticism supposedly dealt with the mechanics by which the soul could become immortal by ascending the divine ladder in the merkabah—the divine throne-chariot of God.

It turns out that the terms *mer, ka,* and *ba* were also words in the Egyptian language. The term *mer,* meaning "pile of stones," was used by the ancient Egyptians to refer to the pyramids. We have already seen that the Ka and Ba were used to refer to two important forms of the soul, both related to human and galactic consciousness. Therefore, we can argue that the Hebrew term *merkabah* may have deep Egyptian roots.

The importance of the two phonemes *ka* and *ba* is also recognized in the tradition of Islam. For example, the most sacred site in all of Islam, located in Mecca, is called the Kaba. In their daily prayers, all Muslims bow their heads toward this site, and all are enjoined to make a pilgrimage there at some point in their lives. Upon arriving in the presence of the Kaba, pilgrims circumambulate it as though they were illuminated stars circling the center of the galaxy.

Given the fact that both Jewish and Islamic traditions trace their roots to Abraham, whose first recorded exploit involved a pilgrimage to Egypt, we can argue that all three traditions—Hebrew, Egyptian, and Islamic—shared, at least to some degree, the same galactic wisdom expressed in terms of the phonemes *ka* and *ba*. Yet these phonemes are not necessarily Egyptian in origin. Thousands of miles away, the Vedic seers also used them to mark the same evolutionary stages of the soul. It appears, then, that we are dealing with a universal spiritual science shared by ancient sages and seers all around the world and expressed in terms of a common phonemic language, which has since been lost. Whereas modern science is expressed in terms of universally accepted mathematical symbols, the ancient science was originally expressed in terms of universally accepted phonemic symbols, such as *ka* and *ba,* which transcend the boundaries of language, culture, and religion.

Although we have come a long way, the realization of galactic consciousness does not mark the end of the spiritual journey. Having cognized the galactic world, the soul must ascend beyond it into the vastness of intergalactic space, like a bird ascending on wings of fire. This leads us to the universal wisdom.

9

The Universal Wisdom

THE VISIBLE UNIVERSE

According to modern theory, there is an observational limit to the universe, which represents the boundary of the visible universe. When scientists began to study distant galaxies during the first half of the twentieth century, they made a remarkable discovery: the light emitted by a galaxy is shifted progressively toward the red end of the electromagnetic spectrum as a function of its distance from the earth. This is known as the cosmological red shift.

At first, this phenomenon had no explanation. One difficulty it presents is that the cosmological red shift is more or less spherically symmetrical. The same red shift phenomenon is observed regardless of the direction in space in which a distant galaxy might lie from the earth. The most widely accepted explanation of this phenomenon was proposed initially by Edwin Hubble, whose name is memorialized in the famous Hubble telescope.

He suggested that the red shift phenomenon is due to a luminous Doppler shift that is comparable to an acoustic Doppler shift, which is part of our common experience and can be characterized by the sound of a train whistle when it passes a stationary observer. Anyone who has experienced this phenomenon has noticed that the sound of the whistle changes as the train passes: As the train approaches, the whistle is higher pitched than after it passes. The seeming change in sound is due to the motion of the train, which serves as the sound's source.

Generally, we can say that any sonic object that moves toward an observer will emit sonic wavelengths that are shorter than those emitted when the object moves away from the observer. In this case, the pitch of the sound is perceived as higher when the object is approaching and lower when the object is receding. The degree to which the wavelengths are shortened or lengthened is related directly to the speed of the moving object as compared to the speed of the sound waves emitted by that object.

Hubble proposed that the cosmological red shift is due to a similar "luminous" Doppler shift, which, in this case, has to do with the light waves emitted by distant galaxies. According to this explanation, these galaxies must be moving away from Earth at a speed that increases with increasing distance, so that emitted wavelengths are lengthened increasingly, or shifted toward the red end of the spectrum, as a function of distance.

Once this proposal was made, theorists were able to predict the recession speeds for different galaxies. In doing so, they found that some of the distant galaxies have recession speeds that are an appreciable fraction of the speed of light. They then calculated the distance at which the recession speed would actually equal the speed of light. This distance scale, estimated to be roughly 10^{28} centimeters, became known as the Hubble radius, or the radius of the visible universe. It represents the radius of that spherical portion of the universe visible from earth. Any galaxy that might lie on the surface or outside the Hubble sphere will not be observable from the earth, even in principle, because its galactic recession speed will either equal or exceed the speed of light. This means that light emitted by such galaxies will never reach Earth.

Whether or not galaxies exist beyond the Hubble radius is still a matter of dispute. Some theorists have proposed that the universe is actually infinite, and that the Hubble radius merely determines the finite portion of the universe visible from Earth. Others have proposed that the Hubble radius marks the boundary of the created universe itself—nothing whatsoever exists outside the Hubble sphere, not even time or space. In actuality, Hubble's explanation of the cosmological red shift is not the only possible explanation; it is simply the most popular. Proposed are a number of complementary explanations that do not require any form of galactic recession and which account for the red shift phenomenon using mechanisms other than a luminous Doppler shift.

No matter which theoretical model is used to explain it, however, the red shift phenomenon itself is not in dispute. It is an empirical fact confirmed by thousands of astrophysical observations. This summarizes our modern scientific understanding of what is meant by the visible universe. Next, we must examine the ancient wisdom concerning the visible universe: the universal wisdom.

PHYSICAL WORLDS AND SPIRITUAL WORLDS

The term *world* is loaded with many different meanings. It can be used to refer to a physical world, such as the planet Earth, which is located at a particular place within the universe. Yet it can also refer to the Cosmos, which represents the physical world as a whole, filled with many billions of galaxies.

The ancients were of the opinion that the universe is filled with many different types of worlds—some corresponding to mundane planets such as Earth, and others corresponding to vast, celestial worlds, such as the solar system or galaxy taken as a whole. In addition to these physical worlds, which are tied to specific locations within the universe, the ancients also held that there is a spectrum of spiritual worlds tied to specific scales of consciousness.

Whereas the physical worlds are manifested by real particles and waves, the spiritual worlds are manifested by virtual particles and waves, which, for all empirical purposes, are unobservable. These virtual spiritual worlds may be compared to universal dream worlds that exist and appear on the level of consciousness even though they cannot be perceived by the physical organs of sense. The ancients referred to these spiritual worlds commonly as the heavens above and the hells below, and believed they represented the worlds inhabited by disembodied souls. These souls, which correspond to point values of consciousness, may not possess a physical body, but they nevertheless possess a conscious point of view, as we do in the dreaming state. Everything revolves around our conscious point of view in this state, and we may perceive ourselves as possessing a dreamlike body or as being little more than a disembodied point of view on various dreamlike events. The images may change from one moment to the next, but our point of view remains constant. This is precisely the type of reality experienced by disembodied souls within a spiritual world.

Unlike those things that exist in the physical world, which appears to possess an objective character so that it seems to exist independently from our individual mind, the things that exist in a spiritual world appear to possess a subjective character. Disembodied souls have the potential to conceive an entire, dreamlike world populated by tangible objects, sights, sounds, sensations, and even other conscious beings. Yet all of these are subject to change at a moment's notice by the slightest alteration in the soul's subjective state of mind. In this way, we may compare a spiritual world to a virtual world, a world within the mind.

Unlike our individual dreaming worlds experienced when we go to sleep at night, however, the universal dreaming worlds appear not as transient realities within the individual mind, but as permanent realities within the universal mind. The virtual phenomena within these worlds may change from moment to moment, but the spiritual worlds themselves are persistent and are tied directly to the imperishable layers of consciousness that constitute collectively the metaphysical Logos.

THE TWENTY-EIGHT HEAVENS AND TWENTY-EIGHT HELLS

According to the Vedic seers, there is a correspondence between the visible physical universe and the invisible spiritual worlds that underlie and pervade the physical universe. The same set of metaphysical layers that uphold the form of the visible universe as a whole also uphold the spectrum of spiritual worlds, which are experienced on different scales of consciousness.

Whereas the visible universe is experienced by the mortal soul while it is in an embodied state, the spiritual worlds are experienced by the soul when it is in a disembodied state, after physical death. According to the seers, this is not a random affair. After death, a given mortal soul will either ascend to a heavenly world or descend to a hellish world in accordance with divine will. The decision depends upon the thoughts, words, and deeds performed by the soul when it was in an embodied state.

If the sum total of all the actions (karma) performed by a soul during life serves to fulfill the purpose of creation, then that soul will be rewarded with a vacation in the heavenly realms. If, however, the sum total of action is contrary to the purpose of creation, then that soul will be punished by a visit to the hellish realms. Heaven and hell were viewed as a system of rewards and punishments.

According to the ancients, the spiritual experience of the mortal soul after death is not so different from our dreaming experience when we sleep. If our minds become filled with pleasant impressions during the day and our actions are born of selfless kindness, then we are likely to have pleasant or heavenly dreams when we go to sleep at night. If, on the other hand, our minds become filled with unpleasant impressions and our actions are born of selfish unkindness, then we are likely to have unpleasant or nightmarish dreams. The same principle holds true after death. Based upon the thoughts, words, and deeds performed during life, some souls ascend to a heavenly spiritual world filled with pleasant dreamlike experiences, while others descend to a hellish spiritual world filled with nightmarish dreamlike experiences.

Rather than having a specific location within the physical universe, these spiritual worlds exist on different scales of time and space. The heavenly worlds exist on scales above the half measure and are filled with the synthetic power of consciousness, while the hellish worlds exist on scales below the half measure and are filled with the analytic power of consciousness. The heavenly worlds are thus more unified and coherent than the hellish worlds, which are diversified and incoherent. Whereas the heavenly worlds exist above, in heaven (the macroscopic half of the spectrum), the hellish worlds exist below, on earth (the microscopic half of the spectrum).

The Vedic seers held that there is a limit to the spectrum of heavens and hells that can be experienced by the mortal soul after death. More specifically, they counted a total of twenty-eight heavens (*nakshatras*) and twenty-eight hells (*narakas*), which represent the spiritual worlds supported by the first twenty-eight layers above and below the half measure. The highest or twenty-eighth heaven was variously called *dyaus* (the shining heaven), *svarga* (the moving world of the self), or *abhijit* (the victorious world). It was also known as the world of Indra, the king of the gods. In the alphabetical model of the spectrum of layers, the highest heaven was represented by the twenty-eighth consonant, the phoneme *la,* which was also viewed as the seed formula (*bija mantra*) of Indra.

This represents the highest heaven that could be obtained by a mortal soul through the performance of action—including the action of thinking. It was not, however, the highest heaven that could be experienced by an immortal or enlightened soul.

THE TELEOLOGY OF THE ENLIGHTENED SOUL

The Vedic seers held that an enlightened soul neither ascends to a spiritual heaven nor descends to a spiritual hell after physical death. At this time, it does not go anywhere. Prior to death, the awareness of an enlightened soul has already begun its spiritual journey, by ascending and descending the divine ladder simultaneously. In the process, it has the potential to cognize the spectrum of spiritual worlds known as the heavens and hells—even during its physical life.

Yet it does not obtain these worlds through the performance of action or thinking. Rather, it reaches them through the practice of tapas—of transcending—that is characterized by tranquillity (*shama*) rather than action (karma). Moreover, the enlightened soul does not experience these worlds in a way that is unbalanced: it does not, for instance, experience a hellish world to the exclusion of a heavenly world. By simultaneously ascending and descending through the spectrum of layers, it experiences both worlds in a balanced fashion.

This results in a completely different type of spiritual experience from that obtained by the mortal soul—one that transcends the notions of good and evil. To the enlightened soul, the hells are not evil and the heavens are not good. Instead, both are viewed as part and parcel of the overall design of creation, which serves to fulfill the ultimate purpose of creation: the realization of immortality in the bosom of the infinite. The spiritual worlds are hidden to the mortal soul during its physical life—but they are not hidden to the enlightened soul. They are experienced as coexisting with the physical world, but on a different level of consciousness. Consequently, when the physical body of an enlightened soul dies, the soul does not have to go anywhere. It does not have to ascend or descend because it has already ascended and descended.

Whatever stage of ascent and descent the enlightened soul has attained during physical life will be preserved after physical death and will serve as the basis for further progress on its spiritual journey. In this regard, physical death was viewed as no obstacle to the attainment of true immortality. The physical body may fall away, but the immortal soul goes on forever, for the enlightened soul is not identified with its mortal, physical body. Instead, it is identified with an immortal body—the metaphysical body of Logos.

The twenty-eighth heaven, the world of Indra, may be the highest heaven that can be experienced by the mortal soul, but it is not the highest that can be experienced by the enlightened soul. The world of Varuna was an even higher heaven, which marked the boundary of the visible universe and everything in it.

THE MYTH OF INDRA-VARUNA

In the Rig Veda, the embodiment of the visible form of the universe was personified by Indra, the king of the celestial gods. Therefore, the gods presided over by Indra correspond to the stars and galaxies that shine within the body of the visible universe.

Yet Varuna, a deity linked closely to Indra, was often described as standing above the whole world. In the mythological accounts provided by the Vedic Puranas, Varuna was known as the regent of the western ocean. The shining heaven of Indra, which encompasses the visible form of the universe, was often compared to the universal sun, because it appears as a sphere filled with luminous galactic particles. When the enlightened soul ascends beyond the world of Indra, however, and arrives in the higher world of Varuna, the visible universe (or universal sun) sets in its awareness. This may be compared to the sun setting in the western ocean in a blaze of reddish light. For this reason, Varuna, the regent of the western ocean, was described with the term *rajasa,* which means both "royal" and "reddish."

The term *varuna* is derived from the compound *va + aruna,* with *va* meaning "ocean" or "pervasive" and *aruna* signifying the reddish color of the sky at dawn and dusk. The phoneme *va* serves as the twenty-ninth consonant of the Sanskrit alphabet—which means it represents the twenty-ninth layer above the half measure. Just as the twenty-eighth consonant, *la,* was viewed as the seed formula of Indra, so *va,* the twenty-ninth consonant, was viewed as the seed formula of Varuna. The implication is that the world of Indra is supported by the twenty-eighth layer above the half measure, and the world of Varuna is supported by the twenty-ninth layer.

The constant association of Varuna with the term *rajasa* (royal redness) can be explained in terms of Samkhya philosophy: All created forms of existence are rooted in three fundamental qualities (*gunas*), called *sattva, rajas,* and *tamas.* The quality of tamas (darkness and inertia) acts as the source of all phenomenal forms of matter, and the quality of rajas (redness and incessant motion) acts as the source of all phenomenal forms of force. The term *sattva,* meaning "the nature (*tva*) of pure existence (*sat*)," represents the quality that acts as the ultimate source of all phenomenal forms of mind.

These three qualities are codependent—they coexist and act together. Yet the theory tells us that one can predominate over the other two. This means that sometimes the field (*kshetra*) can appear as a field of matter displaying the quality of tamas. At other times, it can appear as a field of force displaying the quality of rajas. It can also appear as a field of mind displaying the quality of sattva. It is important to note that these times do not necessarily correspond to sequential moments, but they can correspond to different scales of time and space within the overall spectrum of creation. For example, on the scale of the twenty-fourth layer above the half measure, which marks the boundary of the galactic sphere, the field appears to display the quality of dark matter, with tamas dominating over rajas and sattva. Similarly, on the scale of the twenty-ninth layer above the half measure, which marks the boundary of the universal sphere—the boundary of the visible universe—the field displays rajas (red force), with rajas dominating over tamas and sattva.

In the Rig Veda, the universal field of rajas is described as an "upper mass of light," sustained by Varuna, who is assigned a "reddish" color: "The reddish Varuna of pure vision dwells in the fathomless [space]. He sustains the upper mass of light; the rays [of which] are pointed downwards, while their base is above."[1]

This reddish mass of light represents the proverbial red veil that hides the holy of holies from all mortal eyes and the reddish veil that obscures the higher and larger realities of the universe from all mortal souls—whether they exist in an embodied or disembodied form.

THE LOKA-ALOKA BARRIER

In the Vedic Puranas, this cosmic red veil was also described as the *loka-aloka barrier*. The Sanskrit word *loka*, meaning "world," corresponds to the English term *local*. Its opposite is denoted by the word *aloka*, "nonworld," which corresponds to the English term *nonlocal*. In this sense, the red veil may be understood as the cosmic barrier that separates the local reality of the visible universe from the nonlocal reality of the larger, invisible universe.

The local reality of the visible universe upheld by local cause-effect relations is mediated by real waves that travel at the speed of light. The nonlocal reality of the invisible universe cannot be experienced empirically; it transcends all means of direct empirical observation, and represents the portion of the universe that lies above and beyond the cosmic red veil—that is, beyond the boundary of the visible universe.

In the Vedic texts, the loka-aloka barrier was often compared to a mountain range separating two distinct regions. Although this boundary cannot be seen by any mortal eye, the ancient texts state that it can be perceived by the enlightened eye, the eye of pure consciousness. More specifically, they state that it is experienced as a cosmic field of reddish light, which serves to obscure the visible universe and everything in it. As long as the enlightened soul remains within the highest heaven, represented by the twenty-eighth layer above, the visible form of the universe can be seen. Yet as soon as the soul rises above the highest heaven and enters into the world of Varuna, represented by the twenty-ninth layer, the visible form of the universe is dissolved into an all-pervading field of reddish light. This represents the loka-aloka barrier, which separates the local reality of the visible universe from the nonlocal reality of the invisible universe.

THE COSMIC NOOSE

According to the Vedic texts, the primary characteristic of Varuna is his power to bind: He serves to bind the visible universe and everything in it by means of his cosmic noose (*pashu*), which may be compared to a noose wrapped around the neck of a domesticated animal. In *devanagari* script (script of the gods), the letter *va* is written in the form of a noose attached to a pole.

This noose represents the upper mass of light, the loka-aloka barrier, which serves to create a universal space (loka) in the otherwise realmless space (aloka) of consciousness. It is within this created space that the universal sun (the visible form of the universe) moves and revolves. The Rig Veda states: "The royal (reddish) Varuna verily established a wide space for the shining Sun to follow in its course, a realm in the realmless."[2]

As the lord of the cosmic boundary, Varuna may be described as the Lord of the Noose (*Pashu-pati*), a term that is often used to describe Shiva and that takes us back to our earlier discussion regarding the universal form of Shiva.

THE FIVE FACES OF SHIVA

The Vedic conception of Shiva was synthetic. He was identified not with any particular layer or universal god, but with the entire collection of layers or universal gods that uphold the visible form of the universe and its invisible boundary.

As we have seen, Shiva was viewed as having a galactic torso corresponding to the visible form of our galaxy. He was also viewed as having a blue-black neck, which corresponds to the dark-matter halo that surrounds the visible form of the galaxy. Above the dark neck of Shiva lies his intergalactic head, which, according to tradition, has five faces. These correspond to the five intergalactic layers that extend to the boundary of the visible universe—to the twenty-fifth, twenty-sixth, twenty-seventh, twenty-eighth, and twenty-ninth layers above the half measure.

The tradition holds that the first four faces of Shiva are visible. These correspond to the four intergalactic layers that uphold the visible form of the universe, ending with the highest heaven. The fifth face of Shiva, however, was said to be invisible. This corresponds to the twenty-ninth layer, which upholds the cosmic red veil that is invisible to all mortal eyes, and which serves as the boundary of the visible universe. In this case, the fifth face of Shiva may be viewed as the face of Varuna, the lord of the cosmic noose and the regent of the western ocean. Because this fifth countenance represents his highest face, Shiva was known as Pashu-pati—the Lord of the Noose—a name that is also assigned to Varuna.

In this way, the ancient seers described the reality in different ways, drawing upon different conceptions and names of God, which would prove a labyrinth for those unversed in the ancient wisdoms. Yet, like a diamond that has many facets, the truth is only one.

THE RADIUS OF THE VISIBLE UNIVERSE

This ancient universal wisdom provides the basis for a prediction regarding the radius of the visible universe. If the twenty-ninth layer above the half measure upholds the spherical boundary of the visible universe, then the radius of the visible universe should correspond to the characteristic measure of the twenty-ninth layer. The universal rule of thumb gives this as 10^{28} centimeters. As discussed earlier, modern theorists have also calculated the radius of the visible universe: the Hubble radius, or the radius of the Hubble sphere, is likewise given as 10^{28} centimeters.

Therefore, it appears that the ancient seers and modern theorists are largely in agreement; not only did they arrive at the same conclusion regarding the radius of the universe, but also they reached the same conclusion regarding the quality of light associated with that radius:

red. In modern theory, the redness associated with the cosmological boundary is interpreted in terms of the cosmological red shift, which is explained in terms of a luminous Doppler shift resulting from a galactic recession speed that increases as distance from Earth increases. At the Hubble radius, this speed becomes equal, presumably, to the speed of light. Therefore, the Hubble radius represents the boundary between the local speeds of the galaxies within the sphere and the nonlocal speeds of the galaxies that lie on the surface and beyond the sphere.

The Vedic seers, on the other hand, described the cosmological boundary in terms of an all-pervading force field—the universal field of rajas, which is characterized by redness and incessant motion. As we have discovered, the explanation of the red shift provided by Hubble is not the only possible one. Other competing theories suggest that the electromagnetic wavelengths become lengthened due to a gradual loss of energy as they propagate through intergalactic space over vast distance and time scales. Such theories are described commonly as "tired light" theories. The difficulty with them, however, is that the underlying mechanism that causes this gradual loss of energy remains largely unknown. To account for the energy loss, the vacuum of intergalactic space must be viewed as pervaded by some unknown field, which tends to absorb energy from the propagating electromagnetic waves.

In light of the ancient Vedic theory, this underlying field can be described as the universal field of rajas, which represents a type of force field characterized by redness and incessant motion. This raises a fundamental question: To which of the known force fields does the universal field of rajas correspond?

THE SCALE OF GRAND UNIFICATION

The answer is provided by the system of matched pairs. If the scale of the twenty-ninth layer above the half measure marks the radius of the Hubble sphere, which is pervaded by the field of rajas, then the scale of the twenty-ninth layer below the half measure should mark the scale of the elementary constituents of that field. The universal rule of thumb gives this as 10^{-29} centimeters.

This leads to a prediction regarding the elementary particles of force that characterize the universal field of rajas. The ancient theory predicts that these unknown force particles should have a characteristic interaction scale that is roughly 10^{-29} centimeters. This can also be expressed as a prediction regarding a fundamental transition scale in the quantum vacuum. If the upper cosmological boundary represents a transition between the vacuum of intergalactic space, which is characterized by relations among visible galaxies, and the vacuum of interuniversal space, which is characterized by relations among local or visible universes, then the lower scale should mark a transition between two different types of quantum vacuum states. As we shall see, this prediction has support in modern theory.

In quantum theory, the scale of 10^{-29} centimeters is known as the scale of grand unification: The electro-weak force field becomes indistinguishable from, and hence unified with, the strong force field. The electromagnetic, weak, and strong forces, the three forces described by the Standard Model of quantum theory, serve to uphold all observable forms of matter in the universe. In order for matter as we know it to exist, these three forces must function in a diversified manner—as though they are distinct and independent. On the scale of grand unification, the distinctions among the three forces are obliterated so that they merge into a single, grand-unified force field. As a result, matter as we know it cannot exist. On the scale of 10^{-29} centimeters, all observable forms of matter must dissolve, effectively, into the grand-unified force field.

This reflects the principle "as above, so below." On the scale of 10^{28} centimeters, the observable forms of the material galaxies are drowned in the universal red force field, and on the scale of 10^{28} centimeters, the observable forms of the material particles are drowned in the grand-unified force field. In this way, the two scales form a matched pair so that they represent the macroscopic and microscopic boundaries of the observable universe. The upshot is that we may equate the universal field of rajas described by the Vedic theory and the grand-unified force field described by quantum theory.

THE UNIVERSAL KABBALAH

Although we have relied heavily upon the Vedic tradition in our description of the universal wisdom, this is only because the Vedic literature is by far the largest extent body of writing of the surviving ancient literatures—in fact, it is much larger than all of the other ancient literatures put together. It therefore offers perhaps the clearest insight into the thinking of the ancient seers.

Yet the Hebrew seers—more specifically, the proponents of kabbalah—also possessed this ancient wisdom. The word *kabbalah* (KBLH) means "that which was received." According to traditional sources, the kabbalah was originally received by Adam, the proverbial first man, while he dwelled in the Garden of Eden. More specifically, the tradition holds that Adam received the wisdom from an *elohim* (universal lord) named Raziel, also known as the "keeper of secrets."

Although the Garden of Eden may correspond to a physical and historical place on earth marked by the headwaters of four rivers (Tigris, Euphrates, Pischon, and Gihon), many believe it has a deeper cosmological interpretation in terms of the spiritual heavens. In this expanded cosmological interpretation, the Garden of Eden corresponds to the paradisal spiritual world represented by the highest heaven and realized on the scale of the twenty-eighth layer above the half measure. In this case, Adam and Eve represent archetypal souls inhabiting the highest heaven in the visible universe, and their Fall from the Garden of Eden corresponds to their subsequent incarnation on earth as mortal human beings, when they became clothed in animal skins.

In this case, the Garden of Eden corresponds to the highest heaven, which lies in immediate proximity to the cosmological red veil, hiding from all mortal eyes the higher mysteries of the universe. This interpretation is supported in the doctrine of kabbalah wherein the metaphysical layers are called the *sephirotic emanations*. The tradition holds that each of these emanations has its own presiding deity or lord—the elohim, who are commonly compared to the archangels of God. The elohim called Raziel is listed as the lord of the twenty-ninth emanation (layer) in the ascending direction. In effect, Raziel is just another name for Varuna, the lord of the twenty-ninth layer, who also represents the keeper of the cosmic red veil, which is why Raziel was known as the "keeper of secrets." Apparently, however, Raziel deigned to reveal those secrets to Adam so that he could teach them to human beings on earth in his subsequent incarnation. In this sense, Adam may be viewed as a divine incarnation, a messenger of God who became man on earth in accordance with divine will, in order to teach to his descendants the higher mysteries of the universe so that his progeny might become immortal.

As we have seen, the term *kabbalah* itself is a mantra or a phonemic formula that encodes the first stage of human enlightenment, represented by the phoneme *ka,* and the subsequent stage of galactic enlightenment, represented by the phoneme *ba.* In this sense, the two Hebrew letters *k* and *b* (*ka, ba*) represent a form of galactic wisdom. We can now go further and discover that the three phonemes *k, b,* and *l* (*ka, ba,* and *la*) represent a form of universal wisdom, which pertains to the overall form of the visible universe extending up to the highest heaven. This interpretation is based upon the sequence of consonants in the Sanskrit alphabet, in which the first consonant is *ka,* the twenty-third consonant is *ba,* and the twenty-eighth consonant is *la.* As we have seen, in the Vedic tradition, the phoneme *la* was viewed as the seed formula of Indra, the king of the celestial gods, who was also known as the presiding deity of the highest heaven.

When the human soul first attains enlightenment on the scale of the first layer above the half measure, it becomes identified with the divine Ka. This marks the first major milestone on the path of immortality: the soul cognizes the first universal forms of light and sound to emerge at the beginning of creation. When the soul subsequently ascends to the scale of the twenty-third layer, it arrives at the galactic heaven and becomes identified with the divine Ba. This marks the second major milestone on the path: the soul obtains galactic consciousness and cognizes the visible form of the galaxy within its awareness. When the soul then ascends to the scale of the twenty-eighth layer, it arrives at the highest universal heaven and becomes identified with the divine La, which marks the third major milestone on the path: The soul obtains universal consciousness and cognizes the visible form of the universe within its awareness.

Therefore, the three phonemes *k, b,* and *l* (*ka, ba,* and *la*) represent the first three major milestones on the path of immortality: They correspond to the stages of human enlightenment, galactic enlightenment, and universal enlightenment. Oddly, though, this phonemic understanding of the Hebrew KBLH is rooted in a Vedic interpretation of the Sanskrit alphabet. Once again, this points to the notion that the ancient cultures shared a scientific language expressed in terms of phonemes, which transcended the grammatical differences of their spoken languages. Although this original phonematic language was lost for the most part, it appears that in certain important cases, such as the systematic organization of the Vedic alphabet and the phonemic formula KBLH, the original scientific language was preserved.

At this point, we have reached the boundary of the visible universe—but our journey does not end there. The ancient wisdom extended beyond the boundary of the visible universe to the boundary of the superuniverse, the cosmic egg as a whole. This leads us to the next chapter, in which we examine the superuniversal wisdom.

10

The Superuniversal Wisdom

THE COSMIC EGG

Modern theorists are uncertain as to the full extent of creation. Although there is a general consensus that the smallest scale of creation corresponds to the Planck scale (10^{-33} centimeter), there is an ongoing debate as to whether the Hubble radius (10^{28} centimeter) represents the largest scale in creation. Some theorists hold that the universe is infinite in extent and that the Hubble radius serves merely as an observational limit. Others suggest that nothing exists beyond the Hubble radius—not even space and time.

The ancients differed from both of these opinions. They held that the created universe is finite, but they did not associate the largest scale in creation with the Hubble radius, which corresponds to the scale of the cosmic red veil. The Hubble radius may represent the largest scale of the local or visible universe, but it does not represent the largest scale of the superuniverse taken as a whole.

In the Vedic tradition the superuniverse was called the brahmanda, "the egg of Brahman" and was viewed as the vast celestial body of the Creator, who was referred to variously as Brahma (the living embodiment of Brahman) and Prajapati (the lord of all creatures). The Vedic seers described the overall extent of the cosmic egg in two different ways:

- In relation to the metaphysical layers
- In relation to the various worlds conceived on the basis of those layers

The seers conceived the cosmic egg as being upheld by the first thirty-three layers above and below the half measure—but these thirty-three layers were viewed as upholding seven different types of worlds called the *sapta lokas* (seven worlds). In this regard, the seers distinguished between the first three worlds and the subsequent four worlds: The first three worlds, called the *tri-loki,* were viewed as the three types of mundane worlds bounded by the loka-aloka barrier: the solar worlds, the galactic worlds, and the universal worlds. Therefore, the tri-loki represent visible and physical worlds. According to modern astrophysics, there are some two hundred billion galaxies and twenty trillion stars contained within the visible universe. In this way, the Vedic description is archetypal: It pertains to the three general types of visible worlds and not their specific and numerous manifestations at different locations in space.

Just as the visible universe contains within itself many galaxies and stars, so the superuniverse contains within itself many visible universes, each of which was viewed as a local universal world. Further, all of these universal worlds have an internal observational limit marked by the cosmic red veil. This means that no matter where a physical observer might be located within the superuniverse, he or she will perceive the visible universe as extending no farther than 10^{28} centimeters from the point of observation. On this distance scale, the distant galaxies become obscured by the cosmic red veil so that nothing beyond can be seen by any empirical means.

Described in terms of the loka-aloka barrier, the cosmic red veil serves to separate the three mundane worlds, the tri-loki, from the four supermundane worlds, called the four alokas, which correspond to four nonlocal worlds that exist above and beyond the cosmic red veil. Unlike the three mundane worlds, which are tied to particular locations within the superuniverse, the four supermundane worlds represent invisible, spiritual worlds tied to particular scales of consciousness within the superuniverse.

In the Vedic literature, the four supermundane worlds were designated by the terms *mahah, janah, tapah,* and *satya.* These correspond to the four spiritual heavens that exist above and beyond the loka-aloka barrier and are cognized on the basis of the thirtieth, thirty-first, thirty-second, and thirty-third layers above the half measure, respectively. The highest of these four spiritual worlds was called the world of *satya,* the world of truth. It was also known as *brahma loka,* the world of Brahma, the Creator, because the thirty-third layer represents the station of the Creator.

According to the Vedic seers, this vast, superuniversal world has the form of a luminous sphere or cosmic egg filled with transcendental light—the type of light that illuminates the spiritual worlds throughout the universe. Although virtual light cannot be observed by any empirical means, it can be observed with the enlightened mind, or the eye of pure consciousness. The four supermundane worlds may be hidden to all unenlightened mortal souls, but they are not hidden to enlightened immortal souls. Upon ascending beyond the highest heaven within the visible universe and traversing the loka-aloka barrier, the enlightened soul has the potential to cognize the four higher spiritual worlds, which are filled with virtual forms of reality. The largest such reality takes on the form of the cosmic egg, the vast luminous sphere within which all local, visible universes abide.

According to the ancient science of the gods, the sphere of the superuniversal world is upheld by the thirty-third layer above the half measure. It follows that the radius of this sphere should be determined by the scale of the thirty-third layer above. The universal rule of thumb gives this as 10^{32} centimeters—which leads to a prediction regarding the radius of the cosmic egg.

Unfortunately, this scale lies far beyond the observational limit marked by the Hubble radius. If the Vedic seers are correct, the radius of the superuniverse is some ten thousand times larger than the radius of the visible universe. This immensity is mind-boggling.

THE MINIMUM LIGHT SPAN OF CREATION

The Hubble radius (10^{28} centimeters) may be viewed as the maximum light span of the visible universe. It represents the largest distance that real light—the type of light that can be observed empirically—can travel through space. Its microscopic counterpart corresponds to the scale of grand unification (10^{-29} centimeters), which can be viewed as the minimum light span of the visible universe. It represents the smallest distance that real light can travel through space. These two limits are set by the twenty-ninth layers above and below the half measure, respectively.

The same principles can be applied to the scales of the thirty-third layers above and below the half measure. Yet the thirty-three layers pertain to virtual, not real, light. In this case, the radius of the cosmic egg (10^{32} centimeters) represents the maximum span of virtual light within the universe—the largest distance that virtual light can travel through space. Its microscopic counterpart, which corresponds to the Planck scale, or the scale of superunification (10^{-33} centimeters), therefore represents the smallest span of virtual light within the universe, and the smallest distance that virtual light can travel through space.

Whether light is virtual or real, it is limited by the speed of light. Generally, a speed can be represented as a ratio of space and time. In this regard it should be pointed out that the Planck scale represents not only a minimum distance scale, given by the length $L_p = 1.616 \ldots \times 10^{-33}$ centimeters, but also a minimum time scale, given by the time $T_p = 5.37 \ldots \times 10^{-44}$ seconds. It turns out that the ratio of space and time of the Planck length and Planck time is exactly equal to the speed of light: $L_p/T_p = c$.

This illustrates what we mean by a light span: The Planck length represents literally the distance that light will travel during the Planck time. Because the Planck length and Planck time represent the minimum units of length and time that can be inferred on the basis of the fundamental constants, the Planck length may be understood as the minimum light span in the superuniverse.

In actuality, it is impossible for us to observe empirically an electromagnetic wave with a wavelength on the order of the Planck length or a period on the order of the Planck time. As a result, the Planck length must be viewed as the minimum span of virtual light in the superuniverse, and not the minimum span of real light.

THE MAXIMUM LIGHT SPAN OF CREATION

In accordance with the principle "as above, so below," the Planck length should have a macroscopic counterpart representing the maximum span of virtual light in the universe. We can equate this to the radius of the cosmic egg, which the universal rule of thumb gives as 10^{32} centimeters.

The system of matched pairs, which we have used to examine the various ancient wisdoms, is expressed in terms of distance scales. But we can also view these as time scales so that the distance scales and time scales are linked by the speed of light, as are the Planck length and Planck time.

This understanding is implied in the Vedic texts. Throughout the Vedic literature, a great deal of emphasis is placed upon Para, the supreme time, viewed as the period of time that constitutes the life span of the Creator. It turns out that the ancients equated life and light. This is made apparent in both the Hermetic texts and in the Gospel of John, which describes the life of the Creator by saying: "All that came to be was alive with his life, and that life was the light of men. The light shines on in the dark, and the dark has never mastered it."

This light that shines in the dark corresponds to the virtual light that shines in the darkness of the universal vacuum, which was made equal to the life of the Creator. It follows that we can equate the life span of the Creator and that of the cosmic egg, the celestial body of the Creator. Further, this light span can be expressed in two complementary ways: in terms of a length scale and a time scale. The length scale represents the distance that light will travel over the time scale, while the time scale represents the time it takes for light to travel that distance.

In this regard, it is quite common for modern astronomers to express vast cosmological distances in terms of light-years, with a light-year representing the distance that light will travel over the course of a solar year (365.25 days). It turns out that the period called Para, which represent the life span of the Creator, was also expressed in terms of solar years. The algorithms given throughout the Vedic literature suggest that this period is some three hundred trillion solar years—viewed as the longest period of time in the created universe.

Is it possible that the ancient algorithm provides an estimate of the cosmic radius expressed in terms of light-years? Determining this requires an accurate knowledge of the speed of light. The history of science tells us that the speed of light was first estimated by a European astronomer named Roemer in 1675 through his study of the moons of Jupiter. The Vedic texts were written long before this time, however, so it seems safe to assume that the Vedic seers were unaware of the speed of light.

Nevertheless, we can determine the distance that light will travel over the course of three hundred trillion years: A simple calculation reveals that it will travel roughly 10^{32} centimeters. This is the same estimate obtained from the system of matched pairs whose parameters have been established by the universal rule of thumb. Is this just a coincidence, or does it suggest that the Vedic seers possessed an accurate knowledge of the speed of light thousands of years before it was discovered by modern theorists?

AN ANCIENT ESTIMATE OF THE SPEED OF LIGHT

Although there is no archaeological evidence to suggest that the ancients possessed technological instruments capable of measuring the speed of light, there is textual evidence that they nevertheless possessed an accurate knowledge of that speed long before it was discovered by modern scientists. In a commentary on the Rig Veda dated to the fourteenth century, the author named Sayana recalls a saying that was considered ancient in his day: "Thus it is remembered: you who traverse 2,202 *yojanas* in half a *nimesha*."

This passage occurs in Sayana's commentary on a hymn dedicated to the sun, the primary source of light in our solar system. Because a *yojana* is a Vedic unit of distance and a *nimesha* is a Vedic unit of time, the saying represents an algorithm indicating a speed. Subhash Kak, an electrical engineer at Louisiana State University, wondered if this algorithm might actually be an ancient reference to the speed of light.[1]

We can examine this possibility here. The Vedic units of distance are well documented in the ancient texts:

Units of Distance
8 yava (barleycorns) = 1 angula (digit; $\frac{3}{4}$ inch)
12 angulas = 1 vitasti (hand span or half-cubit; 9 inches)
2 vitastis = 1 aratni (elbow or cubit; 18 inches)
4 aratnis = 1 danda (rod) or dhanu (bow; 6 feet)
2,000 dhanus = 1 krosha (cry) or goruta (cow call; $2\frac{1}{4}$ miles)
4 kroshas = 1 yojana (stage; approximately 9 miles)

The Vedic units of time are also well documented. In the Vangabashi edition of the Vishnu Purana (2.8.55), the units of time are listed as:

Units of Time
1 nimesha = 1 blink of an eye (0.213 seconds)
1 kastha = 15 nimesha (3.2 seconds)
1 kala = 30 kastha (96 seconds)
1 muhurta = 30 kala (48 minutes)
1 ahoratra = 30 muhurta (24 hours)

According to the ancient saying recalled by Sayana, the mysterious speed is 2,202 yojanas per half nimesha. Given the units above, it is apparent that a half nimesha is equal to .1066 seconds. A simple calculation reveals that the speed is:

$$\frac{2202 \times (9 \text{ miles})}{.1066 \text{ seconds}} = 185{,}793.75 \text{ miles per second}$$

Modern calculations tell us that the speed of light is approximately 186,000 miles per second. Therefore, the ancient estimate is extremely accurate—more accurate than the first modern estimate Roemer obtained in 1675, yet this algorithm was recorded in a text written some three hundred years prior to 1675, and even at that time it was remembered as extremely ancient.

Exactly how the ancient seers obtained an accurate estimate of the speed of light without the use of sophisticated electronic equipment or powerful telescopes remains a profound mystery for which we have no answers. Given this algorithm, however, the interpretation of the life span of the Creator (expressed in solar years) as the light span of the cosmic egg (expressed in light-years) becomes inherently plausible.

THE HIDDEN UNIVERSAL SYMMETRY

At this point, we have reached the limits of creation. For all empirical purposes, we may view the created universe as extending over a vast spectrum of space-time scales extending from the Planck scale below to the Para scale above.

Our interpretation of the ancient science of the gods, based upon the system of matched pairs, suggests that the overall spectrum of creation displays a hidden vertical symmetry that remains unknown to modern theorists and involves correspondences between what lies above on macroscopic scales and what lies below on microscopic scales.

To summarize and figure these correspondences, we can assign an exponential layer number L = 1, 2, 3, . . . to each layer so that the sequence of layers above the half measure can be represented by the set of scales 10^{L-1} centimeters, while the sequence of layers below the half-measure can be represented by the set of scales 10^{-L} centimeters. Given this notation, the matched pairs of scales, which relate to the cosmological wholes and their microscopic parts, can be tabulated as follows.

THE HIDDEN UNIVERSAL SYMMETRY

Layer Number	10^{-L} Microscopic	10^{L-1} Macroscopic
L = 12	10^{-12} Nuclear Unification	10^{11} Radius of Solar Sphere
L = 16	10^{-16} Electro-Weak Unification	10^{15} Radius of Heliosphere
L = 24	10^{-24} Dark-Matter Unification	10^{23} Radius of Galactic Sphere
L = 29	10^{-29} Grand Unification	10^{28} Radius of Universal Sphere
L = 33	10^{-33} Superunification	10^{32} Radius of Cosmic Egg

You will not find this table anywhere in the physics literature, because the symmetry outlined above is unknown in modern physics; it has been derived not from modern physical science, but from ancient spiritual science. No doubt, many of the scales represented in the table are known to modern theorists, but the correspondences between the two sets of scales are not. In modern science the small-scale and large-scale laws of nature are studied on the basis of two very different theories: quantum theory and general relativity, which do not see eye to eye. As a result, there is no common theoretical basis to ascertain the relations between the large-scale and small-scale laws of nature. Many hope that the new unified theory will provide this common basis, but at this point; the prospective unified theories are little more than abstract algebraic frameworks, which have yet to be interpreted in a way that allows them to yield accurate empirical predictions.

The ancient spiritual science, on the other hand, can already be used to make accurate predictions regarding the organization of the universe over a vast spectrum of space-time scales. Unlike modern science, however, it was not based upon an objective paradigm, which assigns an insentient, objective nature to the unified field. Instead, it was based upon a subjective paradigm, which suggests that the unified field is ultimately a field of pure consciousness. According to the ancients, the vertical correlations between the large-scale and small-scale laws of nature are mediated not by any known physical force, but by the divine mind, the field of pure consciousness that links all of the vertical layers like so many beads on a string. The correlations are hidden because they exist in consciousness; they exist within the divine mind.

The ancients may have described the overall organization of the universe using spiritual concepts and terms expressed in regards to the gods, but this is just a matter of semantics. The numbers do not lie. The correspondences outlined here provide a convincing argument that the ancients possessed a genuine spiritual science.

Although we have reached the end of the superuniverse, we have not reached the ends of the cosmic spectrum. The first thirty-three layers above and below the half measure represent the layers that are responsible directly for upholding the appearance of the superuniverse in both its real and virtual forms. As such, they are the only layers that we must consider for the sake of empirical predictions. According to the ancient seers, however, the vast superuniverse is but a small part of the infinite reality of the self. There are even larger, uncreated realms that lie beyond the boundaries of the superuniverse, and these are indirectly responsible for its appearance in consciousness. Modern physical science may be limited to the first thirty-three layers above and below the half measure, but the ancient spiritual science was not. It embraced a much larger spectrum of reality extending from the infinitesimal to the infinite. In the remaining chapters we will explore these mysterious, uncreated realms that lie beyond the finite boundaries of the superuniverse.

Although they transcend any scale that can be evaluated on the basis of modern science, the ancient understanding regarding these realms is no less scientific than that supplied for the created realms. Given the fact that the ancient wisdoms provide an accurate description of the overall organization of the created universe, there is good reason to suspect that they also provide an accurate description of the uncreated realms that lie beyond the created universe.

Having reached the shore of this world, we are about to embark upon a spiritual voyage that will take us to the shore of the other world—and beyond. Yet before we set sail, it will be useful to examine in more detail just what the shore of this world represents.

THE CREATED AND UNCREATED ASPECTS OF THE COSMIC EGG

In the Vedic literature, the cosmic egg was a vast superuniversal world called *satya loka,* the world of truth.

Truth is cognized on the level of mind, and not on the level of matter or force. The idea that the superuniverse takes the form of a cosmic egg is quite literal and represents the truth regarding the universe. Yet this truth is twofold: it can be said that the cosmic egg represents both a created and uncreated form of existence.

This duality can be compared to the two aspects of an egg. On one hand, an egg possesses a golden yolk, and on the other, it possesses a surrounding white. In this analogy, the central golden yolk represents the created aspect of the universe, and the surrounding white represents its uncreated aspect. The Vedic seers believed that these two aspects of the cosmic egg are upheld by the thirty-second and thirty-third layers above and below the half measure, respectively. The truth cognized on the scale of the thirty-third layer is that the cosmic egg is both created and uncreated at the same time; it consists of both the golden yolk and its surrounding white. The golden yolk was likened to the supermundane world called *tapo loka* (the world of heating), and the white was likened to the supermundane world called satya loka (the world of truth). The idea was that when the uncreated egg white is heated, it assumes the created form of the golden yolk—otherwise known as hiranyagarbha (the golden womb).

This presents a more detailed picture of the cosmic egg, which is related to the scales of the thirty-second and thirty-third layers. In the alphabetical model, these two layers were represented by the thirty-second and thirty-third consonants of the Sanskrit alphabet: the phonemes *sa* and *ha,* respectively. According to the Vedic rules of phonetic conjunction (*sandhi*), when these two phonemes are joined, they produce the word *om* (*sa* + *ha*), which was viewed as the cosmic hum that leads to the dissolution of the created universe in the divine mind. When the phonemes are joined in reverse, they produce the word *hams* (*ha* + *sa*), which means "swan" or "goose." The cosmic swan was viewed as the vehicle (*vahana*) by means of which the Creator (Brahma) makes the universe from his own divine mind.

This presents two complementary wisdoms regarding the relation between the thirty-second and thirty-third layers: When the enlightened soul ascends from the thirty-second to the thirty-third layer, it experiences the cosmic hum (om), which serves to reduce the created form of the universe to its uncreated constituents. When the soul descends from the thirty-third to the thirty-second layer, it experiences the cosmic swan (hamsa), which serves to create the universe from its uncreated constituents. The cosmic swan represents the proverbial goose that laid the golden egg. In the Egyptian tradition, it was known as the "great cackler."

In the Vedic tradition, the uncreated constituents from which the universe is created were viewed not as elements of force and matter, but as elements of mind stuff (*chitta*). These elements predominated with the quality of sattva, which is responsible for all phenomenal manifestations of mind. As we have seen, in the Vedic system of Samkhya, all states of matter were viewed as evolutes of tamas, all states of force were viewed as evolutes of rajas, and all states of mind were viewed as evolutes of sattva. These three qualities were associated traditionally with the colors black, red, and white, respectively. The implication is that the white that surrounds the golden womb is the superuniversal field of sattva, composed of uncreated mind stuff.

Unlike created particles of force (rajas) and matter (tamas) from which is fashioned the empirical universe, the uncreated particles of mind (sattva) are self-conscious and are therefore capable of responding to the slightest intention of the Creator. By means of pure intention, the Creator creates the universe—he creates from the uncreated by imposing his will upon the superuniversal field of sattva—which represents the cosmic embodiment of his own mind. In the process, the field of sattva becomes "heated." The particles of mind stuff begin to undergo various combinations and permutations, which give rise to created particles of force and matter. These particles, in turn, give rise to the created form of the universe, which appears as the golden yolk of the cosmic egg.

Although the Para scale, the scale of the thirty-third layer above the half measure, represents the largest scale of space and time that has any empirical relevance, it actually transcends the largest form of created existence. The same can be said with respect to the Planck scale, the scale of the thirty-third layer below the half measure: it transcends the scale of the smallest created particles in existence.

This understanding is reflected in modern unification theories. For example, in superstring theory, the elementary particles are modeled as very small quantum strings, similar to vibrating rubber bands, which, on ordinary scales of observation, appear as point particles.

According to superstring theory, the Planck scale (10^{-33} centimeters) represents the scale of superunification, but does not represent the scale of the smallest quantum strings (or elementary particles). The theory suggests that the smallest quantum strings have a characteristic size of roughly 10^{-32} centimeters as opposed to 10^{-33} centimeters. In other words, the smallest created parts of the universe are characterized by the scale of the thirty-second and not the thirty-third layer below the half measure. In accordance with the principle "as above, so below," the same can be said about the largest form of creation, the golden yolk: It is characterized by the scale of the thirty-second and not the thirty-third layer above the half measure. The thirty-third layers above and below therefore transcend the largest and smallest forms of creation. They determine the scales of the superuniversal field of sattva and its elementary constituents, which may be viewed as uncreated particles of mind, rather than created particles of force or matter.

Although the ancient theory is consistent with the principles of superstring theory, it presents a completely different picture of the universe from the one drawn by modern science—a picture rooted in a subjective, rather than an objective paradigm.

THE UNIVERSAL AHA EXPERIENCE

On the scale of the thirty-third layer, the soul cognizes the truth about the universe—that it is both created and uncreated at the same time: created by means of the particles of force and matter, and uncreated by means of the particles of mind, which give rise to the particles of force and matter. This occurs when the field of sattva becomes "heated" by divine will. At that point, the particles of sattva engage in various combinations and permutations that give rise to created particles of force and matter. These two truths—that the universe is both created and uncreated at the same time—are cognized in a balanced manner on the scale of the thirty-third layer.

The thirty-third layer was represented by the thirty-third and final consonant in the classical Sanskrit alphabet, the phoneme *ha*. This was considered the seed formula of Brahma, the Creator, however, the Vedic rules of phonetic conjunction (sandhi) state that if the letter *h*, ordinarily pronounced as *ha*, stands as the final letter in a sequence of letters, then the hard *ha* sound is transformed into the soft vocal sound of *aha*, made by breathing through the letter *h*.

In devanagari script, the final form of *h*, different from an initial *h*, is written in the form of two dots placed one above the other, like a colon (:). These represent the two truths cognized on the scale of the thirty-third layer, the scale of the divine Ha. The lower dot represents the lower truth, that the universe is created, and the upper dot represents the higher truth, that the universe is uncreated. When the soul ascends to the thirty-third layer and cognizes these two truths in a balanced manner, it obtains the ultimate Aha experience regarding the created-uncreated reality of the universe.

THE SUPERUNIVERSAL KABBALAH

We have discovered that the Hebrew word *kabbalah* (KBLH) can be given a human, galactic, and universal interpretation so that the first three phonemes pertain to major milestones on the path of immortality. These correspond to the stage of human enlightenment (Ka), the stage of galactic enlightenment (Ba), and the stage of universal enlightenment (La). We will now see that it can also be given a superuniversal interpretation.

Although the Hebrew and Sanskrit languages are written using different ligatures and expressed using different forms of grammar, there are certain similarities between the two. In both cases, the language is written so that the vowels are largely implied as opposed to being spelled out, as they are in English. In Hebrew, the English word *kabbalah* is written using the four consonants *k, b, l,* and *h* (KBLH); the *a* vowels are omitted in the writing. The same holds true for Sanskrit, in which it is assumed that each consonant is followed by the vowel *a* if nothing else is indicated.

Another similarity between the two languages is related to the treatment of a final *h*. In both cases, if the letter *h* comes at the end of a word or sentence, it is breathed through so that it is pronounced as the softly aspirated sound *aha,* with a barely audible final *a*. In spoken Sanskrit, the *aha* sound is more clearly audible than in spoken Hebrew, where the final *h* more closely resembles a guttural aspirant, but the principle is the same. In this regard, we note that the word *kabbalah* (*kabbalah;* KBLH) ends with a final *h*. This represents the final Aha experience obtained when the enlightened soul ascends to the scale of the thirty-third layer and, in a balanced manner, cognizes the created-uncreated reality of the universe—which represents the fourth major milestone on the path of immortality.

We can therefore conclude that the Hebrew KBLH symbolizes the first four—and not three—major milestones on the path. It represents a sonic formulation of superuniversal wisdom.

THE EGYPTIAN AKH AND SAH

The fact that the Hebrew KBLH can be explicated in terms of the Vedic alphabetical model suggests that the Vedic seers somehow preserved the original meanings of the phonemes used at the dawn of history to record and describe the ancient science.

After the end of the early period, known variously as *satya yuga* (the age of truth) in the Vedic tradition and zep tepi (the first time) in the Egyptian tradition, when men began to babble in various tongues corresponding to grammatical languages, the original phonemic language appears largely to have been lost. In some cases, however—especially with respect to important spiritual concepts and words—the original phonemic meanings shine through.

For example, consider the Egyptian terms *Akh* and *Sah,* which were the words used to denote the immortal soul and its universal body, respectively. In the Vedic alphabetical model, the letter *a* was likened to the infinite self standing above and beyond all the metaphysical layers. When the soul realizes the infinite self and thereby becomes truly immortal, its awareness then extends from *a* to *k*— from the infinite form of the self (the divine A realized at the end of the path) to the first form of the self (the divine Ka cognized at the beginning of the path). This presents the downward-looking view of the self when it becomes established in the infinite.

The upward-looking view, by means of which the self realizes its identity with divine Ha and then becomes identified with the Creator, is represented by the sequence of thirty-three consonants from *k* to *h*. Because the immortal soul includes within itself both views (downward and upward), it can be represented by the sequence of letters $a + k + h = akh$. This presents an explication of the Egyptian Akh (the immortal soul) in terms of the original, phonemic language preserved by the sequence of letters in the Sanskrit alphabet.

The universal body possessed by such an immortal soul was denoted by the Egyptian word Sah. This body corresponds to the cosmic egg, whose two aspects are cognized on the scale of the thirty-second and thirty-third layers above the half measure. These correspond to the letters *sa* and *ha,* which represent the golden yolk and white, respectively. In Sanskrit the word *saha* means "together"—the Sa and the Ha taken together constitute a single cosmic body or a single cosmic egg. In the Egyptian tradition, the cosmic body was thus called the *Sah* ($sa + h$).

These hidden phonemic meanings can be found within a system of correspondences between the phonemes and certain spiritual-cosmological categories of experience related to the metaphysical layers.

Because all the ancient seers experienced the layers in the same way, they shared an understanding regarding the meanings of the phonemes. Here, we are not assuming that the ancient phonemic system was invented by the Vedic seers; we discover only that the system appears to have been better preserved in the Vedic tradition than in the other traditions farther West, perhaps due to its isolation on the Indian subcontinent.

11

The Cosmic Wisdom

THE CREATIVE GODHEAD

The Hermetic texts tell us that the celestial bodies of the gods consist of heads alone in the place of bodily frames. They also tell us that a *head* means a "sphere." Therefore, the great god known as Cosmos was viewed as having a spherical form representing the head of creation—the creative godhead.

This creative godhead, this vast cosmic sphere, is filled with luminous mind stuff. It corresponds to the spherical field of sattva cognized on the scale of the thirty-third layer above the half measure, with the field of sattva being compared to the brain of the creative godhead and the imperishable thirty-third layer of the metaphysical Logos corresponding to the skull.

This understanding is consistent with the Hebrew tradition of kabbalah in which the imperishable spine of Adam Ouila, the first archetypal man, is represented by the 22 + 10 = 32 geometric elements of the diagrammatic Tree of Life. In this system, the highest of the ten sephiroth—Kether, the Crown—represents the thirty-second layer in the ascending direction. More specifically, it symbolizes the crown of the cosmic spine, the atlas upon which rests the cosmic head or skull. This cosmic head itself corresponds to the thirty-third aspect of the Tree of Life—the uncreated whole that exists above and beyond its thirty-two created parts or the thirty-third layer of the metaphysical Logos, which upholds the superuniversal field of sattva, the cosmic brain.

THE SEVEN SHELLS OR SEVEN SKULLS

There is more to this cosmic wisdom than meets the eye. According to the Vedic seers, the Creator of the universe has not one head or brain, but seven. The Creator was thus viewed as possessing a "seven-headed intellect."

In the Vedic literature, the seven heads of the Creator are described as the seven shells (*sapta-kapalas*) of the cosmic egg, which correspond to the seven skulls (sapta-kapalas) of the cosmic head and the seven uncreated foundations (*sapta-talas*) of the created universe.

These seven cosmic shells are like seven cosmic spheres, each of which is filled with its own gradation of uncreated mind stuff and all of which hold up the uncreated picture of the universe. They can be understood as seven cosmic fields of uncreated mind stuff that both pervade and extend beyond the created form of the universe on all sides. The Vedic seers referred to these seven gradations as the seven primordial elements.

THE SEVEN PRIMORDIAL ELEMENTS

In ascending order, the seven primordial elements are earth, water, fire, air, space, ego, and intelligence. These terms are symbolic and cosmic in scope and are related to seven gradations of uncreated mind stuff inherent within the seven cosmic shells (as opposed to created forms of matter-energy).

These seven elements represent different classes of conscious and uncreated particles that abide within the seven shells. As conscious elements, they are capable of responding to conscious intention or visionary imagination. By virtue of the intentions of the Creator, they are roused into activity and united in various combinations and permutations. The end result of this process is the creation of the golden yolk of the cosmic egg. The Vedic texts state:

> From the seven primordial elements, which are roused into activity and united [into combinations and permutations] by the [visionary] presence of the Creator, a golden egg arose. . . . This egg is called the manifestation of matter-energy. Its shells of [earth], water, fire, air, space, ego, and intelligence increase in thickness one after another. Each layer is ten times larger than the previous, and the final outside layer is covered by *pradhana*.[1]

This passage makes clear that the seers were talking about not only the seven shells, but also the imperishable layers that uphold the seven shells so that each shell and each type of primordial element has its imperishable basis in a given layer. These seven cosmic layers extend from the thirty-third to the thirty-ninth layer. The qualities associated with the seven elements—earth, water, fire, air, space, ego, and intelligence—can be viewed in either ascending or descending order. The outermost cosmic shell, which corresponds to the thirty-ninth layer, embodies the most abstract of the seven qualities—*mahat*, cosmic intelligence—and the innermost cosmic shell, which corresponds to the thirty-third layer, embodies the most concrete of the seven qualities—*prithivi*, cosmic earth.

When awareness descends through the seven shells—that is, from the thirty-ninth to the thirty-third layer—the qualities of the previous layer are added to the subsequent layer, so that the earth element consists of all seven qualities and the intelligence element consists of a single quality. This doctrine is made clear in these words: "Among them each succeeding [primordial element] acquires the quality of the preceding one, and whatever place [in the sequence] each of them occupies, even so many qualities is it declared to possess."[2]

When awareness ascends through the seven shells, the reverse holds true. The qualities are stripped from awareness progressively so that, upon reaching the outermost shell, only a single quality remains: cosmic intelligence.

The primordial element upheld by the thirty-third layer is earth because it represents the most concrete of the seven elements and displays all seven qualities. This uncreated mind stuff may be compared to the primordial clay from which are created the actual physical elements. Although this earthen form of mind stuff is conscious, it is not as conscious as the higher gradations associated with the higher shells: water, fire, air, space, ego, and intelligence, which represent progressively more abstract and conscious forms of uncreated mind stuff and are less restricted by their qualitative manifestations.

The doctrine just quoted tells us that the final outside layer (or shell) is covered by pradhana, which denotes not a form of dark matter (tamas) or mind stuff (chitta), but represents the truly imperishable substance of pure consciousness (*chit*), which constitutes the immortal blood (amrita rasa) of the Supreme Being. The immortal substance pervading, transcending, and covering the seven shells can be cognized only when the awareness breaks through the outermost shell of the cosmic egg by ascending to the fortieth layer. Only then do we realize the truly imperishable basis of the seven shells and the seven primordial elements. That imperishable basis corresponds not to the finite field of cosmic intelligence (mahat), but to the infinite field of pure consciousness (chit).

SPONTANEOUS SYMMETRY-BREAKING

In Samkhya philosophy, the imperishable substance of pure consciousness was called *prakriti,* "that which exists prior (*pra*) to creation (*kriti*)." Interestingly, the term *prakriti* was used synonymously with the word *kshetra,* "field," to represent the ultimate unified field, which is cognized on the scale of the fortieth layers above and below the half measure.

In the system of Samkhya, prakriti was defined as the unity of the three gunas held in equilibrium (*gunanam samyavastha*).[3] As we have seen, the three gunas correspond to the qualities of mind (sattva), force (rajas), and matter (tamas). Therefore, the field of prakriti represents the unified field of mind, force, and matter that transcends both the created and uncreated forms of the universe. In this field, the qualities of mind, force, and matter are forever united in homogeneous equilibrium. Yet this unity is different from each of the three qualities themselves: It represents the unqualified or absolute quality of pure consciousness (prakriti; pradhana), rather than the relative qualities of mind, force, and matter (sattva, rajas, and tamas).

According to the seers, the field of unity and homogenous equilibrium cognized on the scales of the fortieth layers above and below is both infinite and eternal; the unified state of homogenous equilibrium is never actually disturbed, though the equilibrium state may appear disturbed when awareness operates on scales that lie in between the fortieth layers.

The apparent nonequilibrium states of the field, which arise on different scales of consciousness, were often compared to mirage water superimposed on a dry desert. Just as mirage water cannot make the dry desert wet, the apparent nonequilibrium states can have no affect on the underlying state of homogenous equilibrium, which is eternal and undisturbable. In Samkhya philosophy, the apparent nonequilibrium states were described as the heterogeneous transformations (*virupa parinamas*) of the field wherein one of the three qualities appears to predominate over the other two. Such transformations were said to provide the basis for the appearance of the universe in consciousness in both its created and uncreated form. Conversely, the transformations associated with the eternal state of homogeneous equilibrium were called homogeneous transformations (*sarupa parinamas*), and were said to preserve the unity and balance of the three qualities in the midst of change.

Both types of transformations coexist—but on different scales of consciousness. The homogenous transformations appear on the scale of the fortieth layers above and below the half measure, and the heterogeneous transformations appear on the scales of the layers in between.

As a result, the symmetry of the field, which eternally exists on the scale of the fortieth layers, appears to become broken spontaneously on the intermediate scales. In modern theory, this type of symmetry-breaking, which arises as a function of a change in the scale of observation, rather than from any dynamic process, is called *spontaneous symmetry-breaking,* and is invoked by modern theorists to explain how various fields of force and matter arise from the unified field.

Both modern and ancient theorists are in agreement regarding the mechanics by which unity becomes transformed into the appearance of diversity: These mechanics involve not a dynamic process, but a change in the scale of observation. These theorists, however, are not in agreement regarding the ultimate scales of unification. Modern science limits itself to the study of force and matter alone; there is no notion in modern theory that in addition to fields of force and matter, the universe is pervaded by fields of mind. As a result, the unification scale is tied to the Planck scale in which the fields of force and matter become unified. This means that the field that arises from such unification can be described as neither a field of force nor a field of matter. It must transcend the dichotomy between force and matter. So what type of field does it represent? According to the ancient seers, it represents the first of seven universal fields of mind, and they equate it with the seven uncreated foundations (or seven shells) of the cosmic egg.

Unlike modern theorists, the ancient seers did not restrict themselves to considering the qualities of force (rajas) and matter (tamas) alone, but included the quality of mind (sattva) in their theoretical descriptions. In this regard, the universal fields of mind associated with the seven shells were viewed as the first seminonequilibrium states of the unified field in which the quality of mind (sattva) predominates over the qualities of force (rajas) and matter (tamas). Given this larger and more complete theoretical description, the ultimate unified field corresponds not to the universal field of mind associated with the thirty-third layer, but to the field of pure consciousness associated with the fortieth layer. It is only on the scale of the fortieth layer that the qualities of mind, force, and matter become truly unified in homogenous equilibrium.

All other forms of the unified field, which appear on scales in between the fortieth layers above and below, were viewed as corresponding only to the nonequilibrium states of the field and arising from a change in the scale of observation, rather than from any dynamic process. In other words, they arise from a process of spontaneous symmetry-breaking. By virtue of this process, the unlimited and unqualified unified field assumes the appearance of various limited and qualified fields. For example, on the scale of the thirty-third layer, it appears as a superuniversal field of mind (sattva); on the scale of the twenty-ninth layer, it appears as a universal field of force (rajas); and on the scale of the twenty-fourth layer, it appears as a galactic field of matter (tamas). All of these are but limited appearances of the ultimate unified field, which transcends, underlies, and pervades them all.

On the scale of the fortieth layers above and below, these relative appearances are dissolved into the ultimate reality of the unified field, the field of pure consciousness. From a Vedic perspective, the ultimate unification scales are 10^{-40} centimeters and 10^{39} centimeters, rather than 10^{-33} centimeters and 10^{32} centimeters. If the behavior of the universe is described in terms of force and matter, then for all practical purposes, the Planck scale (10^{-33} centimeters) and Para scale (10^{32} centimeters) may be viewed as unification scales. If, however, our scientific understanding of the universe extends to the behavior of mind, then we must take into account a more expanded set of scales so that the ultimate unification scales are 10^{-40} centimeters and 10^{39} centimeters.

These scales cannot be inferred directly from empirical data (or the universal constants) because they involve the operation of mind, rather than the operation of force or matter, but the ancients did not derive any of these scales from empirical data. Instead, the scales arose from the operation of the seers' own consciousness over the full spectrum of scales, as represented by the system of matched pairs.

THE SEVEN COSMIC SEERS

The seven cosmic shells were viewed not as insentient fields of force or matter, but as sentient fields of mind, which were personified as seven cosmic persons (*sapta purushas*), also known as the seven seers (*sapta rishis*).

It was held that the seven seers create the universe and everything in it by their mere act of "seeing." The visionary power of each is manifested by intention or will, meaning that each seer, by its own divine will, governs the behavior of a particular type of primordial element. The elements were described as the minute, "body-framing particles" of the seven purushas: By means of their visionary power, the seven purushas frame the created body of the universe—that is, the golden yolk of the cosmic egg—from the seven primordial elements. The Manu Smriti, the oldest and most authoritative of the Vedic books of law, states: "From the minute body-framing particles of those seven very powerful purushas springs this [cosmic egg], the perishable from the imperishable."

The minute, body-framing particles of the seven purushas correspond to the conscious particles of uncreated mind stuff inherent within the seven shells and represent uncreated elements of mind, rather than created elements of force or matter. As a result, such particles are capable of responding to the intentions of the seven seers. By merely envisioning the created form of the universe within their own cosmic minds, the minute, body-framing particles undergo the various combinations and permutations required to give rise to the created particles of force and matter out of which the body of the universe is fashioned or framed.

THE UNBORN CREATOR

According to the Vedic texts, the seven cosmic seers do not act independently from each other; they act as a single cosmic being referred to as Svayambhu, the Self-Existent One.

Svayambhu represents the unborn Creator of the universe and the higher self of Brahma, the born Creator. Whereas the awareness of Brahma is stationed in the lowest and most concrete of the seven shells, corresponding to the shell of cosmic earth, the awareness of Svayambhu is stationed in the highest and most abstract of the seven shells, corresponding to the shell of cosmic intelligence. Therefore, the unborn and born Creators represent two ends of the same sevenfold spectrum.

Unlike the born Creator (Brahma), who conceives his cosmic body in terms of the created form of the cosmic egg manifested over the spectrum of the first thirty-two layers, the unborn Creator (Svayambhu) conceives his cosmic body in terms of the uncreated form of the cosmic egg manifested over the spectrum of the subsequent seven layers, corresponding to the seven shells. Because the body of Brahma corresponds to the created form of the universe, he was viewed as the born Creator, and because the body of Svayambhu corresponds to the uncreated cosmic shells, he was viewed as the unborn Creator. In the final analysis, however, these two aspects of the Creator are one. The Manu Smriti tells us that Lord Svayambhu himself was born as Lord Brahma:

This [universe] existed in the shape of darkness, unperceived, destitute of distinctive marks, unattainable by reasoning, unknowable, wholly immersed, as it were, in deep sleep. Then the divine Svayambhu [the unborn Creator], indiscernible, [but] making [all] this, the great [primordial] elements and the rest, discernible, appeared with irresistible [creative] power, dispelling the darkness. He who can be perceived by the internal organ [of the mind alone], who is subtle, indiscernible, and eternal, who contains all created beings and is inconceivable, shone forth of his own [will]. He, desiring to produce beings of many kinds from his own Self, first with a thought conceived the cosmic waters and placed his seed in them. That [seed] became a golden egg, in brilliancy equal to the sun; in that [egg] he [Svayambhu] himself was born as Lord Brahma, the progenitor of the whole world.[4]

Lord Svayambhu was born as Lord Brahma while yet remaining unborn. The emergence of the cosmic egg from the fields of uncreated mind stuff does not destroy the fields of mind stuff. The uncreated cosmic shells continue to exist along with the created form of the universe, which is born from them. Although the awareness of the unborn Creator embraces all seven cosmic shells, his highest station corresponds to the shell of cosmic intelligence, which is upheld by the thirty-ninth layer above the half measure.

A similar understanding can be found in the Hebrew tradition of kabbalah in which the unborn Creator was called YHVH (Jehovah). Jehovah is likened to the cosmic lord (elohim) who presides over the thirty-ninth sephirothic emanations in the ascending direction. In other words, he represents the presiding deity of the thirty-ninth layer above the half measure. This is the highest station of the unborn Creator, who is identified primarily with the outermost shell of the cosmic egg, though the unborn Creator is actually sevenfold.

In Hebrew, the name of the unborn Creator is represented by the four Hebrew consonants *y, h, v,* and *h* (YHVH), which form the *tetragammon* (or four-lettered name of God). It is understood traditionally, however, that the tetragammon is actually sevenfold due to the unwritten vowels that lie between the consonants. For example, when transliterated in English, the Hebrew YHVH becomes Jehovah, which consists of seven letters. These represent the seven aspects of the unborn Creator—the seven cosmic shells upheld by the thirty-third through the thirty-ninth layers. These seven layers constitute collectively the sevenfold soul of Jehovah, the unborn Creator.

THE COVENANT BETWEEN
HEAVEN AND EARTH

The seven cosmic shells serve a spiritual purpose: they join the perishable and mortal form of the created universe, cognized on the scale of the thirty-second layer, and the imperishable and immortal form of the

Supreme Being, cognized on the scale of the fortieth layer. This is the real covenant between heaven and earth.

The Book of Genesis tells us that the sign of this covenant is the "bow seen in the cloud"—the rainbow, the spectrum of seven colors. The rainbow thus symbolizes the spectrum of seven shells, which serve to join mortality and immortality. The covenant has the form of the seven shells—the seven aspects of the unborn Creator. Genesis goes on to tell us the gist of the covenant, which consisted of a promise: Jehovah Elohim promised to Noah that the earth will never again be destroyed by a cosmic flood.

THE BIBLICAL MYTH OF THE FLOOD

The sign of the covenant was presented to Noah after the Flood, when he emerged from the ark to survey the newly revealed land and offer praises to God.

Although the biblical myth of the Flood may very well have a historical basis in some ancient flood event, the story is much more than it seems on the surface. The ancient process of mythmaking typically involved encoding spiritual truths in colorful, semihistorical tales. Although the myths may seem to be historical accounts, they are actually spiritual allegories designed specifically to convey spiritual truths to those who have the eyes to see and ears to hear. In this way, we can say that the biblical myth of the Flood is related directly to the ascent of consciousness to the fortieth layer above the half measure.

According to the biblical myth, written by Moses and his inner circle, Noah was instructed by God to construct an ark designed to contain pairs of all living creatures so that Noah might ride the rising flood and preserve the seeds of all beings for a new generation to come. It proceeded to rain for forty days and nights. The earth was inundated by a cosmic flood, which destroyed all living creatures other than those on the ark. The ark, however, rode the rising flood, and came to rest eventually on the summit of Mount Ararat—the peak of Mount Salvation. Once the waters had subsided, Noah emerged from the ark and offered praises to God, at which point the covenant between heaven and earth was revealed: God promised Noah that he would never again destroy the earth in a cosmic flood.

In a spiritual context, the ark represents the limited form of enlightened consciousness that ascends through the metaphysical layers—the soul riding a rising flood of consciousness. The nature of enlightened consciousness is such that it embraces the two sets of layers above and below, which are organized into matched pairs (male and female). These layers contain the "seeds" of all created beings, which are preserved in consciousness as the soul ascends (and descends) through the layers. The ascent takes the soul through the seven cosmic shells, and there the qualities associated with the elements of creation become stripped from awareness progressively. In this process, the created form of the universe dissolves in consciousness as though it were submerged in a cosmic flood.

The myth tells us that the rains fell for forty days and nights—symbolic of the forty layers above and below that the soul must traverse in order to arrive at the other shore, the shore of immortality, where a whole new immortal world can be seen. Here, the dissolved world is resurrected in the soul's awareness—but rather than being resurrected out of the seven primordial elements, it is resurrected from pradhana, the imperishable substance of pure consciousness itself. In this case, the duality of the created elements within the cosmic egg and the uncreated elements within the seven cosmic shells is transcended. On the scale of the fortieth layer, both are seen as manifestations of the imperishable substance of pure consciousness itself.

As a result, the reconstructed appearance of the universe is rendered imperishable in the eyes of the soul, which means the soul will never again have to suffer the progressive dissolution of the universe in its awareness, as if by a cosmic flood. This is the real covenant between heaven and earth, and its sign is the sevenfold rainbow. The "bow" symbolizes the spectrum of seven cosmic shells that mediate the relationship between the perishable form of the universe cognized on the scale of the thirty-second layer and the imperishable form of the universe cognized on the scale of the fortieth layer.

In this way, we can see that the biblical myth presents a spiritual allegory related to the ascent of consciousness to the fortieth layer above the half measure, where the covenant between heaven and earth becomes established.

THE EGYPTIAN FLOOD MYTH

Another important flood myth was presented in the Edfu Temple Texts of the Egyptian tradition. These tell us that during the first time (zep tepi), the land of Egypt was surveyed by a mysterious group of seven builder gods or seven sages whose original homeland was an island that was submerged in a cosmic flood. As the only survivors of the flood, the seven sages found their way to the Nile Valley, where they sought to re-create in the land of Egypt an image of their homeland—so that Egypt might be fashioned in the image of heaven. Like the biblical myth, this Egyptian flood myth has a deeper spiritual and cosmological interpretation.

When the awareness of the soul ascends beyond the thirty-third layer, which marks the shore of this world, it enters into the shell of water, which resembles a vast cosmic sea. As the soul proceeds to ascend in sequence through the cosmic shells, the qualities of the primordial elements contained in the shells become stripped. As a result, the created form of the universe, which resembles a luminous island floating in a cosmic sea, becomes dissolved progressively in awareness.

In the end, the created form of the universe, which has served as the homeland of the gods from the very beginning, vanishes from awareness as though it was submerged in a great flood. At this point, the ascended soul is no longer identified with the born Creator, the embodiment of the thirty-three universal gods. Instead, it becomes identified with the unborn Creator, the embodiment of the seven cosmic shells or seven cosmic seers, who are the only survivors of the flood.

In order for the universe to be re-created in awareness, the awareness must become established on the scale of the fortieth layer and then descend through the seven shells. In this way, the qualities of the primordial elements contained in the shells are added to awareness so that the universe reappears magically. This reconstruction of the universe taking place on the basis of the imperishable substance of pure consciousness occurs through the agency of the seven cosmic seers, the seven sages who may be viewed as the builder gods or architects of the universe.

In spite of this deeper cosmological interpretation, the Edfu Temple Texts tie the myth to a specific period, the zep tepi (first time), which predates the first historical dynasties. They also tie it to seven sages or seven godlike men who walked the Nile Valley during that time and surveyed the land of Egypt for the sake of future generations. How do we reconcile the cosmological meaning with the historical meaning?

THE SEVEN COSMIC ADMINISTRATORS

The answer is provided by the Hermetic texts, which were composed in Egypt around the same time as the Edfu Temple Texts, presumably from secret knowledge contained in the scrolls uncovered by the Ptolemies.

These Hermetic texts, which claim to present the older philosophic spirit of Egypt, outline a secret doctrine concerning seven cosmic administrators—cosmic beings who dwell in seven cosmic spheres and whose collective working is called destiny: "The first Mind . . . the Mind which is Life and Light . . . gave birth to another Mind, a Maker of things; and this second Mind made seven Administrators, who encompass in their spheres the [entire] world perceived by sense; and their administration is called Destiny."[5]

Whereas the "first Mind" represents the field of pure consciousness, which serves as the immortal form of the Supreme Being, the second Mind, a "Maker of things," represents the unborn Creator identified with the seven cosmic shells or seers. In the Hermetic texts, the seven seers are called the seven administrators, and their working is called destiny. The texts then go on to reveal a secret about the administrators—a secret kept hidden until this day. It pertained to the first period of human existence on Earth, referred to by the ancient Egyptians as zep tepi:

> Nature mingled in marriage with Man, brought forth a marvel most marvelous. Inasmuch as Man had got from the structure of the heavens the character of the seven Administrators . . . Nature tarried not, but forthwith gave birth to seven Men, according to the characters of the seven Administrators . . . and the Man in them changed from Life and Light into soul and mind, soul from Life and mind from Light. And all things remained so until the end of a period.[6]

This highly suggestive passage seems to refer to a secret Egyptian doctrine of divine incarnation. According to the Hermetic texts, the seven cosmic administrators, identified with the seven cosmic shells, incarnated on the earth as seven men during zep tepi. This amounts to a sevenfold incarnation of the unborn Creator in the form of seven godlike men or seven enlightened sages whose souls reflected the character of the seven cosmic administrators.

A similar doctrine can be found in the Vedic tradition. According to the Puranas, during the first period, satya yuga (the age of truth), the seven cosmic seers—that is, the embodiments of the seven cosmic shells—incarnated on the earth as seven men who were known as the seven seers. These original seers became eventually the patriarchs of the seven families of Vedic seers, which in turn became the elite families of seer-priests and seer-kings that ruled the historical Vedic culture.

The Hebrew sages told a similar story: They placed in the Garden of Eden seven elohim, or lords, who embodied collectively the presence of Jehovah (the unborn Creator) on Earth. It was these seven lords whom

Adam and Eve served while in the Garden, and it was they who banished Adam and Eve from the Garden "lest they become like one of us."

The Sumerians told a similar story of seven *anunnaki*, or sons of heaven, who descended from heaven prior to the advent of the first historical dynasties and instituted kingship on Earth.

Therefore, virtually all of the earliest cultures and civilizations told a similar story: a tale of seven divine men, the incarnations of the seven cosmic seers, who manifested collectively the presence of God on earth at the dawn of human history. Were the ancients caught up in a collective delusion that spanned millennia and continents, or were they recalling a historical event that initiated the dawn of human culture on Earth? Unfortunately, the historical facts have been lost in the sands of time. All that remains is myth and innuendo, but the implications are tantalizing.

THE COSMIC TAROT

In the Agama texts of the Vedic tradition, the thirty-nine layers that lead to the realization of the fortieth layer were known as the thirty-nine *vibhavas* (evolutionary states) of the self.[7] By means of these thirty-nine stages of spiritual evolution, the soul is carried across the sea of mortality and delivered to the shore of immortality.

In these texts, the cosmic being who embodies all thirty-nine layers above and below and serves to carry the soul across the sea of mortality is personified as the universal goddess Tara. The Sanskrit word *tara* means "to carry across."

We can divide into two sets the $39 + 39 = 78$ layers above and below. The first set consists of the $28 + 28 = 56$ layers that carry the soul across the lesser mysteries of the universe. These can be experienced by the mortal soul as the twenty-eight heavens and twenty-eight hells. The second set consists of the $11 + 11 = 22$ layers that carry the soul across the higher mysteries of the universe. They cannot be seen by any mortal eyes.

These seventy-eight layers correspond directly to seventy-eight symbolic cards used in the ancient system of Tarot, which are organized into two sets: The first fifty-six cards, which represent the lower mysteries, are called the Minor Trumps (Minor Arcana) and the subsequent twenty-two cards, which represent the higher mysteries, are called the Major Trumps (Major Arcana). Moreover, each set is divided into two subsets. The Minor Trumps consist of twenty-eight red cards and twenty-eight black cards, and the Major Trumps consist of eleven red cards and eleven black cards. In this way, the Tarot deck reflects precisely the organization of the evolutionary layers as embodied by the goddess Tara. It is highly unlikely that this is a mere coincidence. There is good reason to suspect that the Sanskrit word *tara* is the etymological basis of Tarot.

It turns out that word *tara* can also be found in the very first verse of the Rig Veda in which the first letter of the word, *t*, occurs as the thirty-ninth letter of the verse. In the Vedic tradition, the essence of a god or goddess is viewed as inherent in the first letter of their name. In this sense, it can be said that the essence of the goddess Tara is represented by the thirty-ninth letter of the Rig Veda, which corresponds directly to the thirty-ninth layer above the half measure.

Later, we shall see that the letters in the first verse of the Rig Veda provide an alternate model of the ascending sequence of layers that is different from, but similar to, the alphabetical model.

THE UNBORN DESTROYER

The goddess Tara may be understood as the benevolent aspect of the unborn Destroyer, who is but the flipside of the unborn Creator. These two perspectives of the same set of seven cosmic shells represent the descending and ascending forms of cosmic wisdom, respectively.

When awareness descends into creation, it enlivens progressively the seven shells in descending order so that the qualities of the previous higher shell are added to the qualities of the subsequent lower shell. In this way, there is a progressive building of the qualities that give rise to the appearance of creation. In this case, the seven shells may be viewed as the seven aspects of the unborn Creator.

To go beyond the universe, the awareness must ascend through the seven shells. In this case, the reverse holds true. As awareness ascends through the seven shells the qualities that uphold the appearance of the created universe are stripped. As a result, the created reality of the universe appears to undergo progressive dissolution or destruction, rather than progressive creation. The seven shells may then be viewed as the seven aspects of the unborn Destroyer. In order to attain true immortality, the ascending soul must come face to face with the unborn Destroyer. This particular form of God is terrifying even to those enlightened souls that cannot otherwise be threatened by anything in the created universe.

One of the most colorful descriptions of this terrible form of God is presented in the eleventh chapter of the Bhagavad Gita, which is but a small part of a much larger Vedic text called the Mahabharata. In the Bhagavad Gita, the hero Arjuna (representing the enlightened soul) is given a vision of the unborn Destroyer. Here, the monstrous, cosmic form of God, which pervades the space between heaven and earth, is described as devouring mercilessly all the worlds. In his cosmic vision, Arjuna cries out:

> With infinite power, without beginning, middle, or end, with innumerable arms, moon and sun-eyed, I see thee, with thy blazing oblation-eating mouth, burning all this universe with thine own radiance. This space between heaven and earth is pervaded by thee alone in all directions. Seeing this, thy marvelous and terrible form, the created worlds tremble, O Great Being. . . . Having seen thy cosmic form, which has many mouths and eyes, which has many arms, thighs, and feet, which has many bellies, and the mouths of which gape with many tusks, . . . the worlds tremble, and so do I. . . . Having seen Thy mouths, bearing many tusks, glowing like

the fires of universal destruction, I lose my sense of direction, and I do not find comfort. Have mercy, O Lord of gods, Dwelling of the universe! . . . As moths enter the blazing flame to their destruction with great speed, so also, to their destruction, the worlds swiftly enter thy mouths.

In one sense, this passage should not be taken literally. The Sanskrit terms translated as "arms," "thighs," "bellies," "mouths," "tusks," "eyes," and so forth have multiple complementary and technical meanings related to the types of reality experienced on the scale of the seven cosmic shells.

Yet in another sense, the description of the dissolution of the universe experienced by the soul is quite literal. As the soul ascends through the seven cosmic shells, it experiences the universe and everything in it as being dissolved or destroyed as if by a great conflagration or flood. All the worlds of light and life that have served as its home for billions of years, as well as all the beings that dwell in those worlds, are witnessed as being consumed by the fiery mouths of God and reduced to oblivion. This shakes the soul to its very core, and makes it tremble in fear.

In the Upanishads, it is said that all of the celestial gods—that is, the planets, stars, and galaxies—stay their course out of fear of God. Whereas the celestial gods view the born Creator as their preserver and maintainer, they view the higher, unborn form of God, the being associated with the seven shells, as the cosmic Destroyer, and they tremble in fear lest they be destroyed and reduced to oblivion by transgressing his will.

Yet the Upanishads also state that all forms of fear are born of the conception of another, which appears to be different from the self. Because the other unborn form of God is viewed as alien to the created appearance of the universe, all of the celestial gods and even the enlightened souls tremble in fear of his presence—for he has the potential to destroy all created souls and reduce them to a state of spiritual oblivion, whether or not they are enlightened. Nevertheless, to achieve true immortality, the enlightened soul must be willing to face its deepest fear and offer itself into the fiery mouth of the unborn Destroyer, at which point the created aspect of the soul is drowned, burned to ashes, ripped to shreds, and reduced absolutely to oblivion. This amounts to a cosmic form of spiritual death or ritual suicide, which results in the death of death itself.

THE PROGRESSIVE DISSOLUTION OF THE UNIVERSAL SOUL

The soul is safe as long as it remains in the lowest of the cosmic shells, corresponding to the shore of this world or the shell of earth. As soon as it enters the shell of water, however, the created form of the universe is drowned and the soul becomes caught in the cosmic currents that will lead inevitably to its destruction.

At this point, there is no turning back. Having entered the cosmic sea, the soul is dragged inevitably far from shore by the cosmic undertow, and there, inescapably, it will come to die a cosmic death in silent darkness.

When the soul is drawn subsequently into the shell of fire, it witnesses its own cosmic body, in the form of the created universe, being burned and consumed by the fires of universal destruction—and is helpless to stop it. The shell of fire is the last shell where the form of the universe is seen. Once the universe has been consumed by the fires of total destruction, it is reduced to ashes (point values) and thus assumes a formless condition.

The soul then ascends to the shell of air to which the ashes of the created universe are blown by the cosmic winds, never again to be seen. All that is experienced in that shell is an "indistinct flow" (*apraketam salilam*), which resembles the invisible movement of air in a vast and formless cosmic space. When the soul ascends subsequently to the shell of space, all perceived forms of motion disappear, and all that remains is a dark cosmic void devoid of all light, sound, and motion. This is the cosmic coffin that the soul must enter willingly while still alive—an understanding that is encoded symbolically in the Egyptian myth of Osiris.

In the Egyptian myth we learn that when Osiris returned in triumph from a long journey, he was invited to a welcoming celebration by his brother Set and seventy-two conspirators who had devised a plan to depose the great king. They had constructed a glorious coffin designed to fit perfectly the body of Osiris. When the king arrived, they declared a contest: The coffin would be given to anyone whose body fit its dimensions precisely. When Osiris tried out the coffin to see if it fit, the conspirators sealed him inside. It was then set adrift on the Nile, and from there it floated eventually into the Mediterranean Sea. In the process, Osiris, locked in the sealed coffin, died in total silence, darkness, and isolation.

This myth has a deeper interpretation: The shell of air lying immediately below the shell of space represents the thirty-sixth layer of the metaphysical Logos, counting from the half measure. Because there are thirty-six layers above and below, this shell may be said to have 36 + 36 = 72 aspects, which correspond to the seventy-two conspirators of Set, who himself represents the material nature of the universe.

The ultimate purpose of these seventy-two layers, taken as a whole, is to conspire against the ascending soul: They are designed to lead the soul from the scale of the half measure to the shell of space (the thirty-seventh layer), where it will become locked inside its own cosmic coffin—the coffin of cosmic space. There, it will come to die in total darkness and isolation at the hands of the unborn Destroyer. Once the soul enters into the shell of space, it becomes constrained by its own cosmic coffin and is unable to move. Like a victim bound and prepared for a cosmic sacrifice, the only thing it can do is to wait for its inevitable death at the hands of the cosmic Sacrificer.

The actual sacrifice takes place in the shell of cosmic ego (the thirty-eighth layer), where the universal ego of the soul is slain and the soul loses its universal identity. At that point, the soul experiences a form of cosmic death in the darkness and isolation of its own cosmic tomb. It loses all memory of its individual and universal evolution, which took place over the course of billions of years. Having risen above the shell of space, it also loses all sense of direction. Unable even to think, the soul has no conception of what is up or what is down and is therefore reduced to a state of spiritual oblivion.

After the soul has died in this way, it becomes totally helpless. Being devoid of all forms of ego, whether individual, galactic, universal, or cosmic, it no longer has the potential to do anything. The last stage of the journey is conducted by the benevolent aspect of the unborn Destroyer in the form of the goddess Tara, who carries the dead soul across the sea of cosmic intelligence, represented by the outermost shell of the cosmic egg (the thirty-ninth layer). In the process of being carried across this layer, the dead soul is offered figuratively to the mouth of the unborn Destroyer so that not even the slightest trace of its former existence survives. This marks the end of the evolutionary course of the soul. In the end, the enlightened soul is reduced to the same state from which it began: a state of pure ignorance, which is cosmic rather than individual in scope.

Then, however, a miracle occurs. When the dead soul finally washes upon the shore of the other world (represented by the fortieth layer), it becomes endowed with a new type of existence: It is resurrected from spiritual death as a truly immortal soul, which experiences itself as the same as the supreme self. Because all traces of universal ego have been removed, the soul no longer identifies itself with the cosmic egg or its seven shells. Instead, it becomes identified with the unlimited reality of the Supreme Being, which contains within itself an infinite number of cosmic eggs.

In the Vedic tradition, this infinite reality of the Supreme Being was called the Akshara Brahman, the imperishable reality. Once the soul becomes established in that reality—on the scale of the fortieth layer—it will never again have to endure the process of universal dissolution and spiritual death. It is granted freedom from all forms of death, and it becomes free to ascend and descend through the evolutionary spectrum of thirty-nine layers, while maintaining its imperishable vision on the scale of the fortieth layer.

The ascent to the fortieth layer marks a whole new chapter in the advent of divine wisdom: the advent of the immortal wisdom, which has to do with the immortal and imperishable realms that lie beyond the outermost shell of the cosmic egg.

12

The Immortal Wisdom

THE IMMORTAL AHA EXPERIENCE

If the thirty-third layer above the half measure represents the shore of this world, then the fortieth layer represents the shore of the other world, the imperishable and immortal world of the self.

In the Vedic alphabetical model, the shore of this world was represented by *ha,* the final consonant in the classical Sanskrit alphabet. Due to its final position in the sequence of thirty-three letters (or thirty-three layers), it can be argued that *ha* is transformed automatically into the soft vocalic sound *aha,* which is written in the form of two dots placed one above the other (like a colon).

In actuality, however, *ha* is not the final letter or layer. It is merely the last of the thirty-three letters that pertain directly to the golden yolk of the cosmic egg and its surrounding white. There are six additional layers beyond the thirty-third that the soul must traverse to reach the shore of the other world. In the Agama texts[1] of the Vedic tradition, these additional layers were represented by six extraordinary consonants (or sets of consonants), which were included in the older Vedic alphabet but not in the later classical alphabet. Rather than being simple consonants, these extraordinary letters are complex consonants produced by the process of phonetic conjunction (sandhi).[2] They were used to represent the six additional layers because those layers serve to join the two shores.

In this expanded alphabetical model, the shore of the other world was represented by the unique vowel known as the *visarga* (the emitter), which is pronounced as the softly aspirated *aha*. This is precisely the Sanskrit letter into which *ha* is transformed when it appears as the final letter of a word or sentence, in which case it is written in the form of two dots placed one above the other.

We can say, then, that there are two types of Aha experience: The first is attained on the scale of the thirty-third layer, when the soul stands on the shore of this world and realizes the two truths about the universe (that it is both created and uncreated at the same time). Because this marks the final, thirty-third realization in the soul's ascent through the layers of the created universe, the consonant *ha* can be taken as the final letter in the sequence. As soon as the soul steps into the cosmic sea that lies beyond the shore of this world, however, this thirty-third realization ceases to be final. It becomes instead an initial realization regarding the uncreated reality of the universe. In this case, the thirty-third layer can be represented by the initial form of *ha,* as though it were the first consonant in a sequence of letters.

As the soul traverses the seven cosmic shells represented by *ha* and the six extraordinary consonants, the created appearance of the universe is dissolved in awareness. This means that the universe assumes an increasingly uncreated appearance. When the soul finally washes upon the shore of the other world (represented by the fortieth layer) the dissolved universe is reconstructed in awareness on the basis of pradhana, the truly imperishable substance of pure consciousness.

This reconstructed form of the universe, cognized on the scale of the fortieth layer, was represented by the final form of *ha* as though it were the final letter or layer in the sequence. According to the system of Vedic phonetics, the final form of *ha* represents not a consonant, but one of the sixteen vowels of the classical Sanskrit alphabet, pronounced as *aha* and written in the form of two dots placed one above the other, like a colon.

This unique vowel identified with the fortieth layer was assigned two complementary names: As we have seen, it was called the visarga (the emitter), and it was also called the *visarjaniya* (that which is emitted). These two represent the two complementary aspects of the ultimate Aha experience attained on the scale of the fortieth layer. When the soul ascends to this layer, it realizes simultaneously two truths regarding its existence: that it is immortal and that it is mortal. The immortal aspect of the soul represents the emitter, the one immortal self established on the shore of the other world who emitted all mortal souls in the very beginning and who has never descended into creation. The mortal aspect of the soul represents that which is emitted, the mortal soul that was emitted into creation in the very beginning and covered with the veil of ignorance. After evolving over the course of billions of years and becoming enlightened eventually, the emitted soul ascends the divine ladder and returns to its original source.

When it ascends to the scale of the fortieth layer, the soul realizes its identity with the emitter, that its whole evolutionary journey was but a dream in the night and that it was never actually emitted in the first place. It then realizes two truths: that it is both the one immortal soul that never descended into creation and the mortal soul that has descended into creation. The emitter is immortal, while that which is emitted is mortal. The two truths realized on the scale of the fortieth layer can therefore be summarized by the two opposing statements "I am mortal" and "I am immortal." The paradoxical synthesis of these is represented by the Sanskrit word *tat* (that), which is a synonym for Brahman, the ultimate reality.

This understanding is also reflected in the Hebrew tradition of kabbalah on which the fortieth layer (or sephirothic emanation) counted in the ascending direction is represented by the cryptic formula ESYR AHIH ESYR ("I am that I am")—"I am mortal" and "I am immortal." As in the Vedic tradition, the synthesis of the two opposing statements is denoted here by the term *that*.

In the Egyptian tradition, the fortieth layer was represented symbolically by the Hall of Osiris, where the soul who has just arrived on the shore of the other world is greeted by the family of truly immortal souls (the Grail family) and undergoes its final judgment. This hall was also known as the Hall of Two Truths. The final judgment that takes place there was represented symbolically by a weighing ceremony involving a cosmic balance. On one side was placed the heart of the aspirant, which was then weighed against the feather of Maat, the Egyptian goddess of cosmic truth, harmony, and justice. The heart of the aspirant represents the mortal aspect of the soul, and the feather of Maat represents its immortal aspect. In order to pass the final judgment, mortality must be balanced with immortality. If one aspect outweighs the other, then, according to the Egyptian texts, the soul will be rejected and cast back into the dark abyss of the cosmic shells to be further consumed by the demons of its own false imagining until it attains a cosmic state of balance.

We can conclude, then, that the Vedic, Egyptian, and Hebrew traditions shared a similar understanding regarding the nature of the fortieth layer, which represents the shore of the other world. To become a citizen of the other world, or a member of the immortal Grail family, the soul must attain a state of balance regarding the two truths: that it is both mortal and immortal.

There is a reason for this requirement: If the soul views itself as more mortal than immortal, then it will possess, naturally, an attachment to the cosmic egg from which it has "hatched." In this case, its own cosmic egg will be favored over all the other cosmic eggs that exist within the bosom of the infinite. The Supreme Being, however, shows no such favoritism—all of the cosmic eggs must be treated equally. Conversely, if the soul views itself as more immortal than mortal, then it will view the cosmic eggs as different from the self or unrelated to its immortal existence and will therefore have no interest in maintaining them. The Supreme Being, however, shows no such lack of interest—all of the cosmic eggs must be maintained at all times.

To be identified with the Supreme Being, then, the soul must balance the two truths in its awareness so that both the infinite, immortal world and the finite, mortal world are simultaneously upheld in a state of equanimity.

THE IMMORTAL KABBALAH

We have seen that there is a direct correspondence between the four Hebrew letters *k, b, l,* and *h* that constitute the word *kabbalah* and the four Sanskrit consonants *ka, ba, la,* and *ha* representing the first, twenty-third, twenty-eighth, and thirty-third layers of the metaphysical Logos. Yet because the letter *h* stands as the final letter of the word, it also has an interpretation as *aha,* the sound into which the consonant *ha* is transformed when it stands at the end of a word or sequence of letters.

Whereas the initial sound *ha* denotes the shore of this world (the thirty-third layer), the final sound *aha* denotes the shore of the other world (the fortieth layer). In this sense, the word KBLH may be viewed as a sonic formula that encodes the immortal wisdom extending beyond the first thirty-three layers all the way to the fortieth layer.

In the tradition of kabbalah, these forty layers (or sephirothic emanations) were viewed as organized into four sets of ten and were conceived as the four worlds denoted by the Atziluth, Briah, Yetzirah, and Assiah. The lowest of the four worlds, Assiah, was viewed as the most concrete and physical, and the highest of the four, Atziluth, was viewed as the most abstract and archetypal. The ten layers that make up the Atziluth extend from the thirty-first to the fortieth layers. This was known as the world of spiritual archetypes, and the highest of these layers (the fortieth in the ascending direction) was known as the Great Sacred Seal, the immortal archetype from which are copied all the inferior worlds (upheld by the other thirty-nine layers). The knowledge pertaining to this immortal archetype, however, goes beyond the cosmic wisdom; it is part of the immortal wisdom, which deals with the infinite and immortal realms that lie beyond the outermost shell of the cosmic egg.

THE HOLY GRAIL

The myth of the Holy Grail presents another take on this same immortal wisdom. In this myth, the Holy Grail can be interpreted as either the holy vessel (san greal) or the holy blood (sang real) contained within the vessel.

According to the standard version of the story, the seeker of the Holy Grail must first find the Grail Castle perched on the summit of Mount Salvation, for that is where the Holy Grail can be found. The problem: Mount Salvation is surrounded by a vast wasteland, which hides the sacred mountain from all unworthy eyes.

The summit of Mount Salvation, representing the highest of the thirty-nine layers within the cosmic egg, must be ascended just as we would climb the rungs of a divine ladder or the slopes of a mountain. The summit, however, is hidden from view by the vast wasteland of the cosmic shells wherein is dissolved the created appearance of the universe. According to the Grail myth, when the soul somehow finds the divine mountain and ascends to its summit, it is greeted by the divine Fisher King, who stands guard at the gate of the Grail Castle. This Fisher King is none other than the unborn Creator, whose cosmic station corresponds to the thirty-ninth layer above the half measure—the summit of Mount Salvation.

The myth goes on to tell us that the Fisher King puts the aspiring soul to a test to determine whether it is worthy to enter the Grail Castle and obtain the Holy Grail. The test is: "Whom does the Grail serve?" This can be translated to mean, "Whom does the immortal blood serve?" It is a trick question, and apparently; there are two possible answers. First, it can be said that the immortal blood serves the imperishable reality of God. Second, it can be said that the immortal blood serves the perishable reality of the universe. Yet neither answer is correct on its own. The true answer is that the immortal blood serves both the perishable reality of the universe and the imperishable reality of God. This answer grants immediate access to the Grail Castle and the Holy Grail contained within it.

In other words, to pass the final test, the soul must hold two truths in a state of balance: "I am mortal" and "I am immortal." If there is the slightest imbalance between these two truths so that one outweighs the other, then the soul will answer incorrectly and fail the test. If, how-ever, the two truths are balanced perfectly, then the soul will be admit-ted into the Grail family—that is, the family of immortal souls that abide beyond the outermost shell of the cosmic egg in the mysterious Grail Castle, which is cognized on the scale of the fortieth layer above the half measure and which represents the imperishable reality that rests on the summit of Mount Salvation (the thirty-ninth layer).

To enter the Grail Castle, the soul must "hatch" from the cosmic egg; it must break through the outermost shell and ascend, like the risen phoenix, into the imperishable reality that first dawns on the scale of the fortieth layer. There it cognizes a completely new type of real-ity filled with an infinite number of cosmic eggs similar to our own. These eggs are organized not in a higgledy-piggledy fashion, but ideally, according to the dictates of cosmic intelligence. More specifically, they are organized in the form of an infinite crystalline lattice—the tran-scendental superlattice, which represents a living embodiment of the Logos, the infinite and immortal body of God transcending the finite boundaries of the cosmic egg. That alone is the real Grail Castle, the immortal vessel (san greal) that contains the holy blood (sang real).

We can find here a deep duality: The holy blood corresponds to the imperishable substance of pure consciousness, which pervades and flows throughout the immortal body. Yet in the final analysis, this substance is not different from the immortal body. On the scale of the fortieth layer, the enlightened soul realizes that its own cos-mic egg, in fact, all of the cosmic eggs that make up collectively the immortal body, are ultimately fashioned out of the same imperish-able substance. In this sense, the immortal vessel and the immor-tal blood are one. The mere taste or sight of that immortal blood is enough to render the soul immortal, but it is also enough to make the wasteland whole. Upon cognizing the imperishable substance of pure consciousness, the dissolved universe is reconstructed in aware-ness on that imperishable basis, and the covenant between heaven and earth becomes established.

Although the myth of the Holy Grail is viewed typically as Christian in origin and a product of medieval fantasy, it has a deep resonance in the much more ancient Vedic texts. In the Rig Veda, the divine Fisher King was called Divodasa-Atithigva, "the divine fisherman to whom guests should go." The guests correspond to the aspiring souls who have entered the sea of death—the wasteland of the cosmic shells. They should go to the divine fisherman—that is, the unborn Creator—so that they can be fished from the sea of death and delivered to the other shore.

According to the Vedic seers, when the soul ascends to the station of the unborn Creator, it becomes identified with the unborn Creator and with the sea of cosmic intelligence that abides within the outermost shell of the cosmic egg. Although the soul may transcend that shell by ascending into the imperishable realms that lie beyond, a portion of the enlightened soul identified with the unborn Creator remains behind. In this case, the guest becomes the host: the portion of the soul that remains behind becomes the divine fisherman to whom guests should go and the unborn Creator of the universe who upholds eternally the covenant between heaven and earth and serves to fish aspiring souls from the sea of death.

THE IMMORTAL ARCHETYPE

When the soul breaks through the outermost shell of the cosmic egg and becomes truly immortal, it is marked by the sign of immortality. To use a biblical analogy, this may be compared to the mark of Cain— the mark that prevented Cain from being killed lest his killer be subjected to a sevenfold death.

In the tradition of kabbalah, the sign of immortality was represented by the Great Sacred Seal, the sign of the fortieth layer, which was referred to as "I am that I am." This sign corresponds to the immortal archetype of the immortal body, which is first cognized on the scale of the fortieth layer above the half measure.

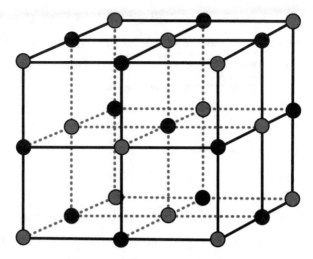

Fig. 12.1. The immortal archetype

Geometrically speaking, the immortal archetype assumes the form of a cosmic cube composed of twenty-seven cosmic eggs. In other words, it corresponds to the unit cell of the transcendental superlattice.

The idea that the immortal archetype assumes the form of a cube can be explained in terms of the Sanskrit: The Sanskrit word for a cube is *aksha,* which also means "eye," "letter," "bead," "salt," and "die" (the noun; plural, "dice"). These various meanings provide the basis for various wisdoms concerning the immortal archetype. For example, the cosmic cube can be compared to the eye of God, because it is from the cosmic cube that the Supreme Being can see all things in the imperishable world. Just as the pupil that sits at the center of the human eye (aksha) provides a point of view for the human self on the perishable reality of the mortal world, so the cosmic egg that sits at the center of the cosmic cube (aksha) provides a point of view for the supreme self on the imperishable reality of the immortal world.

The immortal cube can be compared to a letter because it represents a form of space, and hence a form of speech. This is consistent with the space-speech duality presented throughout the Vedic texts. Just as the sequence of letters (akshas) in the Sanskrit alphabet serve to represent the sequence of layers in the metaphysical Logos, so the same can be represented by a sequence of cubes (akshas) whose parameters are established in terms of the system of matched pairs. In other words, each layer can be assigned its own cubic archetype, which exists on a particular scale of space and time. Yet all of these archetypes reflect the immortal archetype cognized on the scale of the fortieth layer.

The immortal cube can be compared to a bead (aksha), because the archetypal cubes that exist on different scales of time and space are strung together like so many beads on a string by the one eternal self. The sequence of letters (akshas) in the Sanskrit alphabet was thus often compared to a necklace of letters (*aksha-mala*) worn by the Supreme Being.

The immortal cube can be compared to a grain of salt (aksha), because salt crystals have the natural crystalline habit of a cube. To coin a popular phrase, we should take what we read in this book "with a grain of salt," because the understanding presented here is highly subjective and rooted in an underlying cubic geometry. Yet the analogy goes beyond the overall form of a cube. As we have seen, the internal crystalline geometry of the transcendental superlattice is the same as that of ordinary table salt. From a purely geometric perspective ignoring both scale and substance, the transcendental superlattice is identical formally to the sodium-chloride lattice. By extension, the cubic archetype can be compared to the proverbial "salt of the earth"—the underlying metaphysical foundation of the physical universe.

The cubic archetype can also be compared to a die (aksha) because the enlightened soul is endowed with choice regarding its scale of consciousness. It has the potential to ascend by grasping larger cubic forms of reality, and it also has the potential to descend by grasping smaller cubic forms of reality. Each choice may be compared to a roll of the dice, or a "roll of the cubes," because, in the final analysis, all such choices are made by the omniscient Supreme Being, who is the very self of all individual beings. Therefore, in the absence of omniscience, the individual soul will always have some uncertainty about the outcome of its choices—or the outcome of its rolls of the dice. The soul "wins" by ascending the divine ladder, and it "loses" by descending the divine ladder. In this case, the winning roll that results in the attainment of immortality corresponds to the cognition of the fortieth layer above the half measure. This is the ultimate jackpot that makes all other wins and losses pale by comparison. In this way, the term *aksha* provides a multidimensional understanding of the immortal cubic archetype. In actuality, though, this word is a mantra (a phonemic formula) that encodes the entire spectrum of layers.

As we have seen, the letter *a* represents the infinite self, and the letter *k* represents the first form of the enlightened soul, cognized on the scale of 1 digit. Moreover, we have seen that the letter *s* represents the golden yolk of the cosmic egg, cognized on the scale of the thirty-second layer; and the letter *h* represents the surrounding white, cognized on the scale of the thirty-third layer. When the awareness of the self descends from infinity to the scale of the half measure and then begins its return journey by ascending to the scale of the divine Ka, it becomes the embodiment of $a + k$. When it ascends subsequently to embrace the entire cosmic egg, consisting of both the golden yolk and its surrounding white, it becomes the embodiment of $a + k + s + h$. Finally, when it ascends beyond the cosmic egg into the bosom of the infinite, it becomes the embodiment of $a + k + s + h + a = aksha$. In this way, the term *aksha* symbolizes both the descending and ascending paths, which lead from the infinite to the half measure and then back to the infinite.

On the scale of the fortieth layer, this cubic archetype is cognized in terms of cosmic eggs, each of which spans hundreds of trillions of light-years. Yet from the perspective of infinity, these eggs may be compared to tiny atoms in the infinite body of God. The Vishnu Purana tells us that to the Supreme Being, the cosmic eggs seem no bigger than *paramanus* (supreme atoms), and the period called Para, which spans some three hundred trillion solar years, seems no longer than the blink of an eye.

THE BLUE-RED FORM OF THE SUPREME BEING

The Vedic seers referred to the imperishable body of the Supreme Being as *nila-lohita* (blue-red), related to the two types of cosmic eggs from which is composed the imperishable body. To maintain the ideal form of pure geometry, which displays maximum symmetry in three intuitive dimensions, the transcendental superlattice must be composed of two categorically distinct types of point values or cosmic eggs. Yet these cosmic eggs are not different in form or size or with respect to their geometric environment. As far as the category of space is concerned, they are all similar. Their difference lies with the category of time.

This means that when one set of cosmic eggs is in the process of progressive creation, the other is in the process of progressive dissolution so that their cycles of creation and dissolution are 180 degrees out of phase. In other words, the two sets of cosmic eggs are similar with respect to space, but different with respect to time.

The term *nila-lohita* (blue-red) refers to the luminous appearance of these two types of cosmic eggs—as perceived by those who have the eyes to see and ears to hear the imperishable reality of the self. More specifically, the transcendental light emitted by the eggs in the process of creation appears blue shifted, while that emitted by those in the process of dissolution appears red shifted. From the perspective of unbounded awareness, the two types of cosmic eggs thus appear as luminous point values of consciousness colored blue and red.

In accordance with the principle that humans are created in the image of the Creator, we find that throughout the human body there are blue and red blood vessels constituting the circulatory system: The vessels that carry blood from the heart to the extremities are red, and those that deliver blood back to the heart are blue. This corresponds directly to the imperishable body of the Supreme Being. In this analogy, the unit cell of the superlattice may be compared to the archetypal form of the imperishable body, and the cosmic egg that sits at the center of the cell may be compared to the body's heart. The blood of the imperishable body is none other than the immortal blood (amrita rasa), which corresponds to the flowing substance of pure consciousness.

During the process of creation, the immortal blood flows toward the central cosmic egg so that its created form can be nourished and built. Because the egg then appears blue, the converging streams of immortal blood can be assigned a blue color, like the streams of blood flowing toward the human heart. During the process of dissolution, the immortal blood flows away from the central cosmic egg. Because the egg then appears red, the diverging streams of immortal blood can be assigned a red color, like the streams of blood flowing away from the human heart. In this way, there is a color correspondence between the imperishable body of the Supreme Being and the perishable body of the human being.

THE CELLULAR STRUCTURE OF THE IMPERISHABLE BODY

The analogy also extends to the cellular structure of the body. The human body, like all organic bodies, is composed of biological cells. Each of these cells contains DNA, the genetic blueprint from which the human body is built. Similarly, the imperishable body is composed of crystallographic cells. Each of these contains the imperishable blueprint (that is, the point-group symmetry of the superlattice) from which the imperishable body is built.

Each cell also contains a conscious being, the cosmic soul (jiva) identified with the central cosmic egg. This soul is none other than the Creator in both his created (born) and uncreated (unborn) forms. Yet there is not just one Creator; there are an infinite number that are identified with the infinite number of cosmic eggs in the imperishable body of the Supreme Being. Each Creator has an imperishable form, which corresponds to the cubic cell in which the cosmic egg is centrally located. This is a space cell, not a biological one, and it is conceived in terms of the category of transcendental space—the space of consciousness.

Although the imperishable body of the supreme self (atman) is infinite in extent, the cosmic selves (jivas) identified with the cosmic eggs have limited imperishable forms. With respect to the categorical appearance of space, the imperishable forms of the cosmic selves may be compared to space cells. The Vedic seers explained it this way: "Since the atman [infinite Self] appears in the form of jivas [finite cosmic selves] in the same way that space appears in the form of space cells, which are composite things like jars, therefore with respect to the categorical appearance [of space] this is the illustration [to be taught]."[3]

The space cells referred to in this passage are none other than the crystallographic cells of the transcendental superlattice. Each such cell may be compared to a jar that contains a conscious cosmic self—the Creator of the cosmic egg located at the center of the cell."

THE CIRCULATORY SYSTEM OF THE IMPERISHABLE BODY

Like the human body, the imperishable body also has a circulatory system. It is pervaded by flowing streams of the imperishable substance of pure consciousness, which constitutes the amrita rasa, the immortal blood of God.

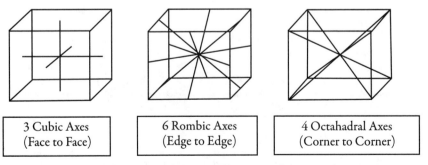

3 Cubic Axes (Face to Face)	6 Rombic Axes (Edge to Edge)	4 Octahadral Axes (Corner to Corner)

Fig. 12.2. The thirteen symmetry axes of the superlattice

These streams are organized not in a random manner, but in terms of the rotational symmetry axes of the superlattice, which correspond to the thirteen rotational symmetry axes of a cube. According to modern crystallography, these axes are organized into three groups: the cubic, rhombic, and octahedral axes.

The terms *cubic, rhombic,* and *octahedral* come from the fact that the three sets of axes may be viewed as connecting the six faces of a cube, the twelve faces of a rhombic dodecahedron, and the eight faces of a regular octahedron, respectively. From the perspective of the cosmic soul located at the center of the cube, these thirteen axes appear as twenty-six rays serving to connect the central egg to the twenty-six other eggs on the surface. Each such ray upholds a circulatory stream of immortal blood, which circulates around the ray as it flows between the cosmic eggs.

The circulatory streams of immortal blood may be compared to cosmic whirlpools or cosmic vortices within the imperishable fluid of pure consciousness. These vortices have a biconical form: As they diverge from one cosmic egg, they expand in radius, and as they converge onto another, they contract in radius, as illustrated from the side.

Because of their biconical forms, the Vedic seers referred to the whirlpools of consciousness using the technical term *parna,* which means "petal," "leaf," or "feather." In accordance to these meanings, the whirlpools were compared variously to the petals of a cosmic lotus, the leaves of a cosmic tree, and the feathers of a cosmic bird.

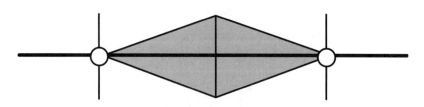

Fig. 12.3. A biconical whirlpool of consciousness

THE LOTUS CUBE

One of the most prominent conceptions of the Supreme Being in the Vedic tradition was that of Vishnu, meaning "all-pervading." According to the Vedic creation myth, in his archetypal form as *pundarika-aksha,* Vishnu grew a cosmic lotus from his navel. From the center of that lotus the Creator (Brahma) was born. For this reason, the Creator was often called Padma-bhavam (Lotus-born). The same notion can be found in the Egyptian tradition in which it was also said that the Creator was born from a cosmic lotus.

The term *pundarika-aksha* is often translated as the "lotus eye" of the Supreme Being—but it also means "lotus (*pundarika*) cube (*aksha*)," referring to the archetypal form of the all-pervading Being cognized on the scale of the fortieth layer above the half measure. This immortal archetype not only has the form of a cube, but also has the form of a fully blossomed cosmic lotus, consisting of twenty-six parnas (cosmic whirlpools) enclosed within the cube. In the Vedic tradition, the immortal archetype was viewed as having the form of a divine lotus cube.

The importance of this archetype within the Vedic tradition cannot be overemphasized. When an individual is initiated into the practice of meditation designed to deliver the awareness to the state of pure consciousness, a sacred verse is recited traditionally at the beginning of the initiation ceremony: "Whether purity or impurity is pervading everywhere, whoever remembers the lotus cube obtains both inner and outer purity."

This remembrance marks the culmination of the evolutionary process. Once the soul has ascended through the thirty-nine layers that represent its evolutionary course and has broken through the outermost shell of the cosmic egg, it then "remembers" the divine lotus cube as the archetypal form of its own eternal and all-pervading self. This is the Great Sacred Seal, the mark of immortality impressed upon the soul when it becomes established in the fortieth layer. At that point, the soul realizes that the archetypal form is all-pervading—it fills the entire evolutionary course of the soul through all thirty-nine layers. This means that every imperishable point value of consciousness in every layer of the metaphysical Logos, no matter what its scale, ultimately reflects the archetypal image of the fortieth layer, the divine lotus cube. On the scale of the fortieth layer, however, that archetypal image assumes an immortal living form: the form of a living cell in the imperishable body of the Supreme Being.

According to tradition, the cosmic lotus has twenty-six aspects. The two cosmic whirlpools that lie along the main axis of vision were called the stem and stamen, and the other twenty-four whirlpools, which lie obliquely to the main axis, were called the twenty-four petals. The cosmic lotus was assigned creative potential: The circulating streams of all twenty-six whirlpools wrap around the cosmic egg like the coils of an enclosing serpent, and these enclosing coils serve to churn out the created form of the universe, much as curds are churned from milk.

As a result, all created forms of existence within the universe display forms of rotation or spin. The stars rotate around the center of the galaxy, the planets rotate around the stars, electrons rotate around the atomic nucleus, and every individual elementary particle spins on its own axis. All of these created forms of rotational motion have their ultimate basis in the twenty-six rotational streams of consciousness that wrap around the cosmic egg and stir the field of cosmic intelligence that lies within. Therefore, the unborn Creator can be said to have twenty-six rotational aspects.

We can find support for this in the tradition of kabbalah in which the deity identified with the outermost shell of the cosmic egg (the shell of cosmic intelligence) was known as YHVH (Jehovah), the unborn Creator. According to the ancient system *gematria,* the Hebrew letters can be assigned numerical meanings so that Hebrew words have an alternate interpretation as numerical formulas. In this way, the four-lettered name of God (YHVH) is assigned a secret number, which, Hebrew scholars tell us, is the number twenty-six. This is representative of the twenty-six rotational aspects of the unborn Creator, which serve to churn the created universe from the field of pure consciousness, the perishable from the imperishable.

TONGUES OF FIRE

We may compare each crystallographic cell in the imperishable body to a habitation of God or a habitation of the immortal soul. These habitations are connected to each other by the circulatory streams of consciousness, which resemble cosmic whirlpools. Like ordinary bathtub whirlpools or tornadoes, these cosmic whirlpools have a hollow center, which is why the Vedic seers compared them to hollow reeds through which the immortal soul could travel from one cosmic habitation to another.

This description was related particularly to Agni, the personification of cosmic fire whose womb was likened to a parna (petal) of the cosmic lotus. In this case, the hollow inside the whirlpool was compared to the hollow of a womb from which Agni was born, the cosmic fire that assumes the form of the cosmic egg.

As the wombs of Agni, the petals of the cosmic lotus were often compared to so many tongues of fire emanated by the fiery form of the cosmic egg. By entering into these tongues of fire, the immortal soul can travel from one crystalline habitation to another within the imperishable body of God. This Vedic metaphor is reflected in the apocryphal Book of Enoch. According to Genesis, the biblical patriarch Enoch, who was the son of Jared and a direct descendant of Adam and Eve, was assigned a unique destiny: It is said that he lived for 365 years (the same number as the number of days in a solar year), and then "was seen no more, because God had taken him away." This implies that Enoch ascended beyond this world into the other immortal world.

The doctrine regarding the ascension of Enoch is presented in the Book of Enoch, which is part of the pseudographia of the Hebrew scriptures. The author, who claims to be Enoch himself, describes his ascent to heaven:

Winds in the vision assisted my flight, accelerating my progress. They elevated me aloft to heaven. I proceeded, until I arrived at a wall built of crystal, surrounded by tongues of fire. . . . I entered into the tongue of fire and drew nigh to a vast habitation built of crystal. Its walls too, as well as its pavement, were formed of crystal, and crystal likewise was the ground. . . . And I looked and saw therein a lofty Throne: its appearance was as crystal.[4]

The "vast habitation" described here is none other than the crystalline habitation of God—the cosmic cube—that is but one cell in the infinite and immortal body of God. The "tongues of fire" correspond to the whirlwinds of cosmic fire that constitute the petals of the cosmic lotus enclosed inside the cube. By entering into a tongue of fire, the soul can travel from one cosmic egg to another. At the end of its journey, it spirals automatically onto the center of a lotus cube, which serves as the throne of God within the crystalline habitation. In the Book of Enoch, both the habitation and the throne are described as crystalline because they are part and parcel of the crystalline body of Logos, the imperishable body of God that is cognized on the scale of the fortieth layer above the half measure.

THE MYTH OF THE RISEN PHOENIX

One of the most prominent of the ancient immortality myths, a story that can be found throughout the old world, from India to Egypt, is the myth of the risen phoenix. According to this myth, the phoenix is a divine bird, which has initially a mortal body. In order to attain immortality, it must offer its body to the sacred fire so that it is reduced to ashes. Yet from those ashes a new immortal body is resurrected. Once the phoenix attains this new body, it then stretches its wings and flies above into the immortal realms.

In effect, the phoenix represents the ascending soul whose mortal body corresponds to the created body of the universe. In the process of ascending through the seven shells, the mortal vestige of the soul is offered to the fire of universal destruction and is reduced to ashes. When the soul finally hatches from the cosmic egg by breaking through the egg's outermost shell, the ashes of the dissolved universe are infused with imperishability and a new immortal body—an imperishable body of Logos—is obtained.

The archetypal form of the immortal body is none other than the divine lotus cube, which is fashioned from twenty-seven cosmic eggs linked together by imperishable whirlwinds of cosmic fire. These may be compared to the outstretched feathers (parnas) of the risen phoenix, which ascends on wings of fire. In the Vedic tradition, the phoenix was thus called *suparna,* the bird with "beautiful feathers."

The feathers of the risen phoenix correspond to the feathers of the Egyptian goddess Maat, the personification of truth, justice, and harmony. In this comparison, we can understand as a measurement ceremony the final judgment scene, which takes place in the Hall of Two Truths. In this interpretation, the heart of the aspirant represents a measure of the cosmic egg itself, while the feather of Maat represents a measure of the relation among cosmic eggs, which is upheld by an immortal feather (parna). If the awareness of the soul can span only the outermost dimensions of the cosmic egg so that its mortal heart outweighs the immortal feather, then the soul is rejected. Yet if it can span both the cosmic egg and the relation among cosmic eggs, then it is accepted—because it has developed the ability to conceive the relations on the basis of which the immortal body is conceived. Those relations were represented symbolically by the immortal feathers (parnas) of Maat.

Metaphorically, the risen phoenix ascends into the immortal realms by stretching its feathers to embrace ever-larger forms of the divine lotus cube, which are stacked one inside the other like an infinite series of concentric Chinese boxes. As the phoenix ascends, the cosmic eggs from which the cubes are composed appear to become smaller and smaller, until they eventually resemble infinitesimal points. Just as an ordinary crystal composed of discrete atoms appears continuous when viewed from a macroscopic perspective, so the crystalline body of God composed of cosmic eggs (or cosmic atoms) appears to assume an increasingly continuous character when viewed from increasingly large, transfinite scales of consciousness. Eventually, the discrete crystalline structure of consciousness, which represents the imperishable body of God, assumes the appearance of the infinite continuum of consciousness, which represents the immortal self of God.

THE ETERNAL FIG TREE

In accordance with the interpretation of a parna as a leaf, the Vedic seers compared the infinite crystalline lattice of cosmic eggs to an eternal fig tree known as the Ashvattha. This is actually the name of a certain type of tree that grows on the Indian subcontinent and whose wood was often used to kindle sacrificial fires.

In this way, the cosmic eggs are compared to the fruits of the tree, or figs, because a fig is spherical and contains many spherical seeds. Similarly, the spherical cosmic egg contains many universal, galactic, and solar spheres, each of which represent the embodiment of a celestial being capable of growing to become the very embodiment of the divine tree itself.

In the fifteenth chapter of the Bhagavad Gita, the eternal Ashvattha tree is described as the living embodiment of the Veda (or Logos):

> They say the eternal Ashvattha tree has its root above and its branch below, such that its leaves (*parnani*) are the (Vedic) hymns. He who knows this is a knower of the Veda. Its form is not perceptible here in this world, nor its end, nor its beginning, nor its staying. This Ashvattha tree, with its well-grown root, should be cut by the strong ax of nonattachment. Then that place is to be sought, from which having gone, they do not return, saying, "In that primordial soul I take refuge, from whence the primeval activity anciently streamed forth."

In this cosmic metaphor, the crystalline layers of the metaphysical Logos are compared to the branches of an eternal tree. These support the fruits of the tree, which correspond to the cosmic eggs, and the leaves of the tree, which correspond to the cosmic whirlwinds that connect the eggs. These leaves are compared specifically to the Vedic hymns or Vedic texts. In this regard, the ancient seers placed a great deal of importance on the organization of the Vedic literature into different sets of texts. In a series of lectures given to several thousand Vedic pandits during the 1980s, Maharishi Mahesh Yogi outlined this ancient organization as involving $26 + 1 = 27$ different types of texts. First he showed that twenty-six types of texts are organized in pairs:

ORGANIZATION OF VEDIC TEXTS

Primary Texts	Subordinate Texts
Four Vedas	Four Upavedas
Upanishads, Aranyakas, Brahmanas	Itihasas, Puranas, Smritis
Six Vedangas	Six Upangas

It turns out that the twenty-six cosmic whirlwinds, which correspond to the leaves of the eternal tree, are also organized in pairs along each of the thirteen symmetry axes. The thirteen axes in turn are organized into three groups, which correspond to the four octahedral axes, the three cubic axes, and the six rhombic axes. We find, therefore, that there is a direct correspondence between the $8 + 6 + 12 = 26$ sets of Vedic texts and the $8 + 6 + 12 = 26$ whirlwinds.

Maharishi, however, pointed out that there is an additional twenty-seventh set of texts, which stands alone $(26 + 1)$. These texts are called the *pratishakhyas,* and they deal with the science of pronunciation within the mouth. This twenty-seventh aspect of the Vedic literature corresponds to the cosmic egg at the center of the cube whose outermost shell may be compared to the mouth of the unborn Creator. It is there that all twenty-six aspects of divine speech are pronounced, thus giving rise to the appearance of creation, which is literally spoken into existence. The idea that the leaves of the divine tree correspond to the hymns of the Veda or to the various sets of Vedic texts is therefore quite precise.

After establishing the correspondence between the leaves of the tree and the Vedic texts, the passage then exhorts the soul to cut the root of the eternal tree with the "strong ax of nonattachment," and to seek that place from which there is no return. If the eternal tree is likened to the Veda, then this amounts to seeking the "end of the Veda," otherwise known as Vedanta. To be admitted into the immortal realms, the soul must first sever its attachment to the fruit of the tree, which corresponds to the cosmic egg from which it has hatched. Yet it still remains attached to the root of the tree, which exists above. This well-grown root is none other than the imperishable crystalline body of Logos cognized above and beyond the scale of the thirty-ninth layer.

In order to transcend the discrete crystalline structure of consciousness and realize the infinite continuum of the self, the well-grown root of the tree must be severed by the "strong ax of nonattachment." This is accomplished by ascending beyond the fortieth layer into the higher immortal realms. In doing so, the distinction between the crystalline body of Logos and the infinite continuum of the self is eventually obliterated.

THE UNOBSTRUCTED BEING AND HIS FOUR IMMORTAL STATES

In the Vedic literature, the crystalline lattice of universes was viewed as the imperishable body of Viraj, the supreme ruler of all the cosmic eggs and their contents. Viraj was also known as Annirudha, the Unobstructed Being, because his vision of the crystalline body of Logos does not obstruct his vision of the infinite continuum of the self.

The awareness of the Unobstructed Being is established on the scale of the forty-third layer above the half measure, the scale of the omniscient, omnipotent, and omnipresent Godhead that rules all of the cosmic eggs and their contents. That supreme Godhead is the supreme self of all beings—whether mortal or immortal. According to the Vedic Upanishads, the supreme self has four immortal states of consciousness, which were compared to the waking, dreaming, sleeping, and transcendental states of human consciousness. Yet unlike human states of consciousness, the immortal states are not cyclical. Instead, they pertain to different scales of consciousness within the immortal realms. More specifically, they pertain to the scales of consciousness associated with the fortieth, forty-first, forty-second, and forty-third layers above the half measure.

In this way, the fortieth layer was viewed as the immortal waking state from which can be seen the crystalline organization of cosmic eggs. In the human waking state, the awareness of the human being is identified with his or her own physical body. Similarly, in the immortal waking state, the awareness of the Supreme Being is identified with its own metaphysical body—the crystalline body of Logos.

The forty-first layer was viewed as the immortal dreaming state. On this scale, the concrete form of the crystalline body ceases to dominate awareness. What dominates instead are glorious and radiant forms of transcendental light that uphold the immortal dream world of the self. In the human dreaming state, we tend to imagine various dreamlike forms and phenomena, which are not part of our waking world. Similarly, in the immortal dreaming state, the Supreme Being imagines various dreamlike forms and phenomena, which are not part of its waking world.

The forty-second layer was viewed as the immortal sleeping state. This was described as a "mass of consciousness" filled with abstract forms of preknowledge (*prajna*). The following addresses the immortal sleep state of the self:

The deep sleep state is that where the sleeper does not desire any enjoyable thing and does not see any dream. The third state [of the self] is called *prajna* [preknowledge], who has deep sleep as his sphere, in whom everything becomes undifferentiated, who is a mass of pure consciousness, who abounds in [abstract] bliss, who is surely an enjoyer of bliss, and who is the doorway to the experience [of waking and dreaming]. This one is the Lord of all. This one is Omniscient. This one is the inner Director of all. This one is the Source of all. This one is verily the place of origin and dissolution of all beings.[5]

Clearly, this passage is referring to the immortal sleep state of the Supreme Being, rather than the mortal sleep state of a human being. Unlike the human sleep state, which is experienced as a state of unconsciousness, the immortal sleep state is experienced as a "mass of pure consciousness" filled with forms of preknowledge (prajna). This preknowledge represents a form of omniscience, which ultimately determines the destiny of all things—including the destiny of all souls. All created souls begin and end on this scale of consciousness. As such, the immortal sleep state was described as "the place of origin and dissolution of all beings."

The forty-third layer transcends all such notions of creation and dissolution. It represents the transcendental state of immortal consciousness. The Vedic texts describe that fourth state:

They consider the Fourth to be that which is not conscious of the internal (dreaming) world, nor conscious of the external [waking] world, nor conscious of both worlds, nor a mass of consciousness [as in the sleeping state]. It is neither consciousness, nor unconsciousness. It is that which is unseen, beyond the empirical, beyond the grasp [of reason], uninferrable, unthinkable, and indescribable, whose valid proof consists in the single intuition of the Self, in which all phenomena cease. It is that which is unchanging, auspicious, and nondual. That is the Self, and that is to be known.[6]

The fourth state of immortal consciousness realized on the scale of the forty-third layer represents the goal toward which tends the entire path of immortality, for it represents the state of all perfection in which the soul becomes identified fully with the omniscient, omnipotent, and omnipresent ruler of all the worlds. When the soul ascends to the forty-third layer, it therefore obtains unobstructed knowledge, power, and presence regarding the entire spectrum of layers. It becomes identified with the very self of the Unobstructed Being.

We can then say that the path of immortality consists of the first forty-two steps on the divine ladder, while the transcendental goal of the path corresponds to the final forty-third step in which the soul becomes finally identified with the very self of the Supreme Being. That supreme forty-third layer represents the absolute form of God who stands at the top of the divine ladder. It marks the end of the way of ways, the end of the path of immortality, and the end of the Veda. Upon ascending to that layer, the well-grown root of the eternal tree is severed automatically by the strong ax of nonattachment. The soul then takes refuge in that primordial soul from whom the primeval activity streamed forth anciently.

Having reached the goal of the path, such souls do not return. They become immune to the cycles of creation and dissolution that plague all lesser souls still on the path.

THE FORTY-THREEFOLD VEDIC WISDOM

From a Vedic perspective, the immortal wisdom can be summed up by the mathematical formula $42 + 1 = 43$. This is presented in the esoteric doctrine called *shri vidya,* the "glorious wisdom," which is considered the most authoritative of all the ancient Vedic wisdoms.

In this doctrine, the Veda or metaphysical Logos is conceived as the divine body of *para shakti* (the supreme mother), who is also known as the mother of the Veda (*veda-janini*). The doctrine revolves around the study of an esoteric diagram called the *shri yantra* (the glorious

श्री यन्त्र

Fig. 12.4. The shri yantra

diagram), considered the king of all esoteric diagrams and consisting of these geometric elements:

- An enclosing square called the *bhu-pura* (the enclosure of existence)
- Twenty-four lotus petals
- Nine large triangles
- Forty-three smaller triangles, which are generated by the intersections of the nine large triangles

• A single point (*bindu*) placed at the center of the central forty-third triangle

First, we note that the entire diagram is enclosed in a square. This is a two-dimensional representation of the cosmic cube that serves as the immortal archetype of the Supreme Being. When this cube is viewed along its main axis, the axis of vision, it appears to enclose a cosmic lotus consisting of twenty-four oblique petals. As we have seen, the lotus cube represents an eternal archetype inherent in each layer. Yet each layer is tenfold, consisting of ten harmonic states of consciousness. According to the Vedic seers, the tenth (or largest) state in each layer represents the self of that layer. This is reflected by the great saying (*mahavakya*), "Thou art the tenth." It is only when the tenth state is realized that the archetypal form of the self, which has the form of a lotus cube, is realized or remembered.

The nine states that lead up to this tenth realization are represented diagrammatically by the nine large triangles enclosed within the lotus cube. These nine states are represented by triangles, because they contain states of pure knowledge involving the unity of three elements: knower, process of knowing, and known. Threefold forms of pure geometry (triangles) were used to represent the threefold states of pure knowledge that lead up to the realization of the tenth state, which has the overall form of a cube.

Yet the diagram pertains to not only the archetypal structure of each layer, but also the overall spectrum of layers. As we have discovered, the type of knowledge possessed by an enlightened soul is holographic. No matter what its operational scale, the enlightened soul has the potential to grasp and envision the whole, at least in principle. This means that the knowledge regarding the entire spectrum of layers is encoded in the archetypal structure of every layer. In the shri yantra, the overall spectrum of $42 + 1 = 43$ layers is represented symbolically by the $42 + 1 = 43$ smaller triangles generated by the intersections of the nine larger triangles. More specifically, the forty-two outer triangles represent the path of immortality, and the central forty-third triangle represents the goal of the path. As such, the central triangle was known as the *sarva-siddhi-pradha,* the "bestower of all perfection." It represents the forty-third layer of pure knowledge in which the soul becomes identified with the self of the Supreme Being and attains all perfection.

The central point (bindu) at the center of the forty-third triangle represents the pointlike reality of the soul, which is contained within and is ultimately nondifferent from the infinite reality of the self. It is from the point value of consciousness that the infinite value of consciousness becomes known.

The shri yantra thus provides a multidimensional symbol that encodes a wealth of information regarding the forty-twofold path of immortality, the archetypal forms of pure knowledge experienced at each stage on the path, and the final forty-third stage, which represents the goal of the path. It presents a concrete geometric embodiment of the mystical formula $42 + 1 = 43$. Yet this formula was not unique to the Vedic tradition. The Egyptian and Hebrew sages used the same mystical formula to encode their own versions of the immortal wisdom.

THE FORTY-THREEFOLD EGYPTIAN WISDOM

As we have seen, in the Egyptian tradition, the immortal wisdom was mapped out by the divisions of the land—the land of Egypt itself was an image of heaven and represented the transcendental ground on which the forty-two layers were conceived. The forty-two nomes therefore constituted the path of immortality. In this sense, the land of Egypt as a whole represents the supreme forty-third layer, the transcendental kingdom of God, which contains the other forty-two lesser kingdoms.

As we have seen, these lesser kingdoms were presided over by the forty-two nomarchs, who were viewed as embodiments of the gods. The land of Egypt as a whole was presided over by the pharaoh, who was viewed as the embodiment of God, the Supreme Being. In this way, the Egyptians strove to create a kingdom of heaven on earth, in accordance with their understanding of the $42 + 1 = 43$ layers of the metaphysical Logos.

This understanding was also reflected in the final judgment scene depicted in the Book of Coming Forth by Day, referred to by modern scholars as the Egyptian Book of the Dead: The heart of the aspirant is weighed against the feather of Maat in the presence of forty-two spiritual judges presided over by Osiris, who represents simultaneously the supreme forty-third judge, and the Lord of Immortality. Immediately prior to the final judgment, the soul must make the forty-two negative confessions by professing its innocence before the forty-two judges. Once all judges are satisfied with the soul's innocence, the heart of the aspirant is weighed and Osiris pronounces his final judgment. This reflects the notion that when the soul ascends to the fortieth layer and enters into the Hall of Two Truths, it comes face to face with all forty-two aspects of the Supreme Being as well as the Supreme Being itself in a type of holographic vision, and is then judged by them all. These forty-three beings constitute collectively the Grail family—the family of the self.

In some Egyptian traditions, the Supreme Being was represented by Thoth, the Egyptian wisdom god. Whereas the rulers of Egypt strove to follow in the footsteps of Osiris, who was viewed as the all-powerful form of God, the priests strove to follow in the footsteps of Thoth, who was viewed as the all-knowing form of God. There was an ancient Egyptian myth that Thoth had composed a set of forty-two secret books containing the knowledge of everything in heaven and earth, but no such books have ever been found. The truth is that the books of Thoth are written in consciousness, and can be "read" only by the soul as it ascends through the forty-two layers that constitute the path of immortality. They represent the forty-two forms of pure knowledge experienced on the basis of the forty-two layers. When the soul ascends to the supreme forty-third layer, it becomes identified with Thoth himself.

We find, then, that the Egyptian seers, like the Vedic seers, conceived the metaphysical spectrum as consisting of 42 + 1 = 43 layers, and sought to copy or model that metaphysical reality by mapping it out on the land and reflecting it in their central myths. The immortal wisdom is not the province of any one culture or religion; it represents a truly universal form of wisdom inherent in every human soul, and it unfolds gradually in ever-greater clarity as the soul ascends the stairway to the sky.

THE FORTY-THREEFOLD HEBREW WISDOM

In the system of kabbalah, the Hebrew sages possessed the same forty-threefold wisdom: There are a total of 42 + 1 = 43 sephirothic emanations, which correspond to the first forty-three layers above the half measure. The first forty layers were viewed as providing the archetypal basis for the creation of the universe, but beyond these, the Hebrew sages counted three additional layers, known as the *ain-soph-aur*.

The highest or forty-third layer was called the *ain*, the Supreme Godhead, from which the other forty-two emanated. As in the Vedic tradition, the Supreme Godhead was viewed as the transcendental basis for an uncountable number of universes. The ain, inconceivable and indescribable, corresponds to the fourth or transcendental state of immortal consciousness. The forty-second layer, the *soph*, represents the omniscient form of the Supreme Godhead, which is filled with infinite wisdom (*sophia*), or preknowledge (prajna). It corresponds to the sleeping state of immortal consciousness. The forty-first layer, the *aur*, is the self-luminous form of the Supreme Godhead, the *aura* of God characterized by transcendental light. It corresponds to the dreaming state of immortal consciousness. These three higher aspects of the Supreme Godhead preside over the lower aspect, represented by the fortieth layer, wherein are seen the immortal archetype and crystalline body of Logos. The fortieth layer thus corresponds to the waking state of immortal consciousness.

The Hebrew sages were therefore in agreement with both the Vedic and Egyptian sages regarding the overall forty-threefold organization of the spectrum. Although this knowledge was made most explicit in the tradition of kabbalah, it was embodied in other forms of Hebrew wisdom as well.

THE UNIQUE DIVINE NAME

In the Hebrew tradition, a great deal of emphasis is placed upon the name of God. Although this name is represented most commonly by the four-lettered name YHVH (Jehovah), the tetragammon, the rabbinical texts tell us that this is but the condensation of an earlier name of God, called the unique divine name, which consisted of forty-two letters. Although the exact spelling of this name has been lost, early commentators believed that it was encoded originally by the first forty-two letters of Genesis.

The Talmud makes clear that this unique name was entrusted not to all, but only to those worthy to receive it: "The forty-two-lettered Name is entrusted only to him who is pious, meek, middle-aged, free from bad temper, sober, and not insistent on his rights. And he who knows it, is heedful thereof, and observes it in purity, is beloved above and popular below, feared by man, and inherits the two worlds, this world and the future world."[7]

The Zohar also discusses this name: The forty-two letters are described as the "ornamentation" of the Holy Name; the entire name represents the whole and the forty-two letters represent its parts: "And the earth was void and without form. This describes the original state, as it were, the dregs of ink clinging to the point of the pen in which there was no subsistence, until the world was graven with forty-two letters, all of which are the ornamentation of the Holy Name."[8]

There are other passages in the Zohar that suggest that the letters of the name are much more than just letters; they are assigned creative power, both in the upper world of unification (synthesis) and the lower world of division (analysis). Moreover, they are described as the supernal mystical principle by which the upper and lower worlds were created.

> "The counsel," he said, "alludes to the sublime mystical knowledge which remains hidden and undisclosed save for those that fear the Lord continuously and thus prove themselves worthy of these secrets and able to keep them. Observe that the world has been made and established by an engraving of forty-two letters, all of which are the adornment of the Divine Name. These letters combined and soared aloft and dived downwards, forming themselves into crowns in the four directions of the world, so that it might endure. They then went forth and created the upper world and the lower, the world of unification and the world of division. . . . These forty-two letters thus constitute the supernal mystical principle; by them were created the upper and the lower worlds, and they indeed constitute the basis and recondite significance of all the worlds."[9]

If the first forty-two layers above and below correspond to these forty-two letters, then the supreme forty-third layer represents the *ain*, the supreme Godhead that embodies the name as a whole. In this way, the *ain* may be viewed as the cosmic speaker to whom the name refers, while the forty-two letters represent the forms of divine speech that lead up to the realization of the name and identification with the cosmic speaker. This presents another version of the 42 + 1 = 43 immortal wisdom, expressed in terms of the unique divine name.

THE STAGES OF THE SONS OF ISRAEL

Yet another version of the same wisdom can be found in the Hebrew scriptures, where it is presented in the form of a historical-spiritual allegory. Many believe that the central, defining story for the historical Jewish tradition is Exodus, which chronicles the liberation of the *ben Israel* (sons of Israel) from their bondage in Egypt and their subsequent journey through the wilderness to Canaan, the Promised Land, where the immortal city of Jerusalem was to be built.

Although there is little doubt that this story describes a real historical event, it is also likely it was embellished and modified by Moses, Aaron, and their inner circle so that it could also be viewed as a spiritual allegory describing the journey of the soul from the state of mortal bondage (Egypt) to the state of immortal liberation (Canaan). In this light, the path that leads from Egypt to Canaan symbolizes the path of immortality.

We can find support for this interpretation in the thirty-third chapter of the Book of Numbers, the fourth book of the Hebrew scriptures, which begins: "These are the stages in the journey of the ben Israel, when they were led by Moses and Aaron in their tribal hosts out of Egypt. Moses recorded their starting-points stage by stage as the Lord commanded him." What follows is a list of the sequential stages in the journey, which may be viewed as the "encampments" of the sons of Israel on their way to Canaan. It is interesting that many of the place names mentioned in this list are completely unknown; indeed, some are not mentioned anywhere else in the Bible. Why was the list compiled—and why was it placed in the thirty-third chapter of the Book of Numbers? The fact that this narrative is recorded in Numbers should tell us to pay careful attention to all the numbers involved. As we have discovered, the number 33 is very important and secret. In kabbalah it signifies the whole of the diagrammatic Tree of Life, which contains a total of 10 + 22 = 32 parts. The whole of the tree of life thus represents the thirty-third implied aspect, which rests upon the 32 parts.

Although most academic scholars believe that the tradition of kabbalah as a whole and the Tree of Life diagram specifically are relatively recent additions to Jewish lore, this assumption is based upon the earliest surviving written texts on the subject, which are not that old. According to its own traditional proponents, however, the kabbalah was passed down orally for a very long time before it was ever written. If the kabbalah was alive in the time of Moses, then it makes sense that a complete synopsis of its teachings would be recorded in the thirty-third chapter of the Book of Numbers, for 33 is the secret number of the whole Tree of Life.

This same number (33) also receives special emphasis in the list of encampments, which is presented unbroken except at one point: Immediately after the thirty-third stage in the journey is recited, corresponding to the encampment at the base of Mount Hor, there is a break in the narrative, followed by the description of Aaron's death: "Aaron the priest went up Mount Hor at the commandment of the Lord, and there he died." This is somewhat odd because the Book of Deuteronomy (10:6) states that Aaron died in Mosera.

We should also note that at this point, the Israelites had just come out of Egypt, where Moses had been raised in the royal court and surrounded by Egyptian symbolism. Hor in the Egyptian tradition refers to Horus, the son of Osiris, who was often conceived as a divine hawk and who was also viewed as having followed in his father's footsteps by ascending beyond the shore (horizon) of this world to the shore (horizon) of the other world. For this reason, Horus was often referred to as the Lord of the Horizon.

This suggests that the story of Aaron's death presented in the Book of Numbers carries symbolic weight. Coming immediately after the recitation of the thirty-third stage, the death of Aaron on Mount Hor appears to be an esoteric allusion to the death of physicality that is experienced when the soul ascends to the thirty-third layer, the shore of this world, and then enters into the cosmic sea of death that lies beyond the physical universe in the hopes of reaching the shore of the other immortal world.

Other than this single interruption, the list continues in an unbroken sequence, marking the stages in the journey from the first encampment just outside of Egypt to the last encampment, which lies just across the river Jordan from the land of Canaan. How many encampments were counted altogether? Exactly forty-two! The land of Canaan itself thus represents the forty-third and final encampment, where the immortal city of Jerusalem was to be built. We can say, then, that there were $42 + 1 = 43$ stages in the journey of the ben Israel, from their first liberated stage outside of Egypt to their final stage in the immortal land of Canaan itself. Just as the Egyptians mapped out the forty-two stages of the path of immortality along the course of the Nile, so the Israelites mapped out the forty-two stages of the path along the course of their journey from Egypt to Canaan.

CULTURAL CORRESPONDENCES

In spite of the fact that the Vedic, Hebrew, and Egyptian sages spoke different languages, had different social customs, worshipped different gods, and practiced different religions, it appears that they all shared the same spiritual map of the layers of the metaphysical Logos and the path of immortality.

Due to the geographic proximity of the Egyptian and Hebrew cultures along with the fact that the Israelites actually lived in Egypt for some four hundred years, we can suppose that the Hebrew and Egyptian traditions came to share the same knowledge through some type of cultural dissemination. We cannot, however, come to the same conclusion with respect to the Vedic culture, which evolved thousands of miles away and employed a language belonging to a completely different language group. Contact between the Vedic culture and the Hebrew and Egyptian cultures was extremely limited.

In addition, each of the three cultures viewed its wisdom as a cultural treasure not to be shared with outsiders. The secret nature of the wisdom precluded it even being shared with the common people of each culture; it was the unique province of the elite classes—the rulers and priests. As we have seen, the common people received only glimpses of the knowledge in the form of childlike myths and arcane symbols. The deeper meanings were passed down by the hereditary tradition of initiates sworn to secrecy. It is almost unthinkable that these initiates would share their secret and immortal wisdom with "foreigners" who spoke a different language, practiced different customs, and worshipped different gods. Yet somehow, all three traditions came to possess the same knowledge.

It seems reasonable to presume that some form of cultural dissemination was necessary for this to occur, but perhaps no cultural dissemination was necessary at all—perhaps the immortal wisdom is inherent in human consciousness, where anyone, anywhere, at any time can tap into it on the basis of pure intuition. Perhaps, then, all three traditions originated the wisdom on the basis of their own enlightened consciousness.

The ancients predicted that eventually their lost wisdom would be rediscovered; at the end of a long cycle of ages spanning thousands of years, human intuition would once again begin to grasp the ultimate purpose and meaning of life, the universe, and everything. The very fact that this book has been written suggests that the immortal wisdom is percolating once again in human consciousness. This percolation may be more conscious in some and more subconscious in others, but we are all in the same boat—and the boat is moving inevitably toward its destination. To illustrate this fact, we can look to an interesting phenomenon in pop culture.

THE ANSWER TO LIFE, THE UNIVERSE, AND EVERYTHING

Typing "the answer to life, the universe, and everything" into Google's search engine produces this result at the top of the list: "The answer to life, the universe, and everything = 42."

Yet this does not necessarily mean that the programmers are aware consciously of the ancient immortal wisdom, which employed forty-two layers to explain the ultimate purpose and meaning of life, the universe, and everything. In actuality, the answer provided by the Google calculator is a parody of the same answer provided by the hypercomputer Deep Thought in Douglas Adams's popular book *The Hitchhiker's Guide to the Galaxy*. Deep Thought, deemed the second greatest computer of all space and time, was constructed by a hyperintelligent race of pandimensional beings to provide the ultimate answer to life, the universe, and everything. After seven and a half million years of continuous calculation, the computer finally arrived at the answer 42.

The two pandimensional beings responsible for overseeing the computer's work were named Loonquawl and Phouchg. Upon hearing the answer, Loonquawl exclaimed: "Forty-two! Is that all you have to show for seven and a half million years' work?" Deep Thought replied: "I checked it very thoroughly, and that quite definitely is the answer. I think the problem, to be quite honest with you, is that you've never actually known what the question is. . . . So once you do know what the question actually is, you'll know what the answer means."[10]

One of the computer operators then asked Deep Thought if it could tell them the question. It replied, "No. But I'll tell you who can." Deep Thought then described the greatest computer of all space and time, which was to be its successor: "a computer of such infinite and subtle complexity that organic life shall form part of its operational matrix." That ultimate computer, designed to provide the ultimate question for the ultimate answer, was called Earth.

The answer to life, the universe, and everything presented in Adams's humorous story has been woven into our popular, computer-based culture and has been embraced by many programmers—including the programmers of the Google calculator. Although it is all a matter of good fun and should not be taken seriously, for some reason the answer provided by Deep Thought has found a deep resonance in the human psyche. It has also spawned a wealth of speculation as to how Adams came up with the number. On one of his discussion forums is a posted Adams reply: "It was a joke. It had to be a number, an ordinary, small-ish number, and I chose that one. . . . I sat at my desk, stared into the garden and thought, 'Forty-two will do.' I typed it out. End of story."

According to Adams, the whole thing was intended as a joke, a par-ody on humankind's endless quest to find the answer to the meaning of life, the universe, and everything. Sometimes, however, our sponta-neous whims, drawn even in jest, provide the best possible answer to a given question. Deep Thought's answer appears to resonate with the human psyche—but why?

Perhaps this resonance is based upon the fact that, after thousands of years of thought, this was the same answer provided by deep think-ers of the ancient past. Yet the answer is more than just the number 42. To understand what it means, 42 must be viewed as a quantity, rather than as a pure number. According to the ancients, the number corre-sponds to the first forty-two layers above the half measure—that is, the path of immortality. Since the ancients viewed the ultimate purpose of life, the universe, and everything as involving the pursuit of immortal-ity, the forty-two layers represent the answer to the ultimate question concerning the meaning of it all.

While Adams may not have had any direct knowledge of the immortal Vedic, Egyptian, and Hebrew wisdom when he composed his book, his wisdom was nevertheless brewing in his awareness and became encapsulated by his spontaneous and whimsical answer. This answer was then embraced by pop culture, because that same wisdom is brewing currently in the awareness of everyone, whether or not we are conscious of it. The implication is that human awareness is ripe for the spontaneous rediscovery of the ancient immortal wisdom. It means simply remembering what has been forgotten, and bringing to conscious awareness what has been submerged in our collective subconscious for thousands of years.

13

The Supreme Wisdom

THE SUPREME ABODE OF IMMORTALITY

Here, we have finally reached the end of the spiritual journey—yet we have not reached the end of spiritual wisdom. The final supreme wisdom concerns the goal of the path more than the path itself.

According to the ancients, this goal represents the very self of the Supreme Being, where all phenomena cease. It was described as neither consciousness nor unconsciousness, yet we would be mistaken to imagine that at the end of the long journey, the soul is reduced to a state of unconscious oblivion.

Although words can scarcely do justice to it, the Vedic seers held that the supreme abode of immortality (*paramapada*) is filled with non-phenomenal forms of immortal existence transcending all notions of duality. The abiding characteristic of that supreme state is not rational knowledge, but divine love—which knows no reason. In that supreme abode, the one supreme self plays eternally with its own immortal forms, and it does so on the basis of divine love, which represents the ultimate expression of the synthesizing power of consciousness.

On that level of reality, all forms of duality are drowned in unity and in the ocean of divine love. The supreme state represents essentially a state of Oneness, yet contains countless virtual forms of duality. The Vedic philosophers referred to this type of virtual reality as nondual (*advaita*). Nonduality represents not absolute Oneness, but a state in which all forms of duality are synthesized into Oneness. In the final analysis, we cannot say much about Oneness. The supreme wisdom pertains to the virtual forms of reality inherent within the Oneness.

THE TWELVE AT THE END

The supreme wisdom suggests that the supreme abode of immortality has twelve internal divisions known in the Vedic tradition as the *dvadashanta,* the twelve at the end. These represent twelve virtual layers inherent within the supreme abode of immortality.

The twelve at the end cannot be viewed as stages on the path. Instead, they represent the internal divisions that characterize the goal of the path, and thereby transcend the forty-two stages of the path.

The essential difference between the two sets of layers is that on the scales of the first forty-two, duality dominates over unity, while on the scales of the final twelve, unity dominates over duality. In this regard, the forty-third layer, which represents the first of the final twelve layers, marks the unique layer where unity and duality attain a state of balance. From the perspective of duality, the forty-third layer represents the end, the nondual reality that characterizes the goal of the path. This is what lies at the basis of the $42 + 1 = 43$ immortal wisdom. From the perspective of unity, however, the forty-third layer marks not the end, but the first of twelve unified layers, which happened to be known as the twelve at the end.

Therefore, the supreme wisdom represents a more expanded and unified form than the immortal wisdom and involves a formulation of $42 + 12 = 54$ layers, rather than $42 + 1 = 43$ layers. Yet just as the forty-third layer stands as representative of the Oneness that lies beyond the first forty-two layers, so an absolute fifty-fifth layer represents the immeasurable reality that lies beyond the first fifty-four layers. The ultimate formulation of the supreme wisdom involved a total of $54 + 1 = 55$ layers.

In truth, the fifty-fifth layer is not at all a layer, but instead represents the immeasurable reality of the self, which is simultaneously "bigger than the biggest, and smaller than the smallest" of the other fifty-four layers (above and below).

THE ALPHABETICAL FORMULATION

In the Vedic tradition, the supreme wisdom was formulated by the letters of the Sanskrit alphabet: The first thirty-three layers above the half measure were represented by the thirty-three consonants in the classical alphabet, and the six joining layers were represented by six extraordinary consonants or sets of consonants formed by the process of phonetic conjunction. These 33 + 6 = 39 consonants symbolize the thirty-nine evolutionary layers that abide within the cosmic egg and its shells.

The immortal realms that lie beyond the outermost shell of the cosmic egg were represented by the sixteen vowels of the Sanskrit alphabet. More specifically, the fortieth layer, which marks the shore of the immortal world, was represented by the visarga (the emitter) pronounced as the softly aspirated *aha.* The immeasurable fifty-fifth layer transcending the other fifty-four was represented by the vowel *a* pronounced as in *father,* which was deemed the immeasurable self (*atman*) of the other 39 + 15 = 54 letters.

In the Agama texts, the sixteen vowels were called the sixteen Nityas, "eternal ones," because they represent the sixteen eternal states of the immortal soul, which lie above and beyond the finite and mortal universe. To illustrate the various gradations of eternal reality that abide within the immortal realms, the seers compared the sixteen eternal ones to the sixteen phases of the moon. In Sanskrit the term *soma* means both "moon" and the imperishable, flowing essence of pure consciousness that serves as the amrita rasa, or immortal blood of the Supreme Being. The sixteen phases of the moon correspond, then, to the sixteen gradations of soma inherent within the sixteen immortal layers.

In this analogy, the fortieth layer, represented by the visarga, was likened to the no-moon phase, when the reflected light of the moon is shadowed completely by the earth. The idea is that when the soul first arrives at the shore of the other world after traversing the thirty-nine evolutionary layers, it does not yet possess the eyes to see the transcendental light of the other world. Just as we are blinded temporarily when we emerge from a dark room into the bright sunlight, so the soul is temporarily blinded when it first enters into the immortal realms. It takes some time for the soul to develop the eyes to see the light of the transcendental realms.

This gradual awakening of transcendental vision is represented by the sixteen phases of the moon, each of which is characterized by a different degree of moonlight, which can also be understood as soma light. On the scale of the fortieth layer, the soma light is present, but can scarcely be seen. Similarly, on the no-moon night, the moon is still present and can be seen if we look closely, but it appears almost empty or devoid of light.

As the soul ascends through the immortal layers, the soma light grows gradually in intensity. On the scale of the immeasurable fifty-fifth layer, represented by the letter *a,* the soma light becomes full. This immeasurable layer was likened, therefore, to the full-moon phase, because the light of soma is fully unshadowed. The other fourteen layers in between were likened to the fourteen phases that lie in between the emptiness of light (no moon) and the fullness of light (full moon).

Here is one version of the supreme wisdom, which pertains to the soma light of the self. Because the sixteen vowels represent the sixteen phases of this light, they were called *svaras,* "the radiances (*ra*) of the self (*sva*)."

THE METRICAL FORMULATION

Another version of the same supreme wisdom is presented by the first verse of the Rig Veda. The Vedic seers held that the first expression of divine wisdom should contain a synopsis of the whole. The first letter in any divine name or the first verse in any sacred text were designed to embody the entire wisdom elaborated by that name or text. The first verse of the Rig Veda, which represents the very first expression of Vedic wisdom, was assigned supreme importance. It was designed to embody the whole wisdom elaborated in the ancient text.

This design involved the use of measured forms of speech to which we can assign nongrammatical meanings. This ancient practice has recently been illuminated by Maharishi Mahesh Yogi, who has suggested that the sequence and number of letters, syllables, words, verses, hymns, and so forth in the Rig Veda, rather than being arbitrary, were designed to encode a hidden science of the Veda that cannot be deciphered using grammatical rules alone.

Maharishi suggests that, in accordance with the ancient tradition, the first verse of the Rig Veda maps out the "unmanifest blueprint of creation" that is inherent in consciousness. Most fundamentally, this blueprint relates to the set of metaphysical layers that constitute the complete spectrum of reality. The most fundamental elements of speech correspond to the letters from which are composed all expressions of speech. The letters in the first verse of the Rig Veda were measured carefully so that the verse contains a precise number. More specifically, the verse was designed to contain fifty-four Sanskrit letters that correspond directly to the fifty-four layers, or grades of divine speech, that abide in the upper sonic half of the spectrum.

Yet the fifty-four letters represent merely the measurable grades of speech inherent within the fifty-four layers. The ultimate immeasurable grade of speech associated with the absolute fifty-fifth layer is implied instead of being represented explicitly. This understanding was made clear in a lecture given by Maharishi in India in 1988: Surrounded by several thousand Vedic pandits, he explained that the first verse of the Rig Veda has at the end an unmanifest letter (*avyakta aksha*) which is to be understood in principle, but not pronounced or written in practice. The traditional Vedic pandits concurred.

This unmanifest letter represents the immeasurable grade of

speech that abides in the immeasurable reality of the self. It can scarcely be called a grade of speech, because it is equivalent to silence. Therefore, it is represented by the silence that arises at the end of the first verse, before the next verse is recited. In this way, the first verse presents an alternate formulation of the 54 + 1 = 55 supreme wisdom. Literally, it encodes the unmanifest blueprint of creation that abides in consciousness.

But there is more. The grammatical meaning of the first verse is expressed in terms of nine Sanskrit words: The first seven, which together contain exactly forty-two letters, describe the process of self-sacrifice by means of which the soul progresses on the path of immortality—that is, by ascending through the forty-two layers. The last two, which together contain a total of twelve letters, describe the fruit of self-sacrifice, the goal of the sacrificial path. The last twelve letters represent the dvadashanta, the twelve at the end. More specifically, the last twelve spell out the two words *ratna dhatamam*, with the transliterated form of *dh* to indicate that it represents a single Sanskrit letter. The word *ratna* means "jewel" or "crystal," and the word *dhatamam* means "supreme upholder."

The grammatical meaning serves as a commentary on the sequence of letters, suggesting that the fruit of all forms of self-sacrifice, or the goal of the path, involves realizing the self as the supreme upholder of the ratna, the crystalline structure of the Veda or Logos. The supreme upholder of the crystalline structure of consciousness is none other than the infinite continuum of consciousness, which represents the supreme self. According to the supreme wisdom, the supreme self has twelve internal divisions, which correspond to the twelve at the end.

Unlike the first forty-two letters, or layers, which represent the external divisions of the self where "another" can be conceived on the basis of duality, the final twelve letters, or layers, represent the internal divisions of the self where all notions of otherness or duality are drowned in unity. When the soul ascends to the forty-third layer, the first of the twelve at the end, the crystalline structure of consciousness becomes indistinguishable from the underlying continuum of pure consciousness, which supports or upholds that structure. As a result, all notions of otherness are transcended.

In this sense, the twelve letters at the end represent the state of Vedanta, which marks the "end of the Veda." The first forty-two letters, on the other hand, represent the very embodiment of the Veda in the form of the forty-two discrete layers, which constitute the adornments of the self. We recall that in the Hebrew tradition the unique divine name was viewed as consisting of forty-two letters that represent the adornments of the name. Traditionally, these forty-two letters are encoded by the first forty-two letters of the Book of Genesis, the oldest and most authoritative of the ancient Hebrew texts. The commentaries make it clear that these represent the forty-two layers that constitute the path of immortality.

We can find that the same practice was employed in the Vedic tradition: The first forty-two letters of the Rig Veda were designed to encode the forty-two layers that constitute the path of immortality. Yet the first verse of the Rig Veda goes beyond the first forty-two layers or letters and was instead designed to encode the complete spectrum of $42 + 12 + 1 = 55$ layers that constitute the supreme wisdom.

The unmanifest letter that abides at the end of the first verse is the unspoken form of the letter *a,* which is also the first spoken letter of the verse. Here, we can say that what is realized in the beginning is also realized in the end, in accordance with the principle "as in the beginning, so in the end." In actuality, there is a mysterious Vedic doctrine regarding the letter *a:* According to the Agama texts, which deal with the science of mantras (sonic formulas) and yantras (geometric diagrams), *a* represents the self (atman) of all the letters. It is therefore assigned three names: the first (*prathama*), the all-pervading (*vyapaka*), and the immeasurable (*aprameya*).[1] The hidden meaning of these names is revealed when the immeasurable and unpronounceable form of *a* is added to the end of the first verse of the Rig Veda. This addition completes the symmetry of the verse.

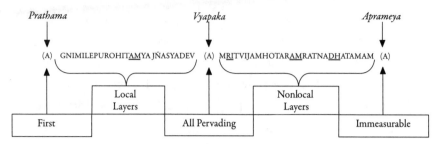

Fig. 13.1. The complete symmetry of the first verse of the Rig Veda

In this diagrammatic representation, the first, middle, and last letters are represented by three forms of the letter *a*. The first (prathama) form represents the first layer above the half measure, where the human soul becomes enlightened—the first state of enlightenment, when the self is filled with both universal light and sound. The middle or all-pervading (vyapaka) form corresponds to the twenty-eighth letter in the sequence and represents the twenty-eighth layer above the half measure, where the ascending soul arrives at the highest heaven within the visible universe and attains universal consciousness. On this level of realization, the self pervades the entire visible or local universe—that is, it becomes all-pervading. The final or immeasurable (aprameya) form represents the immeasurable reality of the self, which transcends all finite names and forms. This marks the supreme or final state, when the pointlike soul realizes its identity with infinity—that which is bigger than the biggest.

By adding an unmanifest letter to the end of the first verse, the bilateral symmetry of the verse becomes complete and the verse becomes a lettered formulation of the supreme wisdom. In this way, the Vedic seers formulated the supreme wisdom in two complementary ways: using letters of the first verse of the Rig Veda and the letters of the Sanskrit alphabet.

THE DIVINE ROSARY

The ancient seers were fond of expressing the truth in many ways. In addition to alphabetical and metrical models, the Vedic seers also employed a practical model involving a rosary-like necklace of beads to illustrate the supreme wisdom.

Even today, throughout India, rosaries consisting of 108 + 1 = 109 beads are used commonly to count the repetitions of a mantra or name of God during the practice of *japa* (repeated recitation). Such rosaries are called aksha-malas (bead necklaces)—but, as we have discovered, the word *aksha* also means "letter." Therefore, the 108 beads of the rosary represent the 54 + 54 = 108 layers that constitute the measurable forms of the self both above and below. The immeasurable form of the self, which is simultaneously "smaller than the smallest, and bigger than the biggest," is represented by a single 109th bead hung as a pendant. This is known as the guru bead.

The number 108 is arguably the most important in the Vedic tradition. Virtually every major conception of God was assigned a list of 108 names, because the Supreme Being was viewed as having 108 fundamental aspects. Moreover, there are 108 Upanishads, because the Upanishads are the texts that deal specifically with the reality of the self. Further, mantras are recited typically 108 times.

To enshrine the supreme wisdom in the daily lives of the people, the seers prescribed the use of rosaries consisting of 108 beads. In the practice of japa, the 108 repetitions are counted by grasping each bead in succession between the thumb (representing the universal self) and the forefinger (representing the individual self). A complete round of 108 repetitions represents a complete cycle of ascent or descent through all 108 layers. The 109th bead, hung as a pendant between the first and 108th bead, marks the beginning and end of each round. When the guru bead is reached, the aspirant is supposed to sit in silence and meditate upon the nameless and formless reality of the supreme self. The 109th bead therefore represents the immeasurable reality of the supreme self, which is simultaneously "smaller than the smallest, and bigger than the biggest" of the 108 layers. It is both the alpha and the omega, the beginning and the end, of each complete cycle through the 108 layers.

Although the alphabetical and metrical models suggest that the supreme wisdom involves a total of 54 + 1 = 55 layers, the fifty-four layers have dual representations in the sense that they exist both above and below the half measure. As such, they can also be counted as 54 + 54 = 108 layers. The immeasurable layer has no such dual representation. It represents the immeasurable Oneness that knows no duality, and corresponds to the fifty-fifth layer as well as the 109th in the two formulations. The divine rosary presents an alternate version of the supreme wisdom, expressed in terms of 108 +1 = 109 layers rather than 54 + 1 = 55 layers.

AS IN THE BEGINNING, SO IN THE END

It turns out that there is a numerical correspondence between the solar wisdom cognized at the beginning of the path and the supreme wisdom cognized at its end. This correspondence can be understood in terms of the ascending and descending paths of the self.

When the self ascends, it starts on the scale of the half measure and then climbs through the twelve solar layers, which correspond to the twelve adityas, or the twelve at the beginning. When the self descends, it starts on the immeasurable scale, and then descends through the twelve supreme layers, which correspond to the twelve at the end. There is, then, a numerical correspondence between the twelve at the beginning and the twelve at the end.

Based upon this correspondence, the seers were fond of comparing the supreme self to the divine sun, whose rays illuminate the universe. These rays are the souls that abide within the forty-two layers of the path. Yet just as the interior of the sun is filled with rays of sunlight, so the interior of the divine sun is filled with its own divine rays, which correspond to the truly immortal souls who have completed the path and taken up residence within the supreme abode. There, in a nondual way, they become identified with the Supreme Being.

The correspondence between the solar wisdom and the supreme wisdom is reflected in many ancient traditions in which the Supreme Being was often conceived as a creator sun god. This is true particularly of the ancient Egyptian tradition.

THE INNER CIRCLE OF THE DUAT

In the Egyptian tradition, the metaphysical Logos was called the Duat, the underworld or underlying hidden world through which the enlightened soul must ascend (or descend) in order to obtain true immortality.

As we have seen, the Egyptians represented the forty-twofold path of immortality with the creation of the forty-two nomes, or ancient divisions of the land, mapped out along the Nile. The goal of the path, on the other hand, was represented by an abstract symbol—the inner circle of the Duat—which was viewed as the supreme abode of all truly immortal souls.

The inner circle of the Duat has twelve inner divisions. Given the correspondence between the solar and supreme wisdoms, these have two complementary interpretations: they can be viewed as the twelve inner divisions of the sun that shines in the lower (physical) sky or the twelve inner divisions of the supreme sun that shines in the upper (metaphysical) sky, the sky of the immortal self.

In spite of its twelvefold inner nature, the symbol used to represent the inner circle of the Duat in inscriptions throughout Egypt was a five-pointed star enclosed within a circle—a potent symbol with several meanings: On one level, it symbolizes the person inside the sun, which is actually a star. This "star person" with its five celestial appendages can be compared to a human with its head, two arms, and two legs. The expanded cosmological meaning, of this symbol pertains to the fivefold celestial body of the Supreme Being, which correspond to the five cosmological spheres:

1. The sphere of the cosmic egg
2. The Hubble sphere
3. The galactic sphere
4. The heliosphere
5. The solar sphere

The Supreme Being dwells ultimately in the inner circle of the Duat. The twelve divisions of the inner circle transcend the fivefold celestial symbol, because they are not celestial. They represent hidden metaphysical divisions, rather than celestial appendages. In this way, the ancient Egyptians, like the Vedic seers, conceived the supreme abode of immortality as having twelve inner divisions, which correspond numerically to the twelve inner divisions of the sun.

THE TWELVE DIVISIONS OF ISRAEL

The Hebrew sages also shared this wisdom. As we have seen, Moses and his inner circle mapped out the path of immortality in terms of the forty-two encampments of the ben Israel on their journey from Egypt (the land of bondage) to Canaan (the land of immortality).

In this spiritual allegory, the land of Canaan or Israel itself represents the supreme abode of immortality reached at the end of the path, and the citizens of that land symbolize the truly immortal souls that live there and the twelve tribes of Israel, who symbolize the twelve classes of immortal souls that dwell in the twelve layers at the end.

Once the twelve tribes arrived in Canaan, they established the kingdom of Israel by dividing the land into twelve pieces, as recorded specifically in the Book of Joshua. By dividing the land into twelve sections, the Hebrew sages established symbolically the supreme abode of immortality on earth, which was called the kingdom of Israel and which was to serve as the abode for all the immortal sons of Israel throughout time.

Therefore, all three traditions—Vedic, Egyptian, and Hebrew— shared the same immortal wisdom regarding the forty-twofold path, as well as the same supreme wisdom regarding the twelvefold goal of the path.

THE IMMORTAL WORLD OF DIVINE LOVE

Wouldn't it be a disappointment if, at the end of the long spiritual journey, the soul was reduced to an abstract, formless, nameless, and motionless state of pure being? In one sense, this is the case, but in another sense, the abstract state of pure being is filled with nonphenomenal forms of reality, which constitute an immortal world—the eternal world of the self described by the ancient seers as a world of indescribable bliss.

In that world, every soul represents an immortal, nonphenomenal form of the Supreme Being so that all distinctions between the individual being and the Supreme Being are drowned in unity. The glue that binds all of these nonphenomenal parts into a single, nonphenomenal whole is none other than divine love—the unifying aspect of pure knowledge, which knows no reason.

In the tenth chapter of the Bhagavata Purana, in the form of spiritual allegory about a divine dance—the *rasa lila* (play of nectar)—the Vedic texts record a metaphorical description of that immortal world. The story revolves around an incarnation of the Supreme Being in the form of Krishna, the god of divine love, who is depicted as an adorable youth of sixteen years. Krishna represents the sixteenfold incarnation of the Supreme Being in the form of the 15 + 1 = 16 immortal layers that lie above and beyond the outermost shell of the cosmic egg.

The immortal souls that dwell within these layers were compared to the female consorts of Krishna, who viewed him as their one true love. Yet the story of the rasa lila presents this as an illicit type of love, which transcends the boundaries of social dictum and reason. Each immortal soul may be viewed as married to the unborn Creator, who presides over the cosmic egg from which it hatched. In this sense, the unborn Creator may be compared to the divine "husband" of the female soul. This marriage upholds both the covenant between heaven and earth and the cosmic eggs as imperishable forms of reality within the self. Although the immortal soul remains married to the unborn Creator, who abides within the cosmic egg, it nevertheless cherishes an illicit love for the Supreme Being, who abides in the immortal realms beyond the cosmic egg. The nature of this love is described metaphorically by the story of the rasa lila.

According to the story, the consorts of Krishna remain dutifully within their homes and serve their husbands. During the night, however, their longing turns to Krishna, their one true love. Wandering in the moonlit forest, Krishna calls to his consorts by playing upon his cosmic flute. Made from hollow bamboo, the flute symbolizes the hollow whirlwinds of consciousness that connect the cosmic eggs and by means of which the soul can travel. When Krishna plays upon his flute, the immortal souls are called to leave their (crystallographic) homes, abandon their husbands, and seek him out in the moonlit forest, filled with fluttering leaves. There, they meet their lover in the adorable form of the sixteenfold whole, and there they engage in the rasa lila, the play of nectar.

Technically, the rasa lila involves the circulatory flow of the imperishable substance of pure consciousness, the soma or amrita rasa. This flow is nonphenomenal in nature and therefore knows no reason. Upon finding Krishna, the consorts dance with him in loving embrace—yet due to their intense love, the consorts actually assume the form of Krishna. The rasa lila thus involves the dance of Krishna with himself, or the dance of the immortal soul with its own supreme self. This provides a symbolic description of the nondual relation between the immortal soul and the Supreme Being that is inherent in the supreme abode of immortality. This relation was presented as a form of illicit love because it transcends all forms of duty and reason. The rasa lila serves no exterior purpose. It plays no role in the creation of the universe and serves only to fulfill the intense desire of the soul for union with the immortal whole. That desire is manifest as divine love for God, the one eternal self.

On that immortal level of reality, "Truth is beauty, and beauty is truth." In other words, the knowledge of God and the love of God are one and the same. That immortal form of God, which embraces the sixteenfold whole, represents the one supreme thing by which, through knowing and loving it, everything else becomes known and loved.

CONCLUSION

Finally, we have reached the end. Beyond the largest and smallest of the 108 layers lies the immeasurable reality of the Supreme Being, which is truly infinite.

As the enlightened soul ascends and descends through the layers, it becomes filled increasingly with the presence of God, and in the end, when it transcends the smallest layer below and the largest layer above, it becomes one with God. What lies beyond that is unknown and unknowable by human beings on Earth.

Yet according to the seers, the expansion of consciousness is endless and eternal. For that reason the supreme reality was called brahman, the ever-expanding reality. Although the ancient spiritual wisdoms may have been expressed in religious terms, we have seen that these wisdoms were also highly systematic, formulated so that the steps on the path of immortality were spelled out literally in the sacred texts and mapped out by the sacred divisions of the land.

Due to this systematic expression, as we have seen, the spiritual wisdoms can be expressed in terms of pure numbers and mathematical formulas that are linked to particular scales of space and time. As we have discovered, encapsulated by the system of matched pairs, this system is genuinely scientific in the sense that it can be used to predict accurately a hidden vertical symmetry in the overall organization of the universe. In the end, however, the ancient spiritual science transcends the boundaries of the finite created universe, and provides a description of the immortal and supreme realities that lie beyond the scope of reason or scientific analysis. It was not, then, just an empirical science; it was also a spiritual science, a science of immortality.

We have discovered that this ancient science was not the province of one culture or religion, but was shared by some of the most ancient traditions of knowledge on earth, including the Vedic, Egyptian, and Hebrew cultures. Although each tradition may have expressed the science in terms of its own symbolic and religious concepts, using its own language, ultimately these traditions were all talking about the same thing.

There is no doubt that this science was kept secret in ancient times, and was passed down exclusively among the elite royal and priestly classes through a process of hereditary and initiatory oral transmission which persisted for thousands of years. Around the time of Alexander the Great, however, these secrets of the elite classes began to be written down and were made available to the public—for example, in the Great Library at Alexandria. Unfortunately, this library was eventually destroyed by a series of fires, and the treasure of ancient wisdom was lost.

Yet this fate was not shared by the Vedic texts, which were preserved by oral traditions for thousands of years, and then were written down eventually in the form of sacred texts. Although only about thirty to forty thousand Vedic texts have actually been cataloged, translated, and studied by Western scholars, these provide an unparalleled glimpse into the minds of the ancient seers and how they viewed the world and what lies beyond the world. Much of our examination of the ancient science has been based upon the Vedic texts because they represent the largest and most complete body of ancient literature that has ever been found on earth—much larger than all of the other ancient literatures taken together.

To be honest, however, we have scarcely begun to explore the vast treasure of ancient knowledge and wisdom that has been left us. The typical view of Western scholars is that the ancient literatures present a bunch of spiritual mumbo-jumbo, which has no relevance to modern society. On one hand, this is true in the sense that modern society has essentially lost its taste and inclination to explore the deeper spiritual reality of the world. On the other hand, as we have seen here, the teachings encoded in the ancient texts may have direct relevance to the most advanced theories being developed today. Moreover, the ancient teachings may have direct relevance to the ultimate destiny of the human soul and its place in the world—something about which modern science remains mute.

Although this knowledge was kept secret in ancient times, here we can find it spelled out in explicit terms and made available to the public in accordance with the spirit of our modern era—the era of the common man. According to the ancients, the advent of the ancient spiritual science on earth took place some twelve thousand years ago, when humankind was still living in caves or in makeshift dwellings beneath the trees. During the last twelve thousand years, the cycle of time has largely erased this science from human memory. The seers predicted, however, that at the end of the cycle, the ancient science would be remembered and a new age of spiritual truth would dawn. If this volume helps to contribute to that remembrance in any way, then it will have served its purpose. Here, we have listened merely to the story as it has been drawn from the ancient texts. What we make of the story is up to each of us.

The fact is that we all see the world through our own tinted glasses. Our modern view of the universe is based upon an objective paradigm, while the ancient view was based upon a subjective paradigm. Here, we have seen that these two paradigms, though mutually opposed, can lead to similar empirical predictions regarding the overall organization of the universe. Which system is more valid, however, cannot be answered here.

A detailed and well-defined mathematical theory of the unified field will be required to determine which paradigm has greater validity. Perhaps this book will inspire great minds to explore the potential for a new type of unified theory, one rooted in subjective rather than objective principles. Whether or not this comes to pass, only time will tell.

Notes

INTRODUCTION

1. Walter Scott, *Hermetica, Vol. 1: The Ancient Greek and Latin Writings Which Contain Religious or Philosophic Teachings Ascribed to Hermes Trismegistus* (Boston, Mass.: Shambhala, 2001), 151–53.
2. Graham Hancock, *Heaven's Mirror* (New York: Three Rivers Press, 1998), 312.
3. R. A. Schwaller de Lubicz, *The Temple in Man: Sacred Architecture and the Perfect Man* (Rochester, Vt.: Inner Traditions, 1988), 106.
4. Ibid., 20.
5. Scott, *Hermetica*, 343.
6. Ibid., 135.
7. Ibid., 461.

CHAPTER I. THE PHILOSOPHY OF ENLIGHTENMENT

1. New English Bible, John 1:1–5.
2. Scott, *Hermetica*, 115–17.
3. Gaudapada, *Mandukya Karika* IV.45.
4. Scott, *Hermetica*, 223.
5. Y. Lee, T. M. Haard, W. P. Halperin, and J. A. Sauls, "Discovery of the Acoustic Faraday effect in Superfluid ^{3}He-B," *Nature* 400, no. 6743 (July 29, 1999), 431.

CHAPTER 2. THE MECHANICS OF ENLIGHTENMENT

1. Scott, *Hermetica,* 131.
2. Isha Upanishad XI.
3. Scott, *Hermetica,* 241.
4. Ibid., 247.
5. Svetashvatara Upanishad II.16–19.
6. Patanjali, *Yoga Sutras,* I.41.

CHAPTER 3. THE SPECTRUM OF CONSCIOUSNESS

1. Scott, *Hermetica,* 221.
2. Shvetashvatara Upanishad V.9.
3. Chandogya Upanishad VII.23.
4. Rig Veda 1.164:18.
5. Ibid., 1.164:19.
6. Genesis 28.
7. Pyramid Texts 1108.
8. Ibid., 773–74.
9. Ibid., 1431.
10. Ibid., 390.
11. Scott, *Hermetica,* 205.
12. Ibid., 515.
13. Jaiminiya Upanishad Brahmana I.23.
14. Bhagavata Mahapurana III.11:41.
15. Svetashvatara Upanishad III.

CHAPTER 4. THE SCIENCE OF THE GODS

1. Scott, *Hermetica,* 457.
2. Ibid., 233.
3. Bhagavad Gita XV.16–17.
4. Bhagavata Mahapurana XII.4:35–37.
5. Ibid., XI.22.

CHAPTER 5. THE FIRST WISDOM

1. Rig Veda X.1:1.
2. Ibid., X.3:1.
3. Ibid., X.2:7.

CHAPTER 6. THE STANDARD COSMOLOGICAL MODEL

1. Scott, *Hermetica,* 205.

CHAPTER 8. THE GALACTIC WISDOM

1. See the Vishnu Puruana and the Bhagavata Mahapurana.
2. Scott, *Hermetica,* 341.

CHAPTER 9. THE UNIVERSAL WISDOM

1. Rig Veda I.24.
2. Ibid.

CHAPTER 10. THE SUPERUNIVERSAL WISDOM

1. Subhash Kak, "The Speed of Light in Puranic Cosmology," *Computing Science in Ancient India,* edited by T. R. N. Rao and S. Kak (Lafayette, La.: USL Press, 1998), 431.

CHAPTER 11. THE COSMIC WISDOM

1. Bhagavata Mahapurana III.26:51–52.
2. Manu Smriti I.19–20.
3. Chandradar Sharma, *A Critical Survey of Indian Philosophy* (London: Rider, 1960), 154.
4. Manu Smriti I.5–11.
5. Scott, *Hermetica,* 119.

6. Ibid., 123–25.
7. See the Ahirbudhnya Samhita of the Pancharatra tradition.

CHAPTER 12. THE IMMORTAL WISDOM

1. See the Lakshmi Tantra and Ahirbudhnya Samhita.
2. These six extraordinary consonants correspond to *ksha,* the retroflex form of *la,* and the *rangas, yamas, jihvamuliya,* and *upadmaniya*—all of which are included in the more expanded and older Vedic alphabet espoused by Panini, the great Sanskrit grammarian.
3. Gaudapada, *Mandukya Karika* III.3.
4. Book of Enoch 14:10–18.
5. Mandukya Upanishad 5–6.
6. Ibid., 7.
7. Talmud, Mas. Kiddushin 71a.
8. Soncino Zohar, Bereshith Section 1, 30a.
9. Ibid., Bereshith Section 2, 234a.
10. Douglas Adams, *The Hitchhiker's Guide to the Galaxy* (New York: Pocket Books, 1979), 181.

CHAPTER 13. THE SUPREME WISDOM

1. See the Lakshmi Tantra.

Bibliography

Adams, Douglas. *The Hitchhiker's Guide to the Galaxy.* New York: Pocket Books, 1979.

Gupta, Sanjukta, ed. *Lakshmi Tantra.* Leiden: E. J. Brill, 1972.

Hancock, Graham. *Heaven's Mirror.* New York: Three Rivers Press, 1998.

Kak, Subhash. "The Speed of Light in Puranic Cosmology." In *Computing Science in Ancient India,* edited by T. R. N. Rao and S. Kak. Lafayette, La.: USL Press, 1998.

Lee, Y., T. M. Haard, W. P. Halperin, and J. A. Sauls. "Discovery of the Acoustic Faraday effect in Superfluid ^{3}He-B," In *Nature* 400, no. 6743 (July 29, 1999): 431–33.

Sargeant, Winthrop, ed. *The Bhagavad Gita.* Albany: State University of New York Press, 1984.

Schwaller de Lubicz, R. A. *The Temple in Man: Sacred Architecture and the Perfect Man.* Rochester, Vt.: Inner Traditions, 1988.

Scott, Walter. *Hermetica, Vol. 1: The Ancient Greek and Latin Writings Which Contain Religious or Philosophic Teachings Ascribed to Hermes Trismegistus.* Boston, Mass.: Shambhala, 2001.

Sharma, Chandradar. *A Critical Survey of Indian Philosophy.* London: Rider, 1960.

Swami Gambirananda, trans. Gaudapads's *Mandukya Karika* from *Eight Upanishads.* Calcutta: Advaita Ashrama, 1973.

Index